Social History of Canada

Allan Greer and Craig Heron,
general editors

Property and Inequality in Victorian Ontario:
Structural Patterns and Cultural Communities in the 1871 Census

Real property was the most important form of wealth in the nineteenth century. The process of acquiring it has recently attracted the interest of historians, sociologists, and economists. The 1871 census of Ontario is a particularly rich source of information, some of it not elsewhere available to researchers. Gordon Darroch and Lee Soltow use this census to study inequalities in socio-economic well-being in nineteenth-century Ontario. They provide the first detailed examination of land and home ownership, and explore related topics, such as the processes of property acquisition, ethnic and religious patterns of ownership, the wealthholding of Canadian emigrants to the United States in 1860 and 1870, and the relationship between literacy and propertied wealth in Ontario.

Mid-Victorian commentators exaggerated the material prosperity that awaited immigrants in Ontario, but this study reveals that, in terms of simple ownership, their perceptions were not far off the mark. Nearly a third of Ontario men owned sufficient property for family security, though this broad base of smallholders was topped by the small, distinct group of the very wealthy and excluded the large group of the virtually propertyless, who were almost all young and unmarried. Darroch and Soltow's analysis of patterns of property ownership and accumulation reveals few limitations on simple ownership, but persistent and significant differences in opportunities to accumulate real estate wealth. Their in-depth study of the framework in Ontario broadens our understanding of previous studies, concerning the United States, Australia, and New Zealand.

GORDON DARROCH is a member of the Department of Sociology, York University, and has published widely in social history.

LEE SOLTOW is a member of the Department of Economics, Ohio University, and author of numerous books, including *Distribution of Wealth and Income in the United States in 1798*.

GORDON DARROCH AND LEE SOLTOW

Property and Inequality in Victorian Ontario: Structural Patterns and Cultural Communities in the 1871 Census

UNIVERSITY OF TORONTO PRESS
Toronto Buffalo London

© University of Toronto Press Incorporated 1994
Toronto Buffalo London
Printed in Canada

ISBN 0-8020-0516-0 (cloth)
ISBN 0-8020-6952-5 (paper)

Printed on acid-free paper

Canadian Cataloguing in Publication Data

Darroch, Gordon
    Property and inequality in Victorian Ontario :
    structural patterns and cultural communities in
    the 1871 census

    (The Social history of Canada ; 51)
    Includes bibliographical references and index.
    ISBN 0-8020-0516-0 (bound)   ISBN 0-8020-6952-5 (pbk.)

    1. Wealth – Ontario – History – 19th century.
    2. Real property – Social aspects – Ontario –
    History – 19th century.   3. Equality – Ontario –
    History – 19th century.   4. Ontario – Economic
    conditions – 19th century.*   5. Ontario – Census,
    1871.   I. Soltow, Lee.   II. Title.   III. Series.

    EC117.06D37 1994   339.2'2'0971309034   C94-930258-9

Social History of Canada 51

University of Toronto Press acknowledges the financial assistance to its
publishing program of the Canada Council and the Ontario Arts Council.

This book has been published with the help of a grant from the Social Science
Federation of Canada, using funds provided by the Social Sciences and
Humanities Research Council of Canada.

Contents

Tables, Figures, and Maps

FIGURES

MAPS

Preface

This study is a collaborative work. It became a joint project as a consequence of mutual interest and chance circumstance. Soltow began the project but put the work aside for some years. Darroch became a colleague in the project through the off-chance of a suggestion by Peter Knights. As the project became fully collegial, it also fostered a friendship.

G.D.
L.S.

Acknowledgments

Like most authors we have accumulated a number of debts in the course of this study. Most are owed to colleagues who gave us general encouragement over a number of years in undertaking this and related work. We hope to repay the favour. Several colleagues and institutions contributed directly to the completion of the study. We thank Edward Stevens for comments on preliminary drafts of some chapters and Ohio University for providing Lee Soltow with release time in the course of the study. We also thank York University for providing Gordon Darroch with sabbatical support during the year in which the joint work began, and the Fulbright Scholar Program for support in 1991–2 at Duke University's Canadian Studies Center, when the manuscript was completed. The members of Duke's Canadian Studies Center provided a marvellous atmosphere of scholarly support.

The careful research assistance of Mrs Elizabeth Vincent in collecting and collating the sample of census data was essential to the study. Peter Knights suggested our collaboration; we hope he is pleased with the product of his idea, and we are certainly grateful that it occurred to him. We have also appreciated the encouragement of Allan Greer, and of Gerald Hallowell of the University of Toronto Press; it helped us through some rough patches. The thoughtful editorial comments of the anonymous reviewer for the Press have also been appreciated.

Portions of chapter 2 were first published as 'Inequality in Landed Wealth in Nineteenth-Century Ontario: Structure and Access,' *Canadian Review of Sociology and Anthropology* 29:2 (1992) 167–90. Additional funding provided by Ohio University and the Faculty of Arts, York University, is also appreciated.

In the latter part of the nineteenth century some friendships were sustained by the postal service between Ontario and Ohio when, as part of the huge southward movement in these decades, so many Ontario folk moved to the northern and midwestern states. Our working relationship has mimicked this communication. We have been sustained in the venture by the complete support and good-humoured incredulity of our wives and families. They have our special thanks.

Gordon Darroch   Lee Soltow
Toronto, Ontario   Athens, Ohio

June 1993

PROPERTY AND INEQUALITY IN VICTORIAN ONTARIO

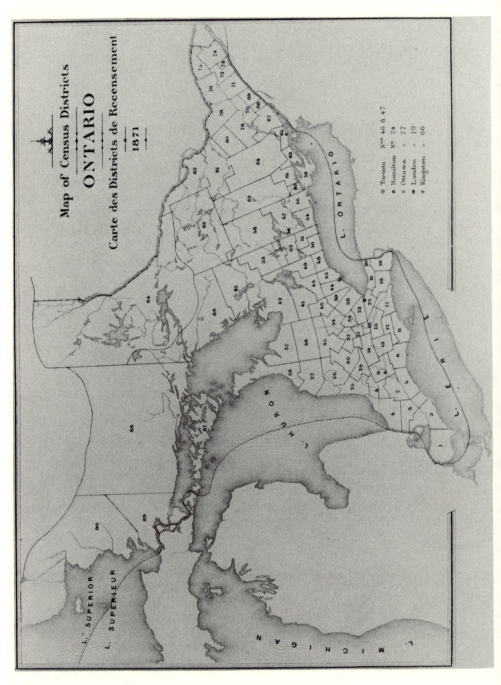

Map 1. Census Districts in Ontario. *Census of Canada, 1871*, vol. I

1

Introduction: Concepts and Contexts

Historically in North America land and home ownership undergirded a social ideal of self-sufficiency that was commonly defined in terms of family security, autonomy, and patrimony. In large measure the pursuit of the ideal fuelled the great migrations from Europe and the spread of settlement across the continent. Accordingly, questions about the distribution of property, about the process of its acquisition, and about the social characteristics of owners and non-owners are fundamental to social history. Despite their importance, the difficulty of addressing the questions systematically has very largely forestalled answers in Canadian studies. Our purpose in this book is to examine closely the acquisition and distribution of property, to determine the social characteristics associated with ownership, and to provide a general appraisal of property inequality in mid-Victorian Ontario. Our primary source is a sample of the manuscript census of 1871. The detailed tabulations of the census provide an unusual opportunity to explore property distributions and their social correlates, including ethnicity and religious affiliations. It is a rare historical document that allows systematic analysis of the implications of cultural communities for material life.

Although the manuscript data of the 1871 census make reference to the ownership and occupancy of land, to private residences, and to a variety of other forms of real property, a full accounting of wealth distributions would have to consider other non-financial assets, such as machinery and equipment, inventories and household furnishings, as well as financial assets, such as bank deposits, shares, and currency. These assets would have to be offset by a knowledge of the debt side of the ledger, mainly mortgages and loans. The present study is not a study of wealth in all its forms, though property was the most important one both economically and socially.

A few studies of nineteenth-century Ontario communities have attempted

'Our home in the woods.' Engraving from the frontispiece of *Life in the Woods*, by Cunningham Geikie, 1872

to assess overall wealthholding and its components.[1] The most recent and comprehensive investigation is that of Di Matteo and George for Wentworth county, at the western end of Lake Ontario, including the city of Hamilton.[2] Their work is based on samples of probate records for the deceased, linked to assessment roll and census manuscript data for the years 1872, 1882, 1892, and 1902. It is also one of the very few studies that provides an estimate of the proportion of total estate represented by real estate. In 1872 the proportion was 0.40, when 40 per cent of the probated decedents also reported farmer as an occupation. The real estate proportion was about the same in each of the other years, with the exception of 1892, when it rose to 0.60. Moreover, between 68 and 72 per cent of the probated decedents reported holding real estate in one form or another from 1872 to the turn of the century.[3] Undoubtedly real estate was the principal form of wealth throughout the last century and was relatively more important in the more rural, farm-based communities. From his careful investigation of early settled, but thoroughly agrarian, Peel county, just west of Toronto,

Gagan concludes that for the nineteenth century 'real property was, apparently, the lowest common denominator of betterment, permanence and social standing.'[4]

Di Matteo and George find that both overall wealth and real estate were quite unequally distributed in Wentworth over the last thirty years of the last century, with some 50 to 60 per cent of total value held by the richest 10 per cent of the samples. They also find that in concert with general economic improvement wealth and real estate inequalites tended to increase, though they declined between 1872 and 1882. Moreover, comparisons with diverse U.S. and Canadian studies suggest to them a surprisingly uniform pattern of unequal distributions of wealth in the nineteenth century.[5]

The combination of probate, assessment roll, and census manuscript records employed by Di Matteo and George is very likely the best approach to estimating wealth and wealth distributions in the last century. But all those who have employed such records readily acknowledge their limitations. There is serious underreporting in assessment records, underenumeration in the census, and problems of the selective population of probated estates and of estimating wealth for the living population from that of the deceased.[6] Historians sometimes envy the apparent accuracy and reliability of contemporary government statistics for establishing wealth distributions. It is instructive, therefore, to note the problems of establishing wealth distributions even for the late twentieth century. To his question posed in 1993 – 'How is wealth distributed in Canada?' – one of the foremost students of wealth distributions, James B. Davies, admits the best answer may simply be 'We don't know.'[7] The surveys that are specifically designed to generate contemporary wealth estimates tend to underrepresent those at the upper end of highly skewed distributions, such as wealth, and are marred by nonresponse (those who refuse to be tallied) and misreporting. Some underreporting is suspected to be as high as 40 to 50 per cent, for example, for assets such as bank accounts.[8] It is certain that even the most scrupulous recovery of wealth holdings for the past is subject to equivalent problems. But ironically, using nominal historical sources, such as probate, assessment, and census records, we may very well be able to establish aspects of wealth distributions for the nineteenth century that cannot be established for the twentieth.

Although a provincial study combining several historical sources at the individual level would be invaluable, it would be a truly formidable research enterprise. The 1871 census data are probably the most representative and revealing historical sources for an examination of real property assets in the last century. We have left the larger project for others to contemplate.[9] We hope this book will serve as a basis and a benchmark for further work.

CONCEPTS OF PROPERTY HOLDING IN ONTARIO SOCIAL HISTORY

Small-property ownership, mainly of farms and homes, remained the basis of Ontario's economy and a central feature of its class structure from early in the century to long after the initial thrusts of urban industrialization in the 1860s and 1870s. Farmers were the numerically and socially, if not the politically, dominant class in nineteenth-century Ontario. Just over half of the male labour force considered themselves farmers when they were enumerated in the 1871 census.[10] The number had decreased by barely 10 per cent from mid-century. From mid-century through the 1880s between 40 and 50 per cent of Ontario's GNP was derived from the primary sector, with some 30 to 40 per cent from agriculture alone. Moreover, agricultural products made up some 40 to 50 per cent of all exports for Ontario between 1850 and 1870. In contrast, manufacturing accounted for less than 20 per cent of GNP in these years, and as late as 1881 just over 20 per cent of the province's labour force was employed in manufacturing, with an only slightly greater proportion in the south-central industrializing core.[11] Despite this dominant rural influence, we know next to nothing about the small-property ownership that characterized the countryside in old Ontario, and, beyond a few specific city studies, relatively little about urban patterns of ownership.

This chapter reviews recent contributions to the social history of Ontario with particular attention to their assumptions about the structure of property ownership and the processes of its acquisition. Though the assumptions are often quite fundamental to the interpretations offered in this literature, historians have frequently noted our limited knowledge of ownership patterns and processes, as well as of wealth more generally.[12] We also describe the design of the sample of the 1871 manuscript census and the organization of the analysis.

A significant body of revisionist social history aimed at recovering the everyday lives and voices of ordinary people in Ontario's past emerged in the 1970s. One of the first and most influential among the studies was innovative research into the origins of public schooling. It was research that carried analysis well beyond the confines of the educational records of the Ryersonian years (1844–76) to questions of the relationships between class society, the growth of an educational bureaucracy, the promotion of schools, school attendance, and teacher training. The new perspective required an interpretation of the relationship between the still dominant rural world and the emerging urban communities, since the studies initially took for granted that interest in schooling radiated from major urban centres. Gaffield has perceptively noted that although the research took several different forms, each project relied on assumptions that resolved the seeming contradiction of an urban-oriented school movement in a predominately rural society.[13]

First, it was taken for granted that in the 1860s and 1870s Ontario was at a turning point in which rural populations were increasingly forced off the land by the settlement process. The key assumption was that the best land was simply 'filled up,' thus rapidly fuelling the growth of urban wage labour. Second, this urban proletariat was further assumed to be swollen by massive immigration, particularly by the supposedly urban-inclined Irish famine immigrants. The perspective largely corresponded to that of contemporary commentators, especially urban school promoters and the propertied class, who viewed an influx of seemingly rootless wage workers and their unoccupied children, especially immigrants, as a growing threat to orderly urban life.

These assumptions implied a working knowledge of the structure and changes of Ontario's rural landed economy, as well as some knowledge of the composition and economic circumstances of immigrant streams and urban populations. But only a very few prior studies took up the relevant arguments or provided evidence.[14] More recent research has raised questions about both key assumptions. For example, McInnis has provided the only systematic overview of Ontario's nineteenth-century distribution of farm property prior to the analysis we undertake here. Based on a sample of farms drawn from the 1861 census, he finds a distribution of farms by size of acreage in which some 60 per cent of farms were between 70 and 170 acres, with very few tiny farms and fewer still over 300 acres. The distribution suggests that owner-occupied family farming was pursued in the absence either of a large class of landless or nearly landless labourers, or of a substantial landed elite.[15] This interpretation of the broadly egalitarian and undivided character of Ontario's nineteenth-century economy does not fit well with the assumptions of early educational history, or with other more general interpretations of the sources of urban labour in Ontario's past. Other recent studies have also questioned common assumptions about the sources and character of wage labouring in Ontario in the formative 1860s and, in particular, have questioned the mainly urban destinations of Irish Catholic immigrants.[16]

With regard to knowledge about the character of nineteenth-century Ontario cities, which also figured in the assumptions, some of the gaps were being filled in by an emerging urban history.[17] One of the most influential and controversial early studies was of Hamilton, undertaken by Katz and his colleagues. Though the work centred on critical interpretations of the growth of public education, it was also innovative in taking up the methods and interests of social science history, especially the analysis of family, mobility, and social structural patterns.[18]

The Hamilton project provided the first systematic analysis of structures of urban inequality and property holding and their relation to the characteristics of individuals and families in nineteenth-century Ontario. The project's evolving interpretive framework came to emphasize a historic turning point in the decades after mid-century, defined by the rapid spread of wage labouring, a deepening urban class divide, and the growth of a web of state-organized agencies and institutions.

Though based entirely on patterns found in this commercial city, the interpretations had implications reaching far beyond one urban area. In addition to the root assumption about the rural and immigrant sources of urban wage labour, to which Gaffield has pointed, there was also the problem of generalizing beyond the city's limits. To what extent did Hamilton's relatively steep inequality in property ownership and wealth represent other cities or the patterns found in the multitude of small towns and rural villages in Ontario? What relation did it bear to provincial patterns as a whole? Generalizing, of course, is both a necessity of community studies aspiring to be more than merely local in significance and a serious potential limitation.[19] One specific objective of this book is to examine provincial patterns of inequality and their urban variations.

Concern about the possible limits of single-city analysis was, it turns out, the least of the criticisms directed at the Hamilton project. Some criticisms simply reflected historiographic conventionality, faced with social science methodologies; others were well founded. The project was criticized for an excessive focus on social structural patterns, its attempts to portray complex social relationships in statistical form, and its inadequate appreciation of local historical context. The harshest judgment was lodged by the new working-class historians, whose early work also focused on Ontario's major cities, Hamilton and Toronto. Palmer and Kealey expressed dismay, especially with the Hamilton project's organizing framework and periodization and with its failure to attend to the evidence of class conflict and working-class cultural formation.[20] The new working-class history, which these authors launched, was also ground breaking, and it was not long before it attracted its critics in turn.

The explorations of working-class history, which were initiated by Palmer's study of Hamilton and Kealey's study of Toronto, established that as early as the 1860s and 1870s capitalist reorganization of production and the labour process had given rise to an early industrial 'revolution' in Ontario. More important, the research also demonstrated how the emerging industrial formation had generated shared forms of class protest and resistance grounded on a moral order of workshop and labour experiences.[21] The critics of this work objected to the core assertion that there was a fundamental unity of class experiences, and they further doubted whether the new studies did more than add to our knowledge of the origins and leadership of the labour movement, as the authors claimed.[22]

In fact, the new working-class history added a strongly revisionist dimension to Canadian social history. In the current context it is of interest that the new interpretations still relied on conventional assumptions about the character of the larger landed economy and, specifically, about structure and change in small property holding. Like the first phase of educational history in Ontario, working-class history has generally assumed that after mid-century large numbers of men and women were forced into towns and cities because good land on which to establish their households was increasingly scarce. We take up the question as part of our analysis of farm ownership, occupancy, and acquisition in chapter 2.

Two other aspects of the distribution of property are of particular interest in the context of Ontario's nineteenth-century working-class formations. First, the moral economy of urban workers was fashioned not only in their workplaces and in their associational life, as the new studies revealed, but within families and household economies as well. Home ownership and the non-wage forms of sustenance it fostered, for example, boarding and gardening, were of fundamental importance to the way of life of urban workers, as recent studies have indicated.[23] We examine mid-Victorian home ownership in Ontario in detail in chapter 3. Our analysis cannot directly address questions about the relation of home ownership to urban working-class culture and movements. We provide the first analysis of provincial patterns of home ownership, however, and we consider their variations among cities, towns, villages, and rural areas, and among broad occupational groups.

Second, from the beginning, social histories using nominal sources revealed that the population of nineteenth-century towns and cities was highly migratory. The early emphasis on the transiency of these migrants is misleading, since migrants were often members of rural, landed households whose remittances from temporary wage work served to underwrite the economies of family farms. Thus, for example, most unskilled and semi-skilled city workers were probably not members of an anchorless floating proletariat, buffeted about by unpredictable changes of the urban labour market. On the contrary, like other sojourners in the north Atlantic economy, many may have had limited commitments to urban labouring and were willing to tolerate low wages and deteriorating working conditions, within limits, for the sake of subsidizing rural family economies.[24] Further, some skilled craft workers, who formed the core of the active defenders of a 'culture of control,' might have been tempted by the idea that an alternative to the defence of their craft was to seek their family's security on the land. Assuredly, there were many who had some immediate family or wider kin connection with Ontario's farm economy. This specific reciprocity between urban working-class and rural household economies has not yet been a subject of analysis in Canadian social history. Such analysis would require very particular and detailed study of individual transitions and family life courses over a wide area. We hope our analysis of the distribution of property ownership and, especially, of the processes of property acquisition provides a context for such work.

The new social histories of urban communities and urban working classes were well established in English Canada before comparable rural community studies began to emerge. John Herd Thompson argues that the new urban histories carried their own subtle anti-rural prejudices, which were offset only by the emergence of a small number of infuential township and county studies.[25] Employing routinely generated nominal records as a basic resource, these detailed studies uncovered close links between the ownership of landed property and family reproduction strategies and inheritance practices. They also highlighted the significance of chain migration and of linguistic and ethnic communities in the settlement and land acquisition processes.

The first thorough study of a rural Ontario community employing nominal sources was Gagan's intensive examination of mid-Victorian Peel county in south-central Ontario.[26] At its core was the persistent question of continuing access to farm land and the associated dilemmas of family inheritance. Gagan argued that the families in the county faced a virtual 'crisis' in access to land. The consequence was a complex series of altered family strategies and inheritance patterns, as well as migration.

Gagan's interpretation drew on and specified the implications of long-standing historical views of the material basis of Ontario's political culture. In these an early abundance of land gave way to comparative scarcity, fostering outmigration, greater reliance on government resource management, and a moderated liberal individualism in comparison with the expansive context of the United States.[27] Despite the path-breaking character of the research, subsequent rural studies both in older farming districts and in more recently settled areas have not generally documented a crisis in land availability. They have tended, rather, to emphasize the complex means by which families attained and maintained landed status, often in combination with intermittent wage work and in the context of ethnic community networks.[28]

Akenson's study of Leeds and Landsdowne township in southeastern Ontario critically assessed the long-standing belief that Catholic Irish immigrants were largely urban bound, locating a large majority in the countryside and documenting their unexpected farm success. Akenson argues that the gaining of title was not only the primary and absorbing motive of the families of the area, but the central thread of the whole institutional fabric of the community.[29]

Studies by Gaffield and Elliott, though very different in focus, have reinforced the view that family reproduction strategies, revolving about the ownership of smallholdings, remained at the heart of the Victorian Ontario experience. Gaffield is primarily concerned with the relation of language conflict and cultural geography to the rise of formal schooling in Ontario. He examines these relations in the hybrid agricultural and forest industry community of Prescott county in the Ottawa valley. His work documents the ways in which schooling and ethno-religious identities were fostered by the material and social contingencies of family reproduction, rather than by provincial public school policy or by ecclesiastical authority. The ownership of homes and land were mainstays of the family, which, Gaffield contends, was 'the unrivalled social institution of Prescott county' from the 1840s to the 1870s.[30]

Similar themes relating migration, landed settlement, and inheritance are pursued in Elliott's unique study concentrating on a population of over 700 immigrant Irish families rather than on a geographically defined locale. Elliott traces the emigration of these north Tipperary families to Ontario and their subsequent migration within the province and beyond. Once again he finds the geographic and social movement revolved primarily about the aim of providing secure futures for family members through the provision of farm land to as many heirs as possible. Migration itself was largely a strategy of landed heirship. Alternatives were sought, when necessary, in sales of original farms and family migration to new Ontario sites and, by the 1870s, in migration to the west. In sum, the accumulating rural studies have underscored the centrality of smallholding and family patrimony to nineteenth-century life in Ontario, though leaving open the question of the nature, extent, and timing of limitations on access to land.

Recent social history of nineteenth-century Ontario, both urban and rural, has been based largely on single-community studies, reflecting a larger intellectual movement. There are clear advantages to the local focus: multiple historical sources can be marshalled to bear on a single site, and a strong sense of place and familiarity with local figures, events, and institutions can facilitate a nuanced interpretation. Though these ideals have not always been fulfilled, in general the enterprise has been conspicuously successful, especially in studies that have used the community in question as a ground for critically examining more general interpretive themes.[31] At the same time, community studies necessarily sacrifice an analysis of the larger context. Local historical patterns were aspects of wider processes and structures – pieces of a larger puzzle. Moreover, they were experienced as such. Very few people in Victorian Ontario lived their lives wholly or even mainly in one locale. Even large numbers of community studies cannot merely be added up to arrive at an understanding of these more diverse experiences and more general contexts. Further, as we have argued above, the more general social and economic structures and experiences often figure in the basic assumptions of the community studies themselves.

One main objective of the current study is to complement the analytic and narrative histories of specific communities with a province-wide analysis. We are also aware that there is a price paid in taking a provincial focus. It necessarily forgoes familiarity with specific community issues, conflicts, and institutional forms in order to concentrate on more general patterns. Nevertheless, we believe it is a strategic time in Ontario's social and economic history to provide a wide-lens view of the structure of property holding, the processes of access to property, and their variations among social and cultural groups.

THE 1871 CENSUS AND THE CONFEDERATION YEARS

Every historical investigation can set out good reasons for the choice of favoured topic, period, and sources. We have discussed above the rationale for our substantive focus. As for our main source, the study is based largely on the especially detailed nominal data furnished by the 1871 manuscript census. The census includes unusual tabulations of individual ownership and occupancy of land, of home ownership and accumulation, and of a variety of social and cultural characteristics of individuals.

It is no mere coincidence that such a rich source of nominal evidence as the 1871 census permits us to examine property distributions shortly after Confederation. Although there were prior population counts and censuses, the 1871 census was the first national tally in Canada, conducted for the four original provinces, Quebec, Ontario, Nova Scotia, and New Brunswick. The new Canadian state had a considerable stake in mapping out population distributions and indicators of economic growth that could serve in the development of public policy, encourage immigration, and generally enhance the nation's claim on a place in the international order.

The 1871 census provides a unique perspective on an era of fundamental change, marked by the end of colonial rule and the achievement of Confederation just four years earlier. In economic terms, the decades immediately after mid-century in Ontario witnessed the significant spread of commercial farming, the rapid growth of a dense network of provincial railways, and the early phase of capitalist industrialization in major cities.[32] The tariff question and the movement towards the National Policy of 1878 were major political issues of the era. The unexceptional people of mid-Victorian Ontario were party to and in some cases deeply affected by these political and economic developments. For the great majority, however, life was organized about the seemingly more mundane questions of starting and maintaining families and making a living, often through the purchase of land, homes, and other small property. Central features of this largely untold story can be recaptured from the census data.

If the 1871 census provides rare historical evidence, it still suffers from the limitations of any single source. In this case, there is the limited perspective of a nineteenth-century, state-sponsored enumeration and the inexperience and biases of the census takers. Of course, the problems of flawed evidence are not unique to historical census analysis; we attempt to recognize their specific consequences for our interpretations. We also enlist a number of other institutional and literary sources to supplement the basic data. Our most systematic use of additional sources occurs in chapter 6, where the aggregate reports of tax assessments for subdistricts are employed as a basis for a series of estimates of taxable real estate wealth distributions from a knowledge of patterns of property holding.

A single census also yields a cross-sectional picture. But further analysis is possible. If one attends to the implications of key assumptions, intriguing inferences can be drawn about the processes of property acquisition and accumulation from age patterns in the census cross-section. Moreover, these patterns provide a perspective on the intersection of individual experience and structural conditions. We pursue the implications of this relationship between experience and structure throughout the analysis. Finally, a census-based, province-wide study has the obvious, but considerable, merit of contributing to the body of recent historical literature that has 'rediscovered the majority' of rural residents who populated nineteenth-century Ontario.[33]

THE CENSUS SAMPLE

A study of the entire province of Ontario in 1871 requires a sampling procedure simply to make the task feasible. The sample must, of course, represent accurately the characteristics of the population and of the social groups of primary interest. Following the method introduced by Soltow in earlier studies, a *film-manuscript* sample of 5,699 individuals was drawn from the first schedule of the 1871 Ontario census on microfilm. Specifically, the microfilms of the first schedule were placed on a reader (the same machine was used throughout), and a sheet of paper, used as a marker, was placed on the read-bin screen. The sampled individuals were determined first by sampling manuscript pages. The reader arm was turned five complete revolutions from the beginning of the film (thus ensuring that the first page of a township had the same chance of being selected as any other page). If the marker coincided with a census page, then all appropriate individuals on that page and on the page following were selected for the sample. If the census page did not coincide with the paper on the screen, individuals on the next two census pages qualified for the sample. In order to equalize probabilities of selection throughout the province, every second microfilm reel was turned in the opposite direction to the one preceding it.

The manuscript census records information for all individuals in households. The first schedule gives the basic personal and demographic information employed in this study: age, sex, occupation, religion, ethnic origin, country of birth, and literacy.[34] Since the study focuses first on property owning, the information of schedule 1 was recorded for *adult men and women (age 20 or over) who were heads of households*. In addition, since the majority of men were prospective household heads, *all other adult men* were included. Women who were not heads of households, but who held property in their own names, were also selected. There were only ten such women who qualified for the sample. Thus, the sample consisted of all men aged 20 or over and all women 20 or over who were heads of households or otherwise property owners.

The procedure was applied to all 116 microfilm reels of schedule one for Ontario. The 5,699 individuals in the sample represented 1.4 per cent of the province's population and about 1,100 of the 80,000 separate manuscript pages. The sample includes 5,386 men over age 20 and 313 women. Among the men, 2,777 considered themselves farmers.

The crucial data on ownership of land, homes, and other real estate and on farm acreage, ownership, and tenancy were recorded on the third and fourth (of nine) schedules of the census.[35] Happily, both schedules include page and line references to schedule 1, so that individuals named on the first can be linked directly to the other two. The data were manually linked.[36]

The results of the sample can be compared with the simple tabulations reported for a number of variables in the published aggregate volumes. Cross-classifications of two or more variables are not presented in these volumes. Table 1.1 gives comparisons for a number of main variables. It can be seen that in every case the distributions of the sample quite closely match those of the aggregate census. Particularly important for this study is the close fit between the tabulations of acreage owned and occupied for the sample and population. The results give us confidence that the sample will represent the population well in the various analyses to follow.

We also report that the sample yields a very close proportional representation of the population of the ninety census districts of Ontario in 1871. A copy of the map from volume 1 of the census of 1871 shows the ninety districts. The close approximation of the geographic distribution results from the fact that the microfilms are arranged by district, and the crank-turning procedure ensures rather uniform selection per running foot of film.

THE STUDY

With a few important exceptions, historical studies of wealth and property holding have tended to examine the upper reaches of the wealth distributions. Usually as a consequence of limited evidence, they often estimate only the holdings of the wealthiest few in a population. Employing a sample of the full census, this study asks both more general and more specific questions.

We begin with an examination of landownership among the majority of Ontario men who were farmers in 1871 (chapter 2). One guiding notion we bring to the analysis follows Laslett's general account and Katz's specific interpretation for nineteenth-century Hamilton that deep and abiding structures of inequality were not only compatible with but sustained by significant opportunity for individual mobility.[37] In the present analysis we consider mobility in terms of the process of land acquisition using the ownership by age distribution, and we review the implications of the numbers who were landless in the context of this process. The evidence throws new light on the question of whether there was a crisis in access to land in the province prior to 1871 and its implications for proletarianization.

Similar expectations regarding stable, but open, structures of inequality are brought tò the analysis of the ownership of homes in chapter 3. Home ownership was the most widespread form of property ownership in nineteenth-century Ontario, and, like landownership, it was a matter both of

TABLE 1.1 Comparisons for selected variables between the film-manuscript sample and published census aggregates for Ontario, 1871

	Census		Sample	
Variable	Number	Per cent	Number	Per cent
	Males 20 and older		Males 20 and older	
1. Age	135,533	34.6	1,802	33.5
20–29	93,173	23.8	1,295	24.0
30–39	69,310	17.7	949	17.6
40–49	48,309	12.3	647	12.0
50–59	28,650	7.3	459	8.5
60–69	13,013	3.3	176	3.3
70–79	3,013	0.8	48	0.9
80–89	418	0.1	10	0.2
90–99	391,493	100.0	5,386	100.0
	Males & females, all ages		Males, 20 and older	
2. Religion	274,162	16.9	894	16.6
Catholic	88,630	5.5	259	4.8
Baptist	330,995	20.4	1,124	20.9
Church of England	462,264	28.5	1,433	26.6
Methodist	356,442	22.0	1,216	22.6
Presbyterian	110,358	6.8	460	8.5
Other	1,620,851	100.0	5,386	100.0
3. Origin	444,711	27.4	1,542	28.6
English & Welsh	328,889	20.3	1,098	20.4
Scotch	559,442	34.5	1,808	33.6
Irish	158,608	9.8	512	9.5
German	75,383	4.7	260	4.8
French	53,818	3.3	166	3.1
Other	1,620,851	100.0	5,386	100.0
4. Occupation	226,883	49.0	2,777	51.6
Farmer	62,179	13.4	660	12.3
Labourer	174,362	37.6	1,949	36.2
Other	463,424	100.0	5,386	100.0
	All		Adult male farmers	
5. Occupiers of land	144,212	83.7	2,318	83.5
Owners	28,046	16.3	326	11.7
Tenant, employee	–	–	133	4.8
Not stated	172,258	100.0	2,777	100.0
6. Average acres of land owned*	$\dfrac{19,605,019}{414,000} = 47.3$		$\dfrac{265,235}{5,699} = 46.5$	
7. Average acres occupied*	$\dfrac{16,161,676}{414,000} = 39.0$		$\dfrac{231,934}{5,669} = 40.7$	

*The number of owners in the population is estimated as 414,000 = 391,493 x (5,669/5,386), where 5,669 is the total number in the sample and 391,493 and 5,386 represent population and sample totals of males 20 and older, respectively. SOURCES: The film-manuscript sample of size 5,669. *Census of Canada, 1871*, vols. I–V. *1.* Table F-I, 36–9, vol. V. *2.* Table II, 142, 143, vol. V. *3.* Table III, 280, 281, vol. V. *4.* Table XIII, 286–97, vol. V. *5.* Table XX, 8, 9, vol. V. *6–7.* Table XXI, 48, 49, vol. V.

family sustenance and of capital accumulation. In mid-Victorian Ontario, as elsewhere in the last century, land and homes had their primary social significance as foundations of household production and family security. At the same time they were the most widespread forms of private capital and wealth accumulation and, thus, represented the multiple, tiny engines of nineteenth-century economic growth. We consider both implications.

In addition to land and homes, the census tabulated a variety of other forms of real and productive property. In chapter 3 the analysis of home ownership is extended to include these other forms of property, for example, barns, shops, factories, warehouses, and vehicles. The analysis is focused on the implications of a division among three main groups: first, those who had accumulated secure or very substantial estates; second, true smallholders of a family residence and small parcels of farm land; and third, those who were quite literally propertyless.

In addition to divisions of property, ethnic and religious communities were central features of Ontario's deeply Protestant culture of the last century. For this reason, throughout the analysis cultural patterns are examined with the broad expectation that they were very influential in shaping the structure of ownership and opportunities for property acquisition. More specific hypotheses are considered in the course of the analysis.

In addition to ethnic and religious groups, there are several minority populations of special interest when property ownership in the nineteenth century is considered. One of these is identified by the census tabulation of illiterates. The census literacy evidence has been fruitfully used in prior studies, despite its acknowledged limitations. In chapter 4 we employ the tabulation for two purposes. First, recognizing that literacy had increasingly become a symbol of Victorian respectability and progress, we provide provincial estimates of the growth of literacy in the province and identify the social pockets of deeply entrenched illiteracy. Further, we use the tabulation to ask about property ownership among this least articulate and visible minority in old Ontario.

Throughout the analysis of chapters 2, 3, and 4 we also consider the patterns of property ownership and illiteracy among the small minority of women who were heads of households or owners in their own right. They are compared with their counterparts, the male heads of households.

Chapter 5 focuses on another minority, Canadian emigrants to the United States. Nineteenth-century emigrants from Ontario are often noted, but wholly obscure, figures in historical analysis. In some cases they have been seen as fleeing a deteriorating landed economy, in others simply as rational economic actors moving to a higher-wage economy, and in others mainly as sojourners passing through the Ontario way station en route to the 'American Dream.' In any case, they have not previously been the focus of systematic study. To provide a context for the Ontario findings in a period of substantial out-migration, Canadians in the northern states are identified and their economic circumstances compared with other immigrants in the United States or with native-born Americans.

As noted above, in chapter 6 we employ the sample data and 1870 dollar values of tax assessments for Ontario's subdistricts to provide a number of estimates of the structure and magnitude of inequality among subdistricts and individuals in the province in 1871. The series of approximations informs us about the overall structure of inequality of nineteenth-century Ontario. Chapter 7 serves to review briefly and to reflect on the preceding analysis.

Finally, the appendix presents a detailed census reanalysis based on the sample data. The census sample provides a unique opportunity to extend the very limited analysis of the 1871 census provided in the aggregate tabulations of the census volumes. For the most part, the published tabulations are limited to a few relationships among two or three variables. The categories used reflect contemporary usage and are often difficult to employ in secondary analysis. In our census re-analysis, population by age profiles are employed to make several estimations of patterns of social and demographic change. These relationships serve as a backdrop for the main analyses of the study, for example, with respect to population growth, rural to urban transitions, ethnic and religious patterns, the characteristics of women heads of households, and new estimates of Ontario's out-migration. As the most detailed evidence yet available on Ontario's nineteenth-century socio-demographic patterns, we hope the appendix may also serve as a background for other historical studies.

A further comment is warranted on what we do not attempt to do. It is clear that in focusing on provincial patterns and selected social groups, the analysis cannot do justice to a full range of subregional and community variations in property holding. The study's main concerns preclude detailed analysis of geographic patterns. We do not deny the salience of a multitude of local variations on the general themes; on the contrary. The provincial focus reflects a judgment on research priorities and a specific design for analysis that follows from it. Different but parallel decisions are made, for example, in the selection of a given community for historical study, involving questions about the availability and quality of sources and about the implications of the specific setting for larger historical issues. Similarly, an adequate analysis of provincial geographic patterns requires a specifically geographic conceptual framework and an alternative methodology and sampling strategy. Sample size is a question both of analytic focus and of available resources. The sample selected here is sufficient for the intended purposes. An additional geographic analysis stretches it too far. We leave that topic to another study.

A last word on our approach is in order. Questions about property distributions invite quantitative answers. We are convinced that a knowledge of these distributions is essential to an understanding of the historical structures that lie behind them. At the same time, within the limits of our evidence and the relevant social historical literature, we have attempted to look beyond the structures to recognize and understand the social processes and cultural experiences that sustained and changed them.

2

Landownership and Land Occupancy in Nineteenth-Century Ontario

INTRODUCTION

If it is true that both merchant and early industrial fortunes could be made in mid-Victorian Ontario, wealth was still primarily in land and farm production and chiefly dispersed among the large numbers of smallholders and their families. Though the early industrial development of the 1860s and 1870s was pregnant with the future, in this sense it remained a relatively slender institutional order resting on a substantial farming base. At the same time, landownership was still very much idealized as the foundation of a largely egalitarian social order of independent yeomen. The Simcoe county farmer and rhymester Alexander McLachlan captured the sentiment in two lines: 'He is King upon a throne / Who has acres of his own!'[1]

In this chapter we focus on the distribution of landownership and land occupancy, first among the majority of men who were farmers and, comparatively, among other occupational and social groups. We also consider the distribution of landed wealth in terms of acreage owned. McInnis's evidence that farming families in Ontario by 1861 constituted a relatively homogeneous class of smallholders is a key point of departure.[2] In contrast, as already noted, Gagan and others have argued that by the end of the 1860s accessibility to farm land had become seriously constricted, at least in some areas, fostering rural depopulation and the growth of a class of landless families.[3]

The fact is we know very little about the distribution of farm wealth in the last century and surprisingly little about property or wealth distributions of any kind in the past, despite recent work.[4] Assessment rolls have been the primary source mined in community-level historical studies to provide evidence of wealthholding for individuals, though some have recently turned

Barrie farmstead, Lanark county, c. 1824

to probate records.[5] For nineteenth-century Ontario, for example, we have studies of Hamilton, Toronto, and Peel and Wentworth counties in south-central Ontario and of Leeds and Lansdowne township in the southeastern corner of the province.[6] Each of these studies, obviously, is limited to a specific locale and population.

In a different tradition there is Gustav Myers's pioneering description of the concentration of economic power in the nineteenth century. Focusing on the select few very wealthy men, he provides a vivid sense of the politics of accumulation but no systematic evidence of the distribution of ownership and wealth.[7]

The census sample for 1871 allows us to draw on evidence from several schedules collated for individuals to explore the key questions of land occupancy, landownership, and tenancy in old Ontario. Since this analysis involves several related issues and a variety of different groups, we outline its organization at the outset. We first focus on landownership and occupancy among farmers, defined by occupational title. The perspective is widened to all adult men in order to compare farmers and other major occupational groups and to consider rural and urban patterns. The analysis of occupancy also raises the question of the extent of tenancy in the province. We then turn to landownership of women heads of households in 1871. The process of land acquisition and its relation to the structure of inequality is next analysed in terms of age by ownership patterns for the male farming population. A similar examination of patterns of landed wealth accumulation follows. We take up the questions of differences in landowning between native-born and immigrant farmers, and in separate analyses we consider variations among religious and ethnic communities. The difference in farm ownership between Ontario's Irish-Catholic and Irish-Protestant groups is pursued in detail. Finally, we examine the overall inequality in landed wealth among farmers in mid-Victorian Ontario and briefly assess it comparatively.

LAND IN POLICY, IDEOLOGY, AND POPULAR CULTURE

The ownership of farm land was at the centre of the web that linked ideology and politics with popular culture and everyday experience in nineteenth-century Ontario. It has been suggested that official policy towards the distribution of land in Ontario promoted inequality in the name of social order and economic progress. Upper Canada's chief justice, John Elmsley, could gravely ask, 'What is capital but property unequally distributed?'[8] The policy has often been characterized as both intentional and effective in ensuring the growth of a landless wage labour force.[9] In fact, one may doubt both the intentionality and the effectiveness of the policies, given the limited consequences for access to land of various changes in the Land Act and the emphasis of state policy on settlement and revenues.[10]

The opening in the late 1850s and 1860s of the Ottawa-Huron tract, between the Ottawa River and Georgian Bay, was the major political response to the concerns that agricultural expansion in the province would be curtailed by the filling up of lands suitable for settlement and cultivation. To twentieth-century observers it seems remarkable that this region of thin soils and rock outcroppings could be thought to hold promise of intense agricultural settlement. That it was testifies to the potent combination in official circles represented by Victorian Ontario's enthusiasm for agricultural expansion and recognition of the drive for landownership. Fewer pioneering farmers actually took up the challenge than had been anticipated by politicians and land agents. The 1868 Ontario Free Grant and Homestead Act represented official re-evaluation of the settlement policy and acknowledged the complementarity of agricultural colonization and timber exploitation.[11]

Whatever the limitations imposed by the Shield lands and the motives behind shifting land policies, the questions of the distribution and access to land remain open and central to our understanding of nineteenth-century Ontario society. In the first place, the ideal of the 'self-made man' continued as a central thread of old Ontario's political culture and was founded largely on the notion of landed independence. Allen Smith has documented the force of these images in the last century: 'As the figure who had been most intimately associated with one of the central features of Canada's existence – the clearing of the land – the pioneer farmer received particularly close attention from Canadian acolytes of the self-made man. By his hard work he at once advanced himself and gave content to his country's development. He was, claimed his literary friends, in the fullest sense his own master, free of all constraint and interference, quite literally able to shape his world as he wished, the heir to an abundant and fulfilling future.'[12] Throughout the last century, at least among the common people, landholding remained the most visible symbol of individual 'success,' – or, in that century's terms, of a measure of competency and autonomy.[13] Ironically, land policy and the ideology of yeoman farming have been far more readily documented than have the historical realities of landholding, to which we turn.

LANDOWNERSHIP AND OCCUPANCY IN 1871

Our first analysis is focused on adult males 20 and older who gave 'farmer' as their occupation on the census. This task is complicated for the 1871 census, since the enumeration instructions specified that sons following their father's occupations and associated with them were to be given their father's occupational titles. Specifically, a farmer's son, working on his father's farm, was to be classified as a farmer.[14] Thus, only 2,117 or about three-quarters of the 2,777 adult male farmers in the sample were the heads of families. The distinction bears directly on interpretations of farm ownership. We consider the implications for estimates of landlessness among farmers and by extension for the probable size of the waged labour pool that had developed by 1871.

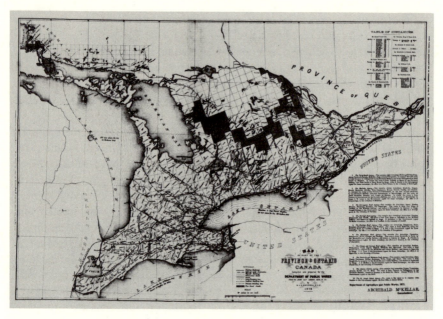

Map 2. Ontario, 1872, free grant lands available for settlement (shaded areas)

Let us ask a simple but telling question: What proportion of Ontario farmers owned land in 1871? The sample evidence indicates that only 62.6 per cent were owners.[15] This figure seems rather low, considering that it is the proportion among *farmers* and that their average age was 40.4 years. To say, alternatively, that the probability of adult male farmers' being propertyless was 0.374 (1 − 0.626) suggests that Ontario's farm economy was quite precarious. The figure might even be cited as evidence that landlessness and incipient proletarianization had spread quite widely across rural Ontario by the time of Confederation. This view is more than just plausible; as we noted above, several prominent interpretations of the growth of capitalist relations in Ontario require that it be taken seriously.[16] There are a number of additional questions to be considered, however, before we conclude that landlessness had become widespread either in fact or in expectation among farmers.

First, it is clear that not everyone could immediately own land at ages 20 or 21 or upon migration to Ontario, nor would any one have had false hopes in this regard. Second, how do we interpret the fact that the estimate includes adult sons working on their father's farms well beyond age 20? Without doubt, most sons worked family farms in the expectation of landed inheritance or due reward for their continuing contributions to the household economy. Simply excluding them eclipses the social dynamic of household economies and the implications of inheritance practices. Finally, tenant families must be considered in addition to the owners of land, since for some farmers the process of land acquisition would have involved tenancy at an early stage.

We can begin to put the simple rates of landownership and landlessness into perspective by estimating the numbers of farming sons at home. The 1871 manuscript census does not record family relationships. One relevant distinction, however, is between the landownership of heads of households and adult male non-heads. We know that non-heads will not normally be recorded as owners, since the census reflected social norms and practice with respect to household organization: 'All properties belonging to the same family are to be entered under one reference to the head of the family.'[17] Thus, farmers' sons at home would be considered owners only if they had title to a separate plot of land. In fact, the contrast is stark: almost all heads of farm households were owners – fully 95 per cent; among non-heads there were virtually no landowners (less than 1 per cent).

The sharp distinction between farm heads and non-heads needs to be qualified further. Among the landless non-heads were farmers' sons who had prospects of landed inheritance, though not yet legal title, and other, single adult farm labourers. Although the 1871 manuscript census does not specify the relationships among members of households, it is very orderly in first listing heads of households and spouses (or widowed and single heads), followed by children (in birth order), other relatives, and unrelated members (visitors, domestic help, hired hands, and so forth). The distinction between farmers and their sons was not one made in drawing the original sample. A second examination of the census manuscripts for every tenth district revealed on the basis of surnames and the order of listing that just about half of the adult, male non-heads of farmers' households were likely to be sons.

A revised estimate for the sample as a whole, then, would leave us with about 12 per cent (half of the non-heads, $(2,777 - 2,117) \times 0.5$, or 330) of those enumerated as farmers actually farmers' sons at home. In terms of their household circumstances and life-cycle experiences, these sons are sensibly considered neither wholly landless nor legally propertied. If one assumed that both heads and all their sons were owners or potential owners, the initial estimate of landlessness among *farmers* would fall to the low estimate of just 15 or 16 per cent.

We emphasize that such an estimate raises largely unanswered questions about the chances of farmers' sons' acquiring land, as well as about the social relationships within farm households. Only a few dependent sons working their family land expected to inherit land directly. Others may have been able eventually to acquire title, but we as yet know nothing of this process. In this context, Gagan's study of Peel county is the most useful to date. He has documented the hybrid inheritance strategy commonly adopted among Ontario farmers. It combined a measure of equality and security for widows and children with an effort to maintain farm property intact. Heirs normally assumed responsibility for the care and provision of their mothers and sisters and for outright cash settlements or annual instalments to brothers. Gagan suggests the burden was often severe and sometimes disabling to an inheritor's capacity to maintain the original farm.[18] In any case, the system ensured that only one dependent son could look forward to immediate landed inheritance, though it may also be the case that other sons were enabled by the arrangements to enter the land market on their own terms.

In sum, we argue that in their social and economic experience farmers' sons straddled the line between smallholder and landless – they occupied a suspended status. Their lifetime experience would be determined largely by their family's capacity to transfer land or confer on them compensating chattels or benefits. We also note, however, that if nineteenth-century landed households were largely collective productive units, they were not unitary in interests and sentiments. Like most adult women, adult men who had not assumed household headship were essential contributors to the household commonweal, but at the same time they were thoroughly subordinate in legal and social status.

Setting aside the question of the landed status of farmers, we enlist both the landownership and the land occupancy records of the census to consider more fully the uses of land in mid-Victorian Ontario, including occupancy among non-farmers and in urban as well as rural areas.

Actual land occupancy was recorded on the agricultural schedule (Cultivated Lands, Field Products, Plants and Fruits), as distinct from the real estate schedule, which recorded land owned anywhere in the dominion. Table 2.1 gives the rates of ownership and occupancy for the three main occupational groups, farmers, labourers, and all others. We have not attempted a more refined classification of occupations; since the proportion of landowners among the non-farm population is relatively small, detailed occupational comparisons would stretch the sample thinly.[19] The table does distinguish the male labour force for rural and urban areas and gives age-standardized rates as well as actual rates.[20]

TABLE 2.1
Acreage owned and occupied among adult males in Ontario, 1871, by occupation and urban-rural residence

Urban-rural residence and occupation	Number in sample	Proportion owning		Proportion occupying	
		Rate	Standardized rate	Rate	Standardized rate
All	5,386	0.377	0.377	0.546	0.546
Farmers	2,777	0.626	0.604	0.730	0.707
Labourers	660	0.048	0.053	0.336	0.355
Others	1,949	0.132	0.142	0.355	0.370
Rural	4,357	0.451	0.447	0.621	0.619
Farmers	2,752	0.630	0.608	0.732	0.710
Labourers	499	0.054	0.060	0.347	0.371
Others	1,106	0.184	0.200	0.468	0.497
Urban	1,029	0.064	0.068	0.228	0.239
Farmers	25	0.240	0.168	0.520	0.407
Labourers	161	0.031	0.029	0.304	0.302
Others	843	0.065	0.069	0.205	0.219

NOTE: The age-specific rates for ages 20–29, 30–39 ... 70–79 have been weighted by the overall population sizes in these classes in obtaining the standardized rates.
SOURCE: The sample of 5,386 adult males from the Ontario census of 1871.

Considering the entire male labour force, the table indicates that men in all three occupational groups owned land, although only 5 per cent (0.048) of labourers and about twice as many, 13 per cent (0.132), of all the various others – journeymen and workers with craft titles, as well as masters, millers, shopkeepers, merchants, and manufacturers – were owners. The table also shows that the occupational differences were not highly age dependent. Since farmers were the oldest group, their age-standardized rate is slightly lower (0.604) than the actual rate, and the age-standardized rates for the other two groups are somewhat higher (0.053 and 0.142). It is important to recall that these are landownership rates only, not rates of ownership of homes, shops, or manufacturing establishments. The ownership of the latter group is taken up in chapter 3.

These data reveal that among all adult men, including farmers, a quite substantial 37.7 per cent owned some plot of land. In the countryside, about 45 per cent of the male labour force owned land, while only 6.4 per cent of adult men in urban areas were landowners.

The ownership rates are compared with those who reported that they *occupied* land in the enumeration district in which they resided.[21] Obviously the latter will exceed ownership rates, but the difference is of considerable interest. Was there a significant class of tenant farmers? Moreover, the census enumerator's instructions made it clear that, in addition to tenant farming, land was cultivated by a wide range of households whose members were not considered farmers at all.[22]

At the outset, we can see that land occupancy considerably exceeded landownership in Ontario in 1871. Over half of *all* adult men in Ontario (0.546) occupied some land for the purpose of cultivation. That over 70 per cent (0.730) of all farmers occupied land is understandable; more striking is the fact that over a third of all labourers and those in 'other occupations' (0.336 and 0.355) were also land occupiers.

The table provides further detail. The rate of occupancy for farmers in rural areas is virtually the same as the total rate (0.732), given their predominance there. Not surprisingly it is also in the rural areas that the largest proportion of labourers and those in the heterogeneous 'other' occupations worked the land. The rates are notably high: about 35 per cent (0.347) of the rural labourers and nearly half, 47 per cent (0.468), of all other men in the rural labour force lived on cultivable land.

The evidence also bears out the impressions of the census officials that even in Ontario's cities, towns, and villages it was very common to cultivate land. The vital importance of gardening for urban household economies in 1871 is underscored by the fact that one in three urban male labourers and one in five of those in other skilled and semi-skilled occupations reported that they occupied cultivable land. The Ontario data confirm that such household cultivation was a widespread practice both among labouring families and among significant numbers of other urban households as well.

Those who occupied and worked land could, of course, be owners, tenants, or, perhaps, merely farm labourers residing on plots separate from their employers. Despite the predominance of rural experience and the agricultural economy in Victorian Ontario, we have very little knowledge of the importance of these distinctions. The census sample permits us to pursue the question, distinguishing owners, tenants, and others who worked farms. The latter were presumably hired labourers. The question of tenancy is of considerable interest, given its implications either as a temporary, initial stage in the process of acquiring landed title or, alternatively, as a form of permanent dispossession, as was the case in so much of Europe by the nineteenth century.

The prevailing, somewhat complacent, view for Ontario has been that in a land of freeholders tenancy was normally a temporary stage, 'not regarded with much favour.'[23] Recently, Marr has addressed the question directly, drawing on debates in the U.S. literature and on both the published census for Ontario in 1871 and the manuscript census data for York county.[24] He begins by noting the wide variation in rates of tenancy among Ontario's counties (0.013 to 0.295). He also provides initial evidence that tenancy was for some, such as the young and the foreign born, a calculated step in entering the land market on the course to owner-occupancy. Marr strongly suggests that tenancy was generally not a form of marginality, but rather a life-cycle stage for aspiring farmers. This interpretation conforms with the experience in the northern United States.[25] Table 2.2 provides relevant distinctions among the occupiers of land in Ontario.

The several census schedules permit a fairly elaborate analysis of the relation of men to the land in 1871, but the different angles make it difficult to bring a single image into focus. In the foregoing table the rates of land-ownership throughout the new dominion were compared with the rates of land occupancy. Here we distinguish owners and tenants among those listed on the agricultural schedules as *occupants*.[26] In this case it is the ownership of the occupied, cultivated land that is at issue, rather than ownership of any land, as recorded on the real estate schedule and considered above. We consider owners and occupiers among all adult men, not only among farmers.

The first portion of the table gives the overall rates of ownership and tenancy. Whereas about 37 per cent (0.373) of all men were owners of land in 1871, only about 11 per cent (0.114) were tenants. According to the aggregate census volumes, this one-tenth of adult men cultivated 16 per cent (0.159) of Ontario's *farms* in 1871.[27] Among *farmers* in our sample the tenancy rate is still only 12 per cent (0.117), as the second row of the table shows. The majority of farmers occupying land were owners, about 60 per cent (0.602). Further, among farming heads 81 per cent were owner-occupiers, whereas only 1 per cent of non-heads were owners, including the farmers' sons discussed earlier.

A small number of those calling themselves labourers also owned land they occupied, around 6 per cent (0.062), and some 14 per cent were tenants (0.138). Approximately the reverse was the case for all those men who were neither farmers nor labourers by occupation: about 15 per cent (0.151) were owners and 10 per cent (0.101) tenants. As in table 2.1, we distinguish the rural and urban populations of the province. Labourers were slightly more likely to be both landowners and tenants in *urban* areas than they were in the countryside, confirming the value of plots of land for subsistence among the least skilled men in Ontario's growing cities and towns.

The table further distinguishes those occupying no acreage or less than one acre from those occupying one acre and those occupying two or more

TABLE 2.2
Proportion of owners and renters among adult males in Ontario, 1871, by acreage occupied, urban-rural residence, and occupation

Urban-rural residence and occupation	Total sample			Landless or occupying less than one acre			Occupying one acre			Occupying two or more acres		
		Proportion			Proportion			Proportion			Proportion	
	Number	Owner	Tenant	Number	Owner	Tenant	Number	Owner	Tenant	Number	Owner	Tenant
All	5,386	0.373	0.114	2,446	0.032	0.059	630	0.152	0.162	2,310	0.794	0.159
Farmers	2,777	0.602	0.117	750	0.023	0.011	64	0.141	0.250	1,963	0.839	0.154
Labourers	660	0.062	0.138	438	0.016	0.080	148	0.088	0.236	74	0.284	0.284
Others	1,949	0.151	0.101	1,258	0.043	0.081	418	0.177	0.122	273	0.612	0.161
Rural	4,357	0.439	0.109	1,652	0.026	0.030	447	0.134	0.161	2,258	0.802	0.158
Farmers	2,752	0.606	0.117	738	0.023	0.009	60	0.133	0.267	1,954	0.840	0.153
Labourers	499	0.058	0.126	326	0.009	0.052	109	0.083	0.239	64	0.266	0.313
Others	1,106	0.197	0.084	588	0.039	0.043	278	0.155	0.108	240	0.633	0.158
Urban	1,029	0.091	0.133	794	0.044	0.121	183	0.197	0.164	52	0.442	0.212
Farmers	25	0.200	0.200	12	0.000	0.083	4	0.250	0.000	9	0.444	0.444
Labourers	161	0.075	0.174	112	0.036	0.161	39	0.103	0.231	10	0.400	0.100
Others	843	0.091	0.123	670	0.046	0.115	140	0.221	0.150	33	0.455	0.182

SOURCE: See table 2.1. Among the 5,386 there were 2,008 who were designated as 'owners,' 614 designated as 'tenants,' and 2,764 others; 78 owners reported no acreage as possessed or occupied.

acres. The distinctions are more or less arbitrary, but they allow us to separate those who were virtually landless from very puny cultivators, whose gardening supplemented other forms of subsistence, and from those who were either subsistence farmers or farmers with marketable surpluses. Later in this analysis we consider in more detail the size distributions of farms.

In these terms, among all adult men in the sample 2,446 or 45 per cent were landless, 630 or 12 per cent had access to just one acre of land, and 2,310 or 43 per cent occupied two or more acres, as shown in row 1 of the table. Thus, landless and puny property occupiers were a clear majority of Ontario's adult men (about 57 per cent), if we ignore the uncertain status of farmers' sons among them. By comparison, among all farmers 27 per cent were recorded as landless, including farmers' sons at home, just 2 per cent were occupiers of the tiny one-acre plots, and 71 per cent occupied two or more acres.

Further strong evidence of the uses of urban land for cultivation in 1871 is found in the rates of ownership and tenancy for both one-acre sites and two or more acres. Among all adult men in urban areas about 18 per cent (183/1,029) occupied an acre of city or town land, and apparently 5 per cent (52/1,029) were recorded as occupying as much as two or more acres, as shown in the third and fourth sections of the table. The experience of Montreal, as revealed in studies by Bradbury and DeLottinville, suggests how population growth and the urban middle-class reform movements of the 1870s would soon press this cultivated land out of the city centres to the urban fringe.[28] There are no comparable Ontario studies, but presumably in the province's major cities there was a similar transition, though smaller places likely tolerated urban gardening and animal raising for some years. Despite the transition, to 1871 the line between urban and rural life in Ontario was blurred by the routine uses of land for family sustenance in both contexts.

In rural areas a bare majority of men, 52 per cent, occupied two or more acres (2,258/4,357), and among them 80 per cent were owners (0.802) and 16 per cent were tenants (0.158). Another 10 per cent occupied just one acre of rural land, with a much lower ownership rate, 13 per cent (0.134), and about the same rate of tenancy as urban areas (0.161). Thirty-eight per cent of rural men were landless (1,652/4,357).

Thus, for Ontario as a whole in 1871 the rate of land tenancy among adult men was relatively low, merely 11 per cent among all men, and around 12 per cent among farmers, and 14 per cent among labourers. By way of comparison with the United States, Atack and Bateman use a large sample of rural townships in the northern states to estimate tenancy rates by states in the midwest and northeast. In the states adjacent to Ontario (Wisconsin, Illinois, Indiana, Michigan, Ohio, Pennsylvania, and New York) the rates of tenancy among *farms* were also quite modest, varying from 20.6 per cent in Pennsylvania to 7.1 and 7.9 in Michigan and New York.[29]

In comparison with tenancy, a much larger proportion of adult men (45 per cent) were virtually landless in Ontario, noting once again that among this group, farmers' sons held an ambiguous, quasi-landed status. Moreover, in a society in which even a small urban plot of land was a significant household resource, one cannot discount the potential liability entailed by landlessness for non-farmers. Despite the numbers who had little or no cultivable land, however, it is still the relatively high rates of landownership that are most striking – 37 per cent among all men over age twenty and some 60 per cent among all farmers.

Cross-sectional patterns of landownership and tenancy, of course, do not reveal the process of property attainment that generated them or the expectations of the young and the dependent in this respect. Nor do they reveal the particulars of the process of settlement and its effects on geographic dispersion and property stratification. But key questions about the property attainment process can be addressed with reference to age patterns, and we do so below. First, we consider the interesting question of the minority of women who were landowners.

LANDOWNERSHIP AMONG WOMEN HEADS OF HOUSEHOLDS

Though the landed status of adult sons of farmers was ambivalent, some had reasonable expectations of inheriting farm land or of making some cash arrangement that would assist them in purchasing their own farms. These expectation's were largely denied to women, either as widows or as farm daughters. Even being a female head of household in 1871 was a rare phenomenon. Yet the sample shows that among these few heads surprising numbers were landowners. The evidence of ownership is given in table 2.3 by the age of women in the sample. To provide an appropriate context for analysis, the proportion of owners among female heads of households is compared with the figures for male heads.

For the sample as a whole, one in three women *heads* owned some land, specifically, 33.5 per cent. Male heads, obviously, were even more likely to be landholders, about 53 per cent. Still, given the prevailing legal and social prejudices, the landownership levels among women exceeded our expectation. The proportions of owners by age suggest that perhaps as many

TABLE 2.3
Proportions of landowners among female and male heads of households in Ontario, 1871, by age

Age	Female heads		Male heads	
	No. in sample	Proportion owning	No. in sample	Proportion owning
20–29	21	0.29	623	0.36
30–39	56	0.18	1,080	0.45
40–49	71	0.38	888	0.60
50–59	70	0.41	611	0.62
60–69	57	0.32	418	0.67
70 and over	38	0.39	186	0.57
	313	0.335	3,806	0.528

SOURCE: The film-manuscript sample.

as four in ten women heads over age 40 were owners of land (for male heads over 40, the rate is over 60 per cent).

Larger proportions of women heads were occupiers of land than were owners. The difference is intriguing. Over half (0.54) the female heads of households reported occupying land in Ontario. In urban areas nearly 30 per cent of the women heads cultivated some plot of land, although most were renters; only 6 per cent actually owned land. The evidence underscores the fact that for urban women land and gardening were of particular value in managing family economies. In rural areas, women heads were obviously better positioned to secure some living from land, with exactly two-thirds (0.67) being occupiers and nearly half being landowners (0.48). Given the relatively high proportions of women occupiers and owners, it bears reiteration that these few female heads of households were a tiny minority of married women. In the following chapter we extend this analysis by examining the home ownership and relative wealth in property of these exceptional few. Home ownership was probably an even more vital resource than land for the maintenance of a female-headed household.

For most women who acquired ownership of land the process was a simple one – they inherited it on widowhood. And in that acquisition they were also exceptional. Current, relatively limited analyses suggest it was unusual for husbands to will legal title of property to their wives. Among men, on the other hand, land inheritance was common; land acquisition was even more widely anticipated and the processes were more predictable.

THE ACQUISITION OF FARM LAND BY MEN IN NINETEENTH-
CENTURY ONTARIO

The process of land acquisition is the key to understanding the social implications of landlessness or tenancy at a given point in time. Using cross-
sectional evidence, we may infer the main process by examining patterns
of landowning by age, with the precaution that such patterns are the product
both of changes over the life cycle of individuals and of structural changes.[30]
We shall argue that the patterns revealed here, in conjunction with other
recent, local social histories, make it very implausible that structural change
could account for the observed 1871 age-by-ownership relationship.

Consider the probabilities of owning land for different age groups of
men. They are given in table 2.4 and figure 2.1. The probability climbs
with age, as expected. The increase is methodical and quite dramatic. The
continuous plot in the upper portion of figure 2.1 indicates that the probability rises from nearly zero at age 20 to about 0.80 at age 40; it changes
little from 40 to 60 or 65 and then declines.

As we have said, age-by-ownership relationships are only a proxy for
actual life-cycle patterns. The age pattern may reflect a tendency for older
men to have had greater opportunity to acquire land in Ontario when they
were young than young men had in the late 1860s and very early 1870s.
In this case, both this structural change and the actual lifetime experiences
of men are reflected in the age patterns. We begin with the assumption that
the observed pattern reveals such a rapid rise of ownership with age that
we cannot plausibly attribute the change solely or mainly to structural changes.
We comment further on this assumption in a moment. But what other
evidence at hand is relevant to the issue?

At present we have only a very few studies of patterns of access to land
in Ontario to 1871. Gagan's study of Peel county is the most notable. Its
central thesis and alternative views were noted in chapter 1. To reiterate,
Gagan argues that there was a virtual crisis in access to land for the generation of farm children coming of age in the 1860s. The crisis in land for
the non-migrating farm families was not necessarily felt in most or every
county in the province, though this effect has often been hinted at. In the
first place, Gagan's study ties the crisis in landed patrimony to the specific
conditions of a long-settled, southern county of the province. Second, Bouchard notes that Gagan's study actually makes reference to two modes of
transmission of landed estate.[31] The first represents the inheritance strategies adopted within the closed system of Peel county, with single male
heirs inheriting undivided property and required to compensate excluded

TABLE 2.4
Proportion of owners and average acres owned among adult male farmers in Ontario, 1871, by age

Class limits of age class	Size of sample Number	Per cent	Average age $\overline{age}$	Landowner proportion, $P_{AC>0}$	Propertyless proportion, $P_{AC=0}$	Average acreage, $\overline{AC}$	Gini inequality index, G_{AC}
20–29	835	30.1	24.3	0.249	0.751	27.8	0.841
30–39	637	22.9	33.9	0.670	0.330	67.4	0.525
40–49	515	18.6	43.9	0.851	0.149	106.3	0.444
50–59	401	14.4	53.9	0.838	0.162	118.1	0.478
60–69	270	9.7	63.2	0.882	0.118	113.0	0.437
70–79	119	4.3	75.7	0.773	0.227	99.4	0.499
All	2,777	100.0	40.4	0.626	0.374	75.8	0.594

SOURCE: The film-manuscript sample of size 5,699, including 2,777 adult male farmers.

family members. For these families the system had the potential for considerable strain. In this sense there was a local crisis in landed patrimony. Even in this case, however, the concept of crisis tends to exaggerate the character of the changes. Gagan emphasizes the variety of altered family strategies that emerged in response to an intergenerational land squeeze in Peel county, rather than an abrupt restriction in access to land.

The second mode of transmission entailed migration out of the county. Gagan cannot systematically follow the migrants, although he cites evidence of Peel county families moving both to the Canadian west and to the U.S. mid-west to allow their children to acquire land.[32] Migration was a common North American mode of accommodation to the problem of matching the desire to bequeath land to children with the numbers of (male) offspring. Moreover, we may add, migration fuels a local land market, even if the price of entry is elevated over time. For Peel, Gagan indicates that those who changed occupations in the county and stayed at least ten years in fact 'showed a single-minded preference for farming.'[33]

Other recent studies also strongly emphasize the variety of accommodations made by families to pursue landed patrimony. They suggest that the land market in southern Ontario was very active in the 1860s and 1870s. And although the Ottawa-Huron tract presented formidable obstacles to settlement, mid-northern Bruce and Huron counties had been filling with astonishing speed since 1850.[34]

In sum, there is no evidence to suggest a sufficiently dramatic change in access to land in Ontario between mid-century and the 1871 census to

FIGURE 2.1 Proportion of owners and average acres owned among adult male farmers in Ontario, 1871, by age

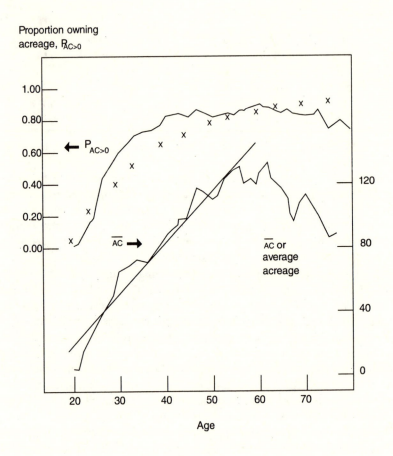

NOTES: The points from age 22–75 represent a five-year moving average of individual age-year averages. The line of Xs represents a binomial calculation stemming from $(P_{\text{AC}=0})^{1/(\overline{\text{age}}-20)} = (0.374)^{1/(20.4)} = 0.953$. The straight least-squares line is $\text{AC}_{\text{age}} = -48.3 + 3.3\text{age}$, $20 \leq \text{age} \leq 59$.

account for the steep incline in landownership reported in figure 2.1 and table 2.4. If the record of the local studies is not definitive, on balance, it is sufficient to encourage a regional interpretation suggested by the age patterns themselves, in which landownership mainly reflects life-cycle changes.

The evidence of table 2.4 shows the increase in landownership was greatest between ages 25 and 35. It appears that farmers entered the land market, either by inheritance or through their own efforts, in a relatively short and early phase of their working lives. In their intensive study of wealth distributions for Wentworth county Di Matteo and George report a confirming pattern. Their four cross-sections for each decade between 1872 and 1902 indicate that, in the first decades especially, individuals began wealth accumulation early in life by acquiring real estate; only later were they able to diversify into other assets.[35]

We can derive a simple model of the land-acquisition process from the provincial data.[36] There is an interesting probability calculation based on $P_{AC=0}$ = 0.374 (the proportion propertyless) and average age of 40.4, which approximates the pattern of figure 2.1. Assume for landless farmers that the chance of *remaining* landless in a given age year, $P_{AC=0,year}$, was *constant* from year to year for a given farmer during his adult life, defined as age $- k \approx$ age $-$ 20. An average adult would have been in the labour force 20.4 years (40.4 $-$ 20), and the probability of being propertyless in a given year might be estimated from the binomial calculation, $P_{AC=0,year} = (P_{AC=0})^{1/(20.4)} =$ $(0.374)^{1/(20.4)} = 0.953$, assuming equal and independent probabilities. Thus, the estimated probability of obtaining property in a given year, if one was propertyless, is $(1 - 0.953 = 0.047)$ or about five chances in 100.

The line representing the binomial model, $P_{AC>0} = 1 - (0.953)^{age-20}$ is sketched as a series of Xs in figure 2.1. The binomial models a process of unchanging chances of becoming propertied for a given individual in every year. The general similarity of the two curves suggests descriptively that there is merit in considering the probability of land acquisition in any year to have been more or less constant from age 20 through age 99.

We further note that the probability of becoming a landowner was greatest in the 22 years between ages 26 and 48. The probability of land acquisition in this age range averages closer to 8 per cent a year than the 5 per cent estimated over the whole age range. After about age 67 there is a significantly reduced chance of making the transition from landless to landowner. The rather advanced age at which the chance of becoming a landowner falls below at least a constant annual probability warrants particular note: it implies that aspiring landowners could actually observe that there were continuing chances of acquiring property throughout their prime years. A further, simple calculation is informative. Assume that the probability of attaining property was some 8 per cent in a year for those over 25 and less than 50 years of age. Since a majority of farming men were in this age range (about 60 per cent), we may tentatively estimate the proportion of farmers becoming 'haves' in a *year* as 0.08 × 0.374 ≈ 0.030, or 3 per cent.

Initially, a rate of land acquisition of 3 per cent suggests a rather slow, nearly invisible process. But this is an estimated *annual* rate of transition to farm ownership. Consider the implications for a hypothetical township of, say, only 200 farmers. Taking our estimates, about 0.374 or seventy-five of the farmers would be propertyless and, as above, we would expect about six (0.08 × 75) of them to attain property *annually*. Even if we apply the rate estimated from figure 2.1 to only the approximately 60 per cent of farmers between the ages of 25 and 50, about three to four (0.08 × 0.60 × 75) men would make the transition from landless to new owner annually in the township. One can see that over a decade or so the conversion of 'have nots' to propertied 'haves' would involve a quite substantial thirty to sixty individuals in this small hypothetical community. If the farming population remained relatively stable, as the propertied everywhere tend to be, what appears to be a more or less constant and modest annual rate of property acquisition would have been a quite visible process of land acquisition in social terms. In sum, over relatively few years in Ontario there were many new owners replacing those who retired or died, or migrated, or who simply had left farming. Others broke new land where that was still possible.

There is a second implication of the relationship. We can derive another estimate of the rate of land acquisition from the landowner proportion by asking the question: 'If the pattern of landowning by age were to hold for the one year from 1871 to 1872 for those now twenty or older, how much above 0.626 would the landowner proportion rise?' In other words, if the male farming population aged one year, *with no new members*, how would the division between propertied and propertyless be affected? Consider the calculation

$$\sum_{age=20}^{98} N_{age,1871} P_{(AC>0,age+1,1871)} = P\triangle,$$

where $N_{age,1871}$ is the relative population of males in the age class in 1871. The calculation for the 2,777 *farmers* in our sample gives a *change* in the landowner proportion of $P\triangle = 0.645$, an increase of 0.019 over our observed proportion of owners in 1871 (0.626), or 3.01 per cent using 0.626

as a base. The specification suggests again a moderate annual 3 per cent rate of increase, one that could well have fostered realistic expectations of eventual landowning among the propertyless in a local community.

Consider further that the population was increasing each year. If it increased 3 per cent per year, with the new adults appearing at age 20, the landowning proportion for *1872* would be approximately, 0.97 (0.645) + 0.03 (0.000) ≈ 0.626, that is, precisely the observed landowner proportion for 1871. Given the assumptions, it follows that an entirely stable *structure* of landowning inequality would result simply from population growth and an equivalent rate of land acquisition by the landless. More generally, significant and visible opportunities for individual mobility into landownership were entirely compatible with the reproduction of a stable structural division between owners and landless.

There is limited relevant evidence with which we can compare the expected pattern. The printed censuses provide only the actual increase in the number of *occupiers* of land (owners, tenants, and others) in Ontario, rather than owners alone; occupiers increased from 99,906 in 1851 to 131,983 in 1861, and to 172,258 in 1871.[37] These figures yield an average annual rate of change of about 2.8 per cent in each decade. They offer indirect confirmation of our estimate based on the age by landowner proportions. The evidence suggests that in mid-Victorian Ontario farmers tended to become landholders at a rate of about 3 per cent per year, while the population of farmers also increased about 3 per cent per year, with few of the youngest having initial ownership. A largely unchanging structure of landed inequality was compatible with relatively visible and open processes of individual and family access to land.

Each of our estimates leads to the conclusion that throughout much of the nineteenth century Ontario experienced a pattern of more or less constant proportions of owners and propertyless among farmers, with a little more than one-third's (0.374) being propertyless at any point in time, including potentially inheriting farmers' sons. Our model has not dealt with the facts that 1 or 2 per cent died each year[38] or 3 per cent population growth is net growth, or with the distinction between property accumulation through inheritance and through new acquisition. These considerations would bear on an interpretation of the key processes by which landownership is maintained and transferred, but they would not alter the general conclusions. Though we can only speculate, these age patterns and our knowledge of family accommodations to shifting land markets hint that Ontario might have had more or less the same landowner proportion in 1861, 1851, and perhaps 1841. This result would conform with estimates for the United

States for 1860 and 1870.[39] As important as the apparent constancy of the structure of landownership itself is the fact that it appears to have resulted from processes of land acquisition that were still open and encouraging to those who sought entry, especially among men between age 20 and 40.

We suggested above that the notion of a genuine crisis in access to land probably overstates the case. In the end, the choice of terms may be a matter of emphasis, though it seems to go well beyond mere nuance. There were contemporary politicians and commentators for whom the term crisis came easily. Recent studies and our evidence indicate that large numbers of Ontario's residents continued to pursue a landed family patrimony as if the option remained viable. Gaffield has sensibly noted that the question of the availability of farm land is complicated by considerations of changing markets, institutional conditions, and shifting social definitions.[40] Our analysis of the implications of the age by ownership patterns for 1871 began with the key assumption that the pattern does not reflect primarily structural change. Since it is a crucial assumption in our interpretation, a final comment is in order.

Suppose we suspend the assumption of limited structural change in the land market. In this case, the pattern of table 2.4 and figure 2.1 implies a sea change, if not a virtual revolution in the character of the Ontario economy in the twenty to thirty years after 1840. If the observed pattern was mainly a consequence of structural change and was not associated with life-cycle acquisition, it implies that almost no young families could have acquired land in the late 1860s and 1870s. We would also expect the record of political agitation and social disruption to be unmistakable. The evidence does not favour this view.

A more moderate interpretation takes the 1871 ownership by age pattern to be the product of both an increasingly restricted market and continuing age-related attainment of ownership. It acknowledges changes both in the dynamics of the market and in aspirations for landownership. On balance, we argue that the census evidence and other recent studies support an interpretation in which families continued to seek land beyond the limits of their townships and counties of origin and found the shifting conditions of land quality, location, and sales could be met with their own altered family strategies. In this view there was no historic turning point or crisis of the basic landed economy at least into the seventh decade of the century.

Despite general continuity, there almost surely were important variations in access to land among social and cultural groups. We examine these questions later in the chapter. Before we do so, however, we turn to the question of the distribution of landed wealth, that is, the acreage held by farmers and the pattern of inequality in farm size. These data are also reported in table 2.4 and figure 2.1.

PATTERNS OF LAND ACCUMULATION

There were nearly 227,000 farmers in Ontario in 1871. On average, they owned 75.8 acres. Agricultural conditions and productivity, of course, varied widely throughout the province. Of greater interest than the average is the distribution of farms by size of landholding. A specific measure of inequality among farmers in acreage owned is undertaken later in the chapter. Initially, we consider the relationship between size of farm holdings and age among male farmers, again with a view to inferences regarding patterns of ownership over time.

Table 2.4 and figure 2.1 present the arithmetic averages for different age groups. The mean for males aged 20–29 was just 27.8 acres; for those aged 50–59, it is 118.1 acres. The lower portion of figure 2.1 plots the relationship of age to average acreage owned by farmers. In comparison with the plot of ownership proportions by age, there is an even greater difference in average size of holdings between ages 20 and 60. Again it seems reasonable to take this pattern largely to represent a life-cycle process of relatively rapid accumulation of farm acreage. There is also a relatively rapid decline in size of holdings after age 60. The decline in average acreage owned suggests a process in which older farmers divested themselves of part of their accumulated land, probably providing for their children prior to inheritance settlements as well as selling to others. It seems surprising, in fact, that older farmers tended to retain such substantial holdings. The likely motive was to maintain family land intact. The average for those over 60 in the sample is 109 acres. Of course, many older farmers had their adult children living with them, still working the land. The entire question begs for further study.

There is another, more direct, implication of these data. People would presumably have drawn some lesson for their own prospects from the visible differences in size of holdings among age groups in a farming community. The evidence of table 2.4 suggests that judging by the experience of others, young men would have had every reason to expect quite steady expansion of their landholdings. Those between ages 30 and 39 had an average of just less than 70 acres (67.4) in 1871, nearly 40 acres more than those in the younger cohort; those 40 to 49 averaged over 100 acres (106.3). Ontario's young landed producers had reason to be optimistic: the accumulated hold-

'Beginnings.' Clearing land in nineteenth-century Ontario

ings of their older neighbours was concrete evidence that the hard pursuit of farming yielded steady, if modest, advancement.

There are also inferences regarding economic change that can be drawn from the age patterns of size of holdings. We have already noted that the pattern of size of holdings by age increases more rapidly in the early years than ownership proportions but decreases more dramatically in old age. Consider the two portions of the age by acreage relationship, that between ages 20 and 59 and that for age over 60. In order to estimate separate implied rates of growth for the two groups, we can fit a regression line to each portion of the relationship. The least squares linear regression equations are as follows:

$\hat{AC} = -48.3 + 3.3$ age $20 \leq$ age ≤ 59, $N = 2{,}388$; $R^2 = 0.12$, $\overline{AC} = 70.4$,
(0.2)

and $\hat{AC} = 188.1 - 1.2$ age $60 \leq$ age ≤ 99, $N = 389$; $R^2 = 0.01$, $\overline{AC}$
(0.7)

$= 109$, (standard errors in parentheses).[41]

The implied increase in acreage can be estimated as the yearly increment divided by the average, or $3.3/70.4 = 0.047$ for those 20–59 and $-1.2/109 = -0.011$ for those 60–99. The first estimate is a positive rate of growth of just less than 5 per cent per year (4.7), and the second estimate, for those over age 60, is a declining rate of about 1 per cent per year (1.1). The implied increment for *all* male farmers might be defined as the difference in the rates for those in the two portions of the curve divided by the average size for the total sample $[3.3 (2{,}388) - 1.2 (389)]/[75.8 \times 2{,}777]$, or 0.035. Thus, we have an estimate of economic growth (in size of farmholdings) of just 3.5 per cent per year. If population increased 3 per cent per year, as we estimated above, the implication is that there was very slight or virtually no change $(0.035 - 0.030 = 0.005)$ in the size of average landholdings with time in Ontario in the decades preceding 1871.

Again, the printed censuses give aggregate figures for 1851, 1861, and 1871 for average acreage *occupied* per farm occupant. The figures are ninety-eight acres in 1851, 101 acres in 1861, and ninety-four acres in 1871.[42] These acreage figures for decades tend broadly to confirm our estimated constancy in size of holdings over time based on the 1871 data. As before, of course, our simple model neglects deaths and inheritances and entails several simplifying assumptions. Still, it provides a first vantage point from which to consider trends in the provincial landed economy of the last century.

The relationship between age and landholding in 1871 suggests, on the one hand, that *individual* farmers and their families would have reason to expect substantial life-time growth in their holdings, both by observing the experience of others and in terms of their own experience. On the other hand, as in the case of our estimates of land acquisition, the relationship of age to size of farm is found to imply almost no change at all in the *structure* of Ontario's landed economy over several decades prior to 1871. Once again, in pursuit of an understanding of the character of nineteenth-century Ontario, we suggest that deeply structured inequality in farm wealth was compatible with, indeed fostered by, a relatively open process of acreage acquisition over the life cycle of farming men.

LANDOWNING AMONG IMMIGRANT AND NATIVE-BORN
FARMERS

The agricultural labour force in Ontario in 1871 was very strongly influenced by European experience, since almost every second person had been born outside the country (47 per cent), primarily in Ireland, England, and Scotland. A strong and reasonable hypothesis holds that aspiring farmers among the immigrant population would be less able to obtain property than native-born Canadians.

It is possible that our conventional image of the initial poverty and dislocation of immigrants suggests too great a disadvantage. Nevertheless, it is easy to enumerate reasons why the foreign born could be heavily overrepresented among the landless. In the long-settled and more fertile agricultural areas most of the land had been patented to individual owners by the 1860s.[43] Presumably, in general the Canadian born had some advantage in this competitive land market, since usually they had the benefit of their family's earlier entrance into the market and of family assistance in raising capital or clearing land.[44] Recent immigrants, even English speakers, would have been less familiar with the institutional procedures for obtaining land, and the German and French speakers in Ontario would have had language handicaps that complicated the acquisition process, for example, in reading local newspapers for land sales or in dealing with land agents. We have already referred to one particularly strong version of the hypothesis that holds that immigration after 1840 in general and that of the famine Irish in particular directly fed landlessness and rising urban wage labour.[45]

The relevant data are provided in the second panel of table 2.5. Despite historical convention and common sense, the hypothesis of a foreign born handicap is *not* sustained by the evidence for landowner proportions. The sample indicates, rather, that foreign-born farmers held a distinct advantage in 1871: about 74 per cent (0.739) of the immigrant population owned land, whereas just over half of the native-born Canadians were owners (0.525).

Akenson's analysis of Leeds and Lansdowne township in eastern Ontario based on the 1861 census also challenges the conventional notion of a foreign-born handicap. He reported that in terms of the average cash value of farms and buildings, for example, the foreign born exceeded the native born by a small margin. The Irish born were the most successful of all.[46] Of course, the local world of an eastern township may not reflect the experience of Ontario as a whole. As it happens, Akenson's local findings of an immigrant advantage do represent the larger Ontario experience a decade later.

We do need to consider the effects of age composition. There was a

TABLE 2.5
Proportion of owners and average acres owned among adult male farmers in Ontario, 1871,
by age and nativity

Classification	Age						
	20–29	30–39	40–49	50–59	60–69	70–79	All
Sample proportion							
Canadian born	0.239	0.136	0.076	0.042	0.025	0.008	0.527
Foreign born	0.061	0.094	0.109	0.103	0.072	0.035	0.473
Land proportion, $P_{AC>0}$							
Canadian born	0.242	0.668	0.840	0.810	0.914	0.826	0.525
Foreign born	0.277	0.673	0.858	0.849	0.870	0.760	0.739
Landowner proportion adjusted for age							
Canadian born							0.626
Foreign born							0.625
Average acreage, $\overline{AC}$							
Canadian born	28	68	108	129	114	79	68.0
Foreign born	25	66	105	114	113	104	90.0
Average acreage adjusted for age							
Canadian born							76.8
Foreign born							72.7
Inequality index, $G_{AC}{}^{*}$							
Canadian born	0.85	0.52	0.43	0.51	0.43	0.33	0.659
Foreign born	0.79	0.53	0.45	0.46	0.44	0.52	0.522
Inequality index adjusted for age							
Canadian born							0.58
Foreign born							0.57

NOTES: The standardized proportion and average for the native born and foreign born
have been computed using the population of adult male farmers for the province (N =
2,777) and five-year age intervals. See the text for age standardization.
*The age-adjusted inequality index or Gini index has been computed as a weighted average
of Gini coefficients for ten-year age groups, using the population of all male farmers as
weights.
SOURCE: The film-manuscript sample of size 2,777. See also table 2.2.

considerable gap in the average age of the foreign and native groups. The
difference in ownership would surely be affected by the difference. Table
2.5 also provides relevant information on ownership proportions and nativity for various age groups. The first row simply gives the age distributions
for native and foreign born.

The Canadian-born population was substantially younger than the foreign born. The modal age for the latter was between 40 and 49 years, a very high figure indeed. The modal age of the native born was the youngest category, 20–29 years. In fact, nearly a quarter of the native-born farmers were between ages 20 and 29, compared with just 6 per cent of the foreign-born farmers. The difference in average age was almost thirteen years (47.1 − 34.4).

As indicated above, a conventional standardization procedure is one way of taking into account the effects of age composition. Specifically, the standardization for the Canadian born can be represented as $P_{AC,\text{Canadian standardized}} = \Sigma_{\text{age}}N_{\text{age}}(P_{AC>0,\text{age},\text{Canadian}}) = 0.6226$, or over 62 per cent, where N_{age} is the relative population in the age class among *all* 2,777 adult male farmers. In other words, the age-adjusted proportion of owners is nearly 10 per cent greater than the actual proportion for the Canadian born (0.623 − 0.527).

A similar calculation for the foreign born produces a virtually identical proportion of owners, 0.6225. In this case, the age adjustment diminishes the landowning proportion by about 12 per cent (0.739 − 0.623). The advantage that immigrants in Ontario had with respect to landownership could be entirely attributed to the differences in age composition. It is worth noting they suffered no disadvantage, however, even when age is taken into account. Indeed, from ages 20 to 60, their actual attainments bespeak a slight advantage, as shown in the third and fourth rows of table 2.5.[47]

The unexpected finding of relative immigrant advantage raises a further question about the immigrant experience.[48] What about farm acreage owned? Table 2.5 also provides the relevant data (the fourth panel).

Again, contrary to conventional accounts, we find that the average land owned is sixty-eight acres for Canadian-born males and ninety acres for foreign-born males, suggesting a significant handicap for the natives. Again, adjustment of the actual averages for the large age gap between the two nativity groups substantially modifies the difference: age-standardized values, as given in the table, are 76.8 acres for the Canadian born and 72.7 acres for the foreign born.

Specifically, the table indicates that for every age group except the elderly (ages 70–79), the average acreage of the Canadian born is slightly greater than that of the foreign born. It also seems that after age 60–69, when average acreage of the nativity groups is almost identical, the Canadian born are a good deal more likely to divest themselves of land than the foreign born. This pattern suggests significant differences in inheritance practices between immigrants and native Canadian farmers. It is a topic that might well warrant analysis within the context of local, rural histories.

In sum, we find that the foreign born suffer a small handicap, on average, in land accumulation. In terms of the previous analysis of age patterns of land acquisition, however, this differential amounts to the accumulation that one might have expected in just one or two years. Immigrant families in Ontario were very nearly as well established in farming as were the native born. The finding not only tends to contradict some common historical assumptions about the disadvantage of immigrants and their tendency to be pressed out of farming, but conflicts with the experience of immigrants in the United States. In contrast to this Ontario experience, dollar-values of real estate in northern states in 1870 showed an immigrant handicap of closer to 20 per cent for farmers.[49]

The main result of the analysis is the relatively small disadvantage detected for immigrants in size of holdings and the virtual absence of a difference in the chances of landownership between native and immigrant groups. Here again Akenson's fine-grained analysis of Leeds and Landsdowne township is relevant. In finding similar evidence to turn conventional arguments on their heads, he suggests immigrants were actually advantaged by their recency of arrival, bringing some capital from the sale of lands overseas or from recent wage earnings. He speculates further that, in contrast to native farmers' sons, immigrants might have found it advantageous to be free of the burden of inheritance arrangements suffered by the native born. Immigrants are more likely to have severed obligations to their siblings. In other ways, as well, native sons may have been more restricted by their family obligations, less free to leave the land for urban jobs.[50] These are intriguing notions which conform with the provincial patterns.

RELIGION AND LANDOWNING

The cultural experience of ordinary men and women in the past remains a most elusive subject of social historical research. Social histories at the community level have tended to bridge the conventional divide between cultural history and economic history, though they have by no means closed it. Still very few studies have examined systematically the cultural stratification of economic well-being, property, or wealth in the past. The questions are fundamental, since church affiliations and ethnic communities were at the core of personal identity and social life in nineteenth-century Ontario. In this chapter we ask how they fostered or retarded landownership. In the next chapter we consider the effects of ethnicity and religious adherence on home ownership and property inequalities more generally.

There are several Ontario community studies that have approached the question of economic inequalities among ethnic and religious groups. They have produced highly variable results. Akenson has traced in detail the economic fortunes of the Irish in Leeds and Landsdowne township, distinguishing Catholic and Protestant in terms of farm values and town occupations. With regard to religion generally, he notes its deep and stabilizing effect on local communities, yet he concludes that existing evidence is too limited to allow close analysis.[51]

Katz, Doucet, and Stern are less hesitant. For Hamilton they conduct a quite elaborate statistical analysis, reporting in the end that religious differentials in wealth and property ownership were minor in the commercial city, with the exception of the distinctive propensity for home ownership among Irish-Catholics.[52] In the very different setting of the nineteenth-century Ottawa valley, however, Gaffield documents quite substantial differences between francophone-Catholic and anglophone-Protestant communities both in the landed basis of family economies and in the growth of waged labour. These distinctions are traced to the intersection of cultural predilections with differences in the timing and location of settlement and propensity to migrate. Gaffield's study has the particular merit of tracing ethno-religious variations in settlement processes.

Community studies like these provide the first invaluable, if piecemeal, views of the relation between nineteenth-century Ontario's cultural communities and the structure of economic inequality. Fortunately, the 1871 census provides a detailed record of two dimensions of the cultural order of Victorian Ontario – religious affiliation and ethnic origin. Of course, an analysis of census variables cannot capture the nuances of cultural expression and community experience of nineteenth-century men and women; this kind of evidence does not get 'under the skin' of social life. But it does provide a rare opportunity to assess systematically the variations among mid-Victorian cultural groups in property acquisition and inequality. We first consider religion.

There are two broad hypotheses we can entertain in taking up the analysis. On the one hand, we might expect abiding religious differences in property holding, not only between Protestant and Catholic but among the Protestant churches as well. On the other hand, there is an argument that by the 1870s the passing of the pioneer phase and the increasing institutionalization of all Protestant churches were accompanied by the social and economic homogeneity of their adherents.

The first hypothesis might be expressed as a version of the 'Weber thesis' regarding the catalytic role of Protestant values on the 'spirit' of capitalism as it developed in the west. In such an account members of a denominational group are seen as sharing distinctive moral attitudes towards self-discipline, work, and profit-making. In turn, personal deportment and conduct are thought to influence directly wealth or land accumulation. Weber attributed to Quakers and Baptists a greater propensity to be imbued with 'this-worldly asceticism' and a methodical regulation of life than he granted Catholics, Lutherans, or Anglicans.[53] The evangelical communities took to heart the dictum that work itself was part of one's duty to God in this world – a religious calling.

In a different perspective we might emphasize that class divisions were in formation throughout the nineteenth century and had a powerful religious component. In England the nineteenth-century heritage of the evangelical movements had made the faith and practices of Protestant Christianity hallmarks of the respectable middle classes.[54] Although the opportunities for landownership differed hugely from those in England, the aspiring middle class of Victorian Ontario likely shared this concern with social respectability. They may also have sought its expression through evangelical forms of Protestantism, especially as the taint of the early sectarianism of the poor and the pioneer faded. Johnson and Ryan, for example, have offered persuasive accounts of the role played by evangelism in the formation of middle-class cultures and in the definition of middle- and working-class divisions in the northern United States prior to mid-century.[55] The influences were present, though modified, north of the border.[56]

Apparently in direct contrast to the foregoing interpretations of persistent religious differences, it has been suggested that the deep liberal and individualistic influences of nineteenth-century North Atlantic Protestantism did not so much distinguish denominational groups as assimilate them. For example, in emphasizing the formative cultural continuity of pre-Confederation Ontario, Harris and Warkentin write, 'In stressing individual freedom before time and community, most Ontarians held values that were liberal in the classic sense ... Tradition and continuity were weakened in such settings, as were the value systems that did not emphasize individual initiative and freedom. For this reason groups of different background tended to merge in Ontario.'[57]

The view gathers strength from the tendency for both sects and churches in Ontario to become increasingly institutionalized after mid-century. In this development they paralleled the structural institutionalization of the market, politics, education, and welfare. All religious groups witnessed organizational and ecclesiastical convergence in terms of territorial concentration of their congregations, the appointment of permanent clergy, and the building of formal church structures.[58] The assimilationist view suggests that by 1871 denominational differences in economic values and their consequences for economic accumulation might be quite limited or non-existent.

The film-manuscript sample allows us to examine the competing interpretations for Catholics, members of the Church of England (Anglican), Presbyterians, Baptists, Methodists, and adherents classified as other religions. In this analysis we focus again on the landowning, farming majority, leaving the question of religious stratification more generally to the next chapter. Table 2.6 gives the distribution of the sample by religious affiliation, nativity, age, and three measures of material condition – landownership, acreage owned, and inequality in ownership.

First, reviewing basic demographic characteristics, we see that the Baptists and Methodists were the smallest and largest groups among farmers, respectively (about 5 per cent and 28 per cent), and both were more likely than other religious groups to be native born.[59] Although the average ages of both native- and foreign-born groups were similar, the Baptists were marginally older and the Methodists marginally younger (43 versus 39 years; the average for all groups is 40.4 years). The landowner proportions for the groups are given in the third panel of the table, and the last panel gives the landowner proportions standardized for age differences among the denominations (using the age distribution of the total population of farmers as a standard).

Our first observation is that there is a striking similarity among groups in the proportions owning land: the lowest proportion is 0.60, for the Church of England or Anglican group, and the highest proportion is 0.67, for the other more or less sectarian Protestant churches, representing just 9 per cent of all farmers. There is a somewhat greater range of ownership among the Canadian-born groups. Again the Church of England group has the lowest proportion: less than half of the Canadian-born farmers of this group are owners (47 per cent). In comparison, 61 per cent of the Canadian-born Baptist farmers own land. The differences among the foreign born are slighter, ranging from a low of 68 per cent among Anglicans to a high of 78 per cent for both Methodists and the other Protestant church adherents.

These modest differences are in the general *order* one might predict in emphasizing the tendency for more evangelical churches to promote self-discipline and a work ethic. Only the largest differences among church groups are statistically significant even when other variables were also considered.[60] There is, at least, an indication in these data that the relatively large body of adherents of the Church of England were less likely to be farm owners than the members of the smaller Baptist and 'other' more evangelical congregations. It is possible that these differences are due to

TABLE 2.6
Proportion of owners and average acres owned among adult male farmers in Ontario, 1871, by religion and nativity

Classification	Religious denomination							
	Catholic	Baptist	Church of England	Meth-odist	Presby-terian	Other	Protes-tant	All
Sample proportion								
All	0.153	0.049	0.180	0.283	0.245	0.089	0.847	1.000
Canadian born	0.077	0.035	0.071	0.190	0.107	0.047	0.450	0.527
Foreign born	0.076	0.014	0.109	0.093	0.138	0.042	0.397	0.473
Average age								
All	41	43	42	39	40	42	40	40.4
Canadian born	35	36	33	35	32	36	34	34.4
Foreign born	47	52	47	46	47	48	47	47.1
Landowner proportion, $P_{AC>0}$								
All	0.63	0.65	0.60	0.63	0.62	0.67	0.63	0.626
Canadian born	0.52	0.61	0.47	0.55	0.47	0.58	0.53	0.525
Foreign born	0.73	0.74	0.68	0.78	0.74	0.78	0.74	0.739
Average acreage, $\overline{AC}$								
All	71	85	72	77	78	78	77	75.8
Canadian born	55	74	53	70	55	74	64	63.0
Foreign born	86	112	85	91	99	83	91	90.0
Inequality index, $G_{AC}{}^*$								
All	0.59	0.63	0.62	0.61	0.56	0.58	0.59	0.594
Canadian born	0.65	0.61	0.70	0.66	0.64	0.65	0.66	0.659
Foreign born	0.53	0.65	0.56	0.49	0.49	0.50	0.52	0.522
Adjusted for age								
Landowner prop., All	0.64	0.66	0.59	0.63	0.62	0.64	0.62	0.626
Average acreage, All	72	84	71	79	77	71	75	75.8

*See the text for a description of the Gini index of inequality.
SOURCE: The film-manuscript sample of size 2,777.

other factors, such as the relative advantages conferred by the timing of settlement and location patterns, rather than to religious convictions and the practices they engendered. In the absence of an opportunity to examine the effects of these other conditions, the religious differences stand as intriguing. In later statistical analysis some economic and social conditions are considered along with the cultural variables.

What is more striking is the lack of notable difference in farm ownership between the Catholic and Protestant populations generally; 63 per cent of each are owners. And there is virtually no difference among either the foreign-born or the Canadian-born Catholics and Protestants. Given the large Irish and small francophone components of Ontario Catholics, one would have expected a quite substantial Catholic disadvantage in farm ownership. Moreover, standardizing the proportions of owners for age differences of the religious groups does not alter these patterns, as shown in the second-last row of the table.

Broadly, then, the relatively slight differentials in ownership proportions tend to suggest relative material parity among religious communities of farmers in the province by 1871: being a landowner rather than a hired hand or tenant is not strongly related to religious preference. In clear contrast, table 2.6 shows that there are wider religious variations in the size of farm holdings, the basis of farm wealth.

The average acreage held for the various denominations varies from a high of eighty-five acres for the Baptists to a low of seventy-one acres for the Catholic population. Standardization for age differences among the groups does not much alter the pattern, with the exception of the adherents of the small, other Protestant churches. The standardized values, given in the last row of the table, reveal that the slight differences in landowning are translated into much larger differences in farm acreage. The Baptist group has a standardized average of eighty-four acres per male farmer. They are followed in order by the Methodists, the Presbyterians, and then by the Catholic and Church of England groups. Most notable is the distinct Baptist advantage: as a group they exceed the Catholics and Anglicans by a margin of 15 to 20 per cent in amount of farm acreage. The Methodists follow with a 10 per cent margin over Catholics and Anglicans. Under the conditions of mid-Victorian farming in Ontario these figures could have represented considerable differences in investments and in margins of potential production.

The general pattern corresponds to S.D. Clark's argument that the established diocesan churches were more thoroughly urban and institutionalized after 1860. In contrast, in the 1860s the Baptist community of adherents apparently remained the most rural and sectarian.[61] This continued rural dispersion among Baptists suggests that the pattern of farm holdings reflects differences not so much in moral order among the groups but rather simply in the settlement patterns among farmers. The most obvious hypothesis would be that greater acreage resulted from the tendency of some denominations to settle in the newer, still largely pioneering counties. As we have noted, our sample is too limited to explore such small groups in terms of their geographic locations. But an examination of the geographic patterns by census district reported for denominations in the published census volumes does not, in fact, lend support to the idea. The evidence bears citing.

According to the aggregate census tabulations, Baptists comprised just 5 per cent of Ontario's male population in 1871. They were overrepresented in only two broad areas, both early and thoroughly settled – in the western peninsula, where they averaged about 11 per cent of the district populations, and in the band of districts stretching from London along the north shore of Lake Erie to Niagara, where they made up an average of 14 per cent of the district populations. They were significantly underrepresented east of York county and Toronto and in the north. In contrast, the adherents of the two churches with the smallest average holdings, the Catholic and the Anglican, did not share settlement patterns. The former were heavily underrepresented everywhere except in districts close to the Quebec border and in the north, where they were greatly overrepresented. They constituted approximately 20 per cent of Ontario adult males, but made up over 40 per cent of the population north and west of Ottawa. The Church of England congregations were rather evenly dispersed throughout the province, though slightly underrepresented in south-central Ontario and overrepresented in York county and east and north of it. In sum, the aggregate census data give no reason to think that the denominational differences in size of farm holdings reflect geographic patterns. This fact encourages a cultural interpretation.

We consider one other implication. The differences in size of holding among the groups also raises the intriguing prospect that there were systematic differences in inheritance practices among denominational groups. Is it possible that, say, sons of Ontario Baptist farmers routinely had larger inheritances than their peers in other denominations? Our data allow us to consider the question only indirectly. Presumably such differences in inheritance practices would be manifested mainly among the native born. The comparisons of native and foreign born in table 2.6 show clearly, however, that if native-born Baptists exceeded all the native born, foreign-born Baptists also exceeded all the foreign born in average acreage owned, and by a greater margin. These data make differences in inheritance practices an unlikely source of the land accumulation patterns among denominations and lead us back to an emphasis on more general differences in ethos and cultural practices.

ETHNICITY AND LANDOWNING

If religious conviction was a primary element of self-identity and community formation in the mid-Victorian era, ethnicity was a more ambiguous, though still influential, basis of both social cleavage and solidarity. Recent revisionist studies of ethnic communities and cultures have de-emphasized the significance of old-world ethnic heritage and the trauma of the transatlantic voyage to focus on ethnic communities as emergent, relatively autonomous cultural formations.[62] Gaffield, Mannion, Elliott and others have shown for nineteenth-century Ontario how 'chain' migration and settlement patterns engendered ethnic community ties and institutions.[63] These mainly rural studies have treated the relationship as nuanced and variable. A number of urban studies have tended, in contrast, to find class and economic differences to be virtually synonymous with ethnic differences – especially with the division between Irish and non-Irish.[64]

As in the case of religious communities, we pose the question of whether there were differences in landownership among those of differing ethnic origin in old Ontario as a whole. A later analysis considers the joint implications of religion and ethnicity. Table 2.7 provides the evidence for ethnicity and landowning that parallels that for religion. With reference to male farmers, the first two panels of the table give the distributions for six ethnic groups, the average age of each group, and their Canadian- and foreign-born composition. The Irish origin group is the largest, 36 per cent of male farmers, followed by the English and Welsh group (26 per cent) and then by the Scottish (22 per cent). The groups are of nearly identical average age, with the Canadian born more than ten years younger on average for all groups except for the very small (4 per cent) French-origin population.

The crude landowner proportions of the third panel indicate that, as in the case of denominational groups, there was an elementary equality among the groups in their capacity to become farm owners. The age-standardized proportions of the last panel of the table, which take account of the age differences, confirm the conclusion with one exception. The large Irish group appears to have a slight *advantage* in landownership (66 per cent were owners, compared with 60 and 61 per cent for the English and Welsh and Scottish groups). The advantage is confirmed in multiple regression analyses in which age, religion, and nativity are entered as competing variables. That analysis shows that the Irish farmers had a statistically greater likelihood of being landowners than the English and Welsh origin group, which served as the comparison population.[65] It is especially striking that only the Irish among origin groups stood out as being more likely to be farm owners than the English and Welsh, given the still common assumption that the Irish-Catholics among them were largely deprived economically.

The result takes us to the heart of a fascinating question in Canadian

TABLE 2.7
Proportion of owners and average acres owned among adult male farmers in Ontario, 1871, by country of origin and nativity

Classification	England, Wales	Scotland	Ireland	Germany	France	Other	All
	Country of origin						
Sample proportion							
All	0.256	0.217	0.357	0.107	0.039	0.024	1.000
Canadian born	0.135	0.098	0.167	0.077	0.033	0.017	0.527
Foreign born	0.121	0.119	0.190	0.030	0.006	0.006	0.473
Average age							
All	40	41	40	41	41	41	40.4
Canadian born	34	32	32	39	42	38	34.4
Foreign born	47	47	47	47	36	50	47.1
Landowner proportion, $P_{AC>0}$							
All	0.61	0.61	0.64	0.63	0.63	0.68	0.626
Canadian born	0.52	0.47	0.49	0.60	0.66	0.69	0.525
Foreign born	0.70	0.73	0.78	0.71	0.50	0.67	0.739
Average acreage, $\overline{AC}$							
All	67	79	83	73	53	76	75.8
Canadian born	58	56	65	76	56	81	63.0
Foreign born	77	99	99	66	38	63	90.0
Inequality index, $G_{AC}*$							
All	0.61	0.58	0.59	0.58	0.58	0.55	0.594
Canadian born	0.66	0.65	0.71	0.60	0.57	0.54	0.659
Foreign born	0.55	0.52	0.49	0.52	0.60	0.58	0.522
Adjusted for age							
Landowner prop., All	0.60	0.61	0.66	0.63	0.60	0.64	0.626
Average acreage, All	65	80	85	71	50	73	75.8

*See the text.
SOURCE: See table 2.6.

historiography. The prevailing, and until recently almost exclusive view of the Irish in Ontario had been that they were a people who shunned rural life in the last century or were too limited in capital and skills to take up farming in any great numbers. The image followed a well-established historical view of the urban and non-farm orientation of the Irish in the United States. Studies of the last few years, most prominently those of Akenson, have shown that the image was adopted virtually in the absence of evidence.[66] The Ontario Irish were, in fact, predominantly rural residing and farmers. That our provincial evidence reveals Irish origin farmers were also by 1871 rather *more* likely to be landowners than any other origin group simply underscores the extent to which the earlier historical fiction reversed the historical record.

The immediately related question has been whether the rural and farm orientation of the Irish was mainly a Protestant pattern, with the Catholic Irish more often confined to urban areas. As noted above, both conventional interpretations and some new urban history have taken the Irish-Catholic experience to be largely urban and economically deprived.[67] We can pose the question directly using the sample data regarding farm ownership within the province.

A precise specification of the issue can take the form of a regression analysis which allows us to separate statistically the effects of several variables on farmers' landownership, including religious affiliation and ethnicity. The following ordinary least squares regression equation predicting farm ownership includes independent variables representing age cohorts (each compared with the age 20–29 group), foreign birth (compared with the native born), Catholic religious affiliation (compared with all Protestants) and Irish origin (compared with all other origin groups).[68]

$$P_{AC>0} = 0.229 + 0.420\text{age}30\text{–}39 + 0.601\text{age}40\text{–}49 + 0.587\text{age}50\text{–}59$$
$$(.022) \qquad (0.024) \qquad (0.026)$$
$$+ 0.629\text{age}60\text{–}69 + 0.518\text{age}70\text{–}99 + 0.008\text{RC} + 0.045\text{Irish}$$
$$(0.030) \qquad (0.042) \qquad (0.023) \qquad (0.017)$$
$$+ 0.008\text{FB}, \qquad N = 2{,}227 \text{ and } R^2 = 0.29.$$
$$(0.017)$$

The equation first records the strong effects of age on increased landownership, with each coefficient being several times the value of the standard error. In contrast, the difference between Catholics and Protestants is minuscule and non-significant, as is the difference between native and foreign born. The difference between farmers of Irish origin and those of all other origin groups, however, is statistically significant, though of less consequence than age differences. The analysis confirms that farmers of Irish origin were more likely to be landowners than others, quite independent of their age *and* whether they were Protestant or Catholic.[69] The penchant of the Irish for homeownership, which has been documented for the last century, seems to have been matched by their desire to own farm land.[70]

With the exception of the Irish, the major ethnic groups in nineteenth-century Ontario cannot be distinguished in terms of farmers' propensity to own land. It will be recalled that in the case of religion there were more marked differences in the average size of farms than in ownership proportions. We present a similar analysis for the origin groups. The fourth panel of table 2.7 provides the average acreage figures for the groups. The last row of the table gives these farm size differences standardized for age. They provide the most relevant comparisons. Once again, confirming Akenson's analysis for 1861 and contrary to conventional images, it is the Irish-origin population of the province that tended to own the most farm land in 1871, averaging eighty-five acres. The Irish are followed by the Scottish farmers (eighty acres), the small 'Other' origin group (seventy-three acres), the German-origin population (seventy-one acres) and, finally, by the English and Welsh farmers. The latter, who were also least likely to be landowners, tend to have quite small average holdings (sixty-five acres). Finally, the tiny group of French-origin farmers trail far behind, owning just fifty acres on average in the province. The differences between Irish-Catholic and Irish-Protestant are examined below.

Neither these data nor other Ontario studies can fully inform us about the significance of farm size for family subsistence, marketable surpluses, or social status. The overlap in the distributions of farm sizes for the various ethnic groups and the dispersion of the groups over the province probably made the relatively small average differences more or less invisible in everyday life. Nevertheless, some of the differences suggest manifest social and economic gaps. Judging from other studies, even in the most productive areas of the province, a farm of fifty to sixty acres may have been sufficient for family subsistence, but it was not likely to permit much marketable surplus.[71] Thus, the modestly larger holdings of many Irish and Scottish farm families would have conferred a significant measure of greater economic security than that enjoyed by their neighbours of English or German origin. And the small French-origin (and almost entirely Catholic) group of Ontario was clearly the poorest. One might also imagine a number of unmeasured factors that could moderate the observed relationship between acreage owned and ethnicity. For example, a sceptic of a cultural interpretation might argue that the early chain migration patterns of, say, the Irish or Scottish farmers happened to allow them to acquire more acreage than those of English or German background. In any given community such differences might be readily detected, though the fact that we here observe a provincial pattern suggests that settlement history alone is not a sufficient account of the ethnic differences.

Table 2.7 also shows that the foreign-born Irish and Scottish acquired greater farm acreages than their native-born counterparts by a wide margin; both foreign-born groups had an average of ninety-nine acres, while the next highest average was seventy-seven acres for the English and Welsh immigrants. Moreover, the three largest immigrant groups (Irish, English and Welsh, Scottish) considerably exceeded the three smaller groups in average farm size. Apparently, the earlier settlement of the families of native-born members of these groups did not tip the balance in their favour. In contrast, there is an acreage advantage on average for the Canadian-born members of the smaller German, French, and 'Other' ethnic groups.

Again the question of whether the Irish-Protestants exceeded Irish-Catholics arises with respect to the size and possible prosperity of farms.[72] If we employ data not reported in the table, the answer is clear. In terms of farm acreage owned there was some, but not much, difference between the groups in 1871: the Irish Protestant average was eighty-five acres and the Irish-Catholic average was eighty acres, with both groups having the same average age. Rather than Ontario's Irish-Catholic farmers' being limited in the accumulation of farm land in 1871, they matched the Scottish and exceeded every other ethnic group.

LANDOWNING, ETHNICITY, AND RELIGION

We have found that there were systematic differences among nineteenth-century Ontario's religious and ethnic communities in land accumulation and have explored the implications of the Catholic-Protestant divide among the large Irish-origin population. Clearly religion and ethnicity are related attributes. It is feasible that the apparent variations in farm land for one, say, ethnicity, are largely artefacts of the other, religion. The most effective means of disentangling measurable effects is to employ both as variables in a multiple regression analysis.

We present the results of a further multiple regression equation in which age, religion, origin, and nativity (native versus foreign born) again appear as independent variables in the form of simple dichotomies. As before, each category of the variable, say, Irish or Catholic, appears as a separate factor contrasted to a selected comparison category of the same variable (those that are implicit and are not recorded in the equation). Thus, all of the religious and ethnic origin groups appear in the equation, and in this specification they compete with age and nativity in accounting for the variations in farm acreage owned among members of the sample. The ordinary least squares regression equation is as follows:[73]

$$AC = 9.9 + 41.0 age_{30-39} + 81.5 age_{40-49} + 94.5 age_{50-59}$$
$$(5.4) \qquad (5.9) \qquad (6.5)$$

$$+ \ 89.0\text{age}_{60\text{-}69} + 75.3\text{age}_{70\text{-}79} + 1.8\text{Cath} + 18.3\text{Bapt.} + 12.3\text{Meth}$$
$$(7.5) \qquad\quad (10.2) \qquad\quad (7.2) \qquad (10.1) \qquad\quad (5.9)$$
$$+ \ 3.9\text{Pres.} + 10.2\text{otherreligion} + 17.5\text{Scot} + 23.1\text{Irish} +$$
$$(7.0) \qquad (8.2) \qquad\qquad\quad (6.8) \qquad\quad (5.4)$$
$$+ \ 2.6\text{German} + 10.6\text{French} - 1.9\text{otherorigin} - 5.3\text{foreignborn}$$
$$(7.2) \qquad\quad (11.6) \qquad\quad (13.2) \qquad\qquad\quad (4.5)$$
$$N = 2{,}777 \text{ and } R^2 = 0.12.$$

An example of the coding of the variables is that $\text{age}_{30\text{-}39}$ is 1.0 if an individual is 30–39 years; otherwise it is zero and so on. The values in parentheses are the standard errors of the coefficients. Roughly, a variable can be considered statistically significant if the value of the coefficient is two times the standard error. If all explicit variables were zeros, we would have a regression value for individuals who are in all the selected comparison groups. The comparison groups are those aged 20-29, members of the Church of England, those whose origins are English or Welsh, and the native born. Though the three factors account for only some 12 per cent of the variance in owned acreage, it is the differences in the coefficients for the categories that is of interest. Each coefficient can be directly interpreted in the partial derivative sense. For example, we can read the equation as indicating that being aged 30–39, in comparison with those aged 20–29, increases expected landholdings by 41.0 acres, *with the effects of all other variables being taken into account statistically.* Or we see that being a Baptist instead of a member of the Church of England (the comparison group) increases expected holdings by 18.3 acres, again holding age, origin, and nativity constant. Or further still, we can conclude that the advantage of the Church of England adherents over the Catholics is nil, just 1.8 acres (not statistically significant).

The main object in presenting the relatively complicated regression analysis is to consider the possible reduction or elimination of the effects of religion or ethnic origin on the ownership of farm acreage when the effects of the other variables are considered. Broadly the results are clear. Some, but not all, origin and religious groups have separate, significant effects on the size of holdings, and these effects are not accounted for by other variables in the equation. Specifically, members of the Baptist or Methodist churches had an important advantage in landholding in comparison with the Church of England congregation, and those of Irish and Scottish heritage had an advantage over the English and Welsh. It is also the case that age or life cycle is by far the most important of the measured effects on a farmer's accumulated landholding, as all our earlier analyses indicated: all the age coefficients are positive, sizeable, and significantly different from zero.

The model could easily be made more complicated, say, by including combinations of categories reflecting the joint effects of variables, for example, the effect of being young and Catholic. We had no strong hypotheses of this kind to consider, and the inclusion of a number of complications can seriously compromise our ability to interpret a statistical model. On balance the analysis provides clear evidence that membership in the Baptist and Methodist congregations and, independently, in the Irish and Scottish ethnic communities significantly increased a man's chances of landholding in mid-Victorian Ontario.

LANDHOLDING INEQUALITY AMONG ONTARIO'S FARMERS

Despite recent valuable studies, there remain large gaps in our knowledge of the social and economic circumstances of Ontario's farmers. We still know relatively little about, for example, the household economies of farmers, family life, labour requirements, inheritance patterns, or occupational mobility in and out of farming. Moreover, if farmers made up Ontario's most significant class throughout the nineteenth century in sheer numbers and in shared conditions and ethos,[74] they were surely not a homogeneous group in their landholding wealth. What was the extent of inequality in ownership among farmers in 1871?

The foregoing tables 2.5, 2.6, and 2.7 provide relevant information. Each shows a series of Gini coefficients, the common summary measure of inequality in wealth distributions.[75] In table 2.7, for example, the second-to-last panel reports Gini indices (G) for all farmers in acreage owned, by nativity, and by ethnic-origin group. The index for all farmers is 0.59, suggesting comparatively modest inequality. It is also shown that the inequality was greater among the Canadian born than among immigrants, but the indices do not vary much by origin group; the greatest inequality is among the Canadian born of Irish origin, and the least is among the foreign-born Irish.

Table 2.5 gave the pattern by age group and table 2.6 by religious denomination. Inequality in holdings was greatest among the youngest men, otherwise varying little by age. And there was little to distinguish the religious groups.

The general pattern of inequality for the province can be presented in more detail. A sorting of the amount of acreage owned from highest to lowest for the 2,777 farmers in the sample yields the results of the table 2.8. In these data the landless population is equivalent to those with no acreage (lower class limit of 0, representing 0.374 of all farmers).

The very largest landowners, holding over 1,000 acres, represented only

TABLE 2.8
Proportions of farmers and of acreage by size of acreage, Ontario, 1871

Lower class limit acreage class, AC	Proportion of farmers above class limit, N_{AC}	Proportion of total acreage, A_{AC}
1,000–	0.0004	0.014
500–	0.0065	0.064
200–	0.098	0.376
100–	0.393	0.826
50–	0.580	0.982
1–	0.626	1.000
0	1.000	1.000

SOURCE: See table 2.6.

a tiny fraction of all farmers – about 4/100 of 1 per cent (0.0004). The calculations for proportions of total acreage show that these privileged few owned 1.4 per cent of the province's farm land (again, strictly, of the land reported as owned in the dominion). Those with large holdings, over 500 acres, including the very largest landowners, made up less than 1 per cent of all farmers, including the landless third. However, those owning 200 or more acres represented 9.8 per cent of the total. To be more precise, the top 1 per cent of all farmers held 8.5 per cent of land, the top 2 per cent had 14 per cent, the top 10 per cent had 38 per cent, and the top 20 per cent had 57 per cent. Thus, one-fifth of Ontario's farmers controlled nearly three-fifths of the land. Calculating the concentrations of property at the top shows that the structure of inequality among farmers in landholdings was steeply pitched. At the same time, the base of this distribution was also very wide. In these terms a contemporary would likely have been struck more by the relative moderation than by the depth of the inequality in landholding: only 39.4 per cent of farmers held 100 acres or more of land, as shown in table 2.8, and only 16.4 per cent of all men did so. There is scant evidence of how this inequality was perceived by contemporaries, but some points of comparison can be cited.

For Wentworth county in southern Ontario, Di Matteo and George report a Gini index of 0.72 or 0.73 in real estate holdings for 1872 and subsequent decades to the turn of the century, though the figure is somewhat lower in 1882. Their finding corresponds to the fact that the top 10 per cent of decedents held between 48 and 60 per cent of real estate wealth, somewhat greater inequality than we find for landed wealth in the province as a whole.[76]

From recent systematic studies of the same period, it seems sure that urban wealth inequality, at least in larger cities, was greater than the inequality in farm holdings over the province generally. Assessment roll data for Hamilton and Toronto show that the reported values of real estate and personal estate in those cities after 1851 was very concentrated. For example, the top 10 per cent of householders in Toronto held 54 and 56 per cent of *assessed* estate and personal wealth in 1861 and 1871.[77]

Data for farm areas in the United States provide another relevant point of comparison. As one would expect, inequality in Ontario's farm landholdings was moderate in comparison with that of dollar values of real estate or dollar values of total estate among males in similar rural areas of the United States.[78] If we convert size of farms for Ontario to approximate real estate values, a more direct comparison can be made. Using indirect correlations for 1860, a relationship between the value of real estate holdings per farm and size of farm can be derived from the U.S. data and then applied to Ontario. For the United States it is known that real estate values per farm were related to acres per farm by the relationship $RE = \$10 \times AC^{1.3}$. If we transform our Ontario acreage into a distribution of values using this coefficient and assuming $AC_{RE} = AC^{1.3}$ or $AC^{1.4}$, we obtain a pattern of inequality measured by a Gini coefficient of 0.66 or 0.70. The coefficient reflects a Lorenz curve of inequality among farm men – plotting the proportions of farmers by the proportions of land owned – which is quite similar to that in the northern states in 1870.[79]

These are limited comparisons. Still, if we consider nineteenth-century Ontario's heavily immigrant and very mobile population, we must assume that people could draw direct and generally favourable comparisons with the more limited opportunities for farmownership in Europe and apparently comparable opportunities in the northern United States. They also would have known that the structure of wealthholding in major cities was even less favourable. Moreover, as we have argued earlier, the processes of individual land attainment gave many people reason to think they could gain some measure of the security and independence promised by family landowning.

OVERVIEW

Landownership patterns in Ontario in 1871 reveal that less than two-thirds of farming men were owners. Considering that this figure includes large numbers of farmers' sons at home qualifies the first impression that it represented a deep structural divide between owners and landless. These sons occupied an ambiguous, suspended status between owner and dispossessed, but they were landless in terms of title. More important, the proportion of owners increased directly and rapidly with age and there are sound reasons to think that the age pattern largely reflects the historical process of land acquisition over individual life cycles. The pattern indicates that from the 1840s and 1850s to the early 1870s the chances were quite good that a propertyless farmer would become a landowner: about 3 per cent of all landless adult farmers could expect to become owners in every year. In 1871 by age 50 over 85 per cent of farmers were in fact owners.

A further implication is that the proportion of landed farmers by age very likely remained constant from year to year, since the farm population also grew about 3 per cent per year in this period. Thus, it is not a contradiction that there was a persistent age-graded divide in the landed economy between owners and landless and considerable individual opportunity for land acquisition. The one, in fact, entailed the other: the landless proportion was annually fed by the youngest entrants to the farm economy, who had very reasonable expectations of gaining a 'competency' in land. The analysis further suggests that on a provincial level no dramatic crisis in access to land had been experienced two decades after mid-century, though the term may be an appropriate description of the circumstances of a core of stable and aspiring farmers in a given locale, as Gagan has observed for Peel county. Migration, both within Ontario and beyond, and lively land markets in areas that had been long settled by the middle of the last century were the other major features of land transmission in mid-Victorian Ontario.[80]

In general, the possession and use of land remained the fundamental economic and social resource in Victorian Ontario. In addition to farmers, many others owned or rented land. Although tenancy rates were actually fairly low, representing only about 11 per cent of adult men, fully one-half of all Ontario's adult men occupied some cultivable land in 1871. These petty owners included significant numbers of labourers, whose family economies presumably were wholly or partially dependent on land for their survival. Especially large numbers of people occupied plots of land in *urban* areas, attesting to the vital importance of cultivation and gardening for urban household economies. In a related context, very few women were ever heads of households, but among them nearly one-third owned land and four in ten over age 40 were owners.

Regarding landed wealth we find that average acreage owned increased from age 20 to age 60 in 1871 and then decreased significantly. Again it is shown that the pattern implies a steady process of increasing farm size over the life cycle and that the average size of farms was virtually constant over several decades prior to 1871. The finding is consistent with existing aggregate census data for 1851 to 1871.

In addition, farm size differed considerably among some of the province's main ethnic and religious communities, and the differences could not be accounted for by demographic and settlement factors, as far as we are able to determine. Baptists had a 15 to 20 per cent advantage in farm acreage per capita, and Methodists had 10 per cent more land per capita than either Catholics or members of the Church of England. Thus, there is some evidence to suggest the continuing importance of an evangelical moral order in fostering an emergent agrarian middle class. Among ethnic groups, the Irish as a whole had 20 per cent more land per farmer and the Scottish had 15 per cent more than those of English, German, and French origin. A closer analysis of Protestant-Catholic differences among the Irish revealed them to be minor with respect to landownership and farm size, reinforcing recent revisionist interpretations of the Irish-Catholic experience in the province.

Ontario was hardly a promised land in the late nineteenth century, but the comparatively modest landed inequality and, especially, continuing access to land for the young would have encouraged many families to believe their quest for landed security, independence, and patrimony would be rewarded. The prospect was neither mere ideology nor illusion.

3

Home Ownership, Secure Property, and the Propertyless: Structural Patterns and Cultural Communities

INTRODUCTION

In Ontario in 1871 family land and family economies were the pillars of a way of life closely tied to the ethos of independent yeomanry. As the analysis of the previous chapter has demonstrated, the prospects that a farming man would become a landowner before his fortieth birthday were remarkably good in Victorian Ontario. For these families the farm home was the taken-for-granted centre of household production and of the social reproduction of family life. Home ownership was also a vital resource for mid-Victorian non-farm families in their attempt to ensure a measure of competency. In Doucet and Weaver's words, 'A home that one could improve, even build, on freehold land made "the New World" a meaningful term' in the last century.[1]

Once considered of only passing interest, the question of home ownership has been revealed in recent studies to be central to our understanding of nineteenth-century family and class.[2] Although age and class conditioned the chances of urban ownership, people of very modest means strove to establish a secure base for their families in the face of much insecurity. For this reason working-class men and women may have had the very strongest aspirations for a 'home of their own.' Katz, Doucet, and Stern cite a revealing quotation from the *Ontario Workman* of 1872: 'Next to being married to the right woman, there is nothing so important in one's life as to live under one's own roof, ... there is no landlord troubling us with raising the rent, and expecting this and that. There is no fear in our bosom that in sickness and old age we will be thrown out of house and home, and the money saved to pay the rent is sufficient to keep us in comfort in the winter days of life.'[3]

In recent urban history, a focus on the value of home ownership for family economies and security has displaced in large measure the consideration of houses as a form of economic accumulation: use value apparently predominated over exchange value, to borrow Katz, Doucet, and Stern's rendering. The emphasis is not misplaced, but clearly the two are not mutually exclusive. Even for those with modest means, if good fortune and resources allowed, the purchase of a second house probably appeared to be the most promising way to supplement family income and hedge the uncertainties of the economy, health, and old age in the last century. It may not, in fact, have been an optimal investment, as a continuing debate indicates.[4] But from the point of view of ordinary familes, coupling the relative independence and personal satisfaction of home ownership with the home's potentially appreciating value was a sensible, perhaps compelling, strategy. Of course, accumulating a number of houses was an even more obvious investment for those who had the financial means.

In the following analysis we are concerned both with the general distribution of home ownership and with the accumulation of houses as a form of wealth. Like land, of course, houses represent only real estate, not personal estate. And some groups were better placed to invest in other forms of wealth, including other forms of real estate. Shopkeepers or craftsmen were more likely accumulate merchant or industrial capital than farmers, clerks, or labourers were. Less obvious, but no less intriguing, is the prospect that some cultural or denominational groups may have taken advantage of financial or non-residential investment opportunities in preference to real estate, as a reflection of common experiences and cultural practices. Some, like Jews, may have preferred to rent accommodation, as a consequence of discrimination. Like other historical analyses to date, our study is unable to trace such specific patterns in wealthholding, though it does concentrate on ethnic and religious variations in home ownership later in this chapter. In any case, studies of the northern part of the United States and of Ontario indicate that there were quite high correlations between real and personal property holding in the nineteenth century.[5] We analyse home ownership, then, first recognizing the diffuse economic and social value of freehold dwellings for family economies on and off the farm and, second simply as a basic real estate investment.[6]

The sample data permit the first province-wide analysis of home ownership in nineteenth-century Ontario. The analysis includes an examination of ownership among women heads of households and is then extended from the ownership of homes to a variety of other forms of real estate: shops, stores, warehouses, barns, vehicles, and acreage. This analysis distinguishes those with minimum holdings from the 'securely propertied' and from the literally propertyless. Finally, the main conditions contributing to ownership are assessed in a multivariate analysis, including life cycle, ethnicity, and denominational differences.

HOME OWNERSHIP, ONTARIO, 1871: DISTRIBUTIONS AND
PATTERNS OF ACQUISITION

Our first analysis of home ownership focuses on patterns among adult males. Figure 3.1 shows the proportion of male home owners by age and, for comparison, the proportions of all adult men (not just farmers) who owned land or were tenants, which is drawn from the analysis of chapter 2. Home ownership exceeds the age-specific rates of landownership at virtually every age. One reason, of course, is that the ownership of land tended to confer the ownership of a dwelling as a condition of farming for a livelihood. The age patterns of land and home ownership are strikingly similar. The pattern for the latter, however, rises even more rapidly with age. Almost no men owned homes at age 20, but almost 50 per cent did so at *age 30* in 1871. The data suggest there was, simply, a quite remarkable rate of home acquisition in the province. Over three-quarters of men could reasonably expect to own homes by their early forties if the 1871 pattern held over time. As in the case of land acquisition, the pattern is taken to reflect mainly life-cycle experiences, rather than structural change. The assumption is based on the very rapid rise of home ownership with age and the lack of reason or evidence to suggest that the opportunities for home purchase or building had been dramatically curtailed in the twenty years after mid-century.

With some levelling in the rate of increase after age 45, home ownership attained a peak rate exceeding 80 per cent of all men in their late fifties. The rate declined fairly rapidly after age 60 but never fell below about 50 per cent, even for men in their late seventies. The data also indicate that *land* 'possession', that is, tenancy and ownership combined, tended to parallel home ownership rates closely. Home ownership was notably higher than land possession for men until their early sixties. That it fell below land possession for men in their seventies suggests that non-farm rates of ownership declined quite steeply for this older group.

The striking conclusion to be drawn from these age patterns is that owning one's own home would have been an expectation of virtually all heads of households in the mid-Victorian era in Ontario: no resident could have failed to notice that few men in their middle years did not own a home of some description. Of course, this situation poses the question of the variety

FIGURE 3.1 Proportion of home owners, landowners, and land 'possessors' among adult males in Ontario, 1871, by age

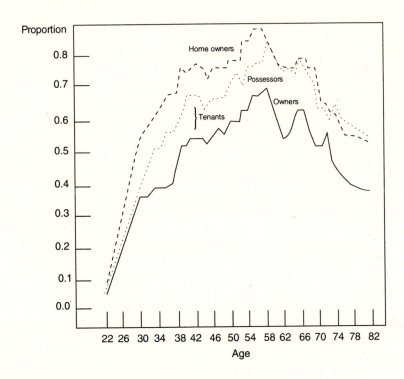

of types of construction represented by the simple census record of 'dwelling houses owned.' They varied from urban shanties to city mansions and the fine three-storey brick and wooden 'gingerbread' houses that began to dot the farm communities of the 1860s and 1870s. No evidence is available for systematic analysis of house types in 1871, but in appendix B of the chapter we consider the unique information on types of housing construction from the census of 1851–2 to provide some purchase on the question.

More generally, the expectation that a home of some description was attainable by many was tempered by other economic and social differences, such as urban or rural location, farm or non-farm occupation, birthplace, religion, and ethnicity. We consider these factors in turn. First, we examine more closely the process of home acquisition.

Log house built in 1859

Home of William and Jane Scott, built in 1858, South Dumfries township

What was the likelihood of a man's owning a home in Ontario in 1871? The census data indicate that the proportion of *all* adult males owning homes was 0.473, slightly less than half. As we have just seen, the non-owning half was composed largely of the young. We consider the age patterns of ownership for farm and non-farm groups and for native and immigrant populations. Table 3.1 presents the relevant data. Among the immigrants we further distinguish between the largest group, the Irish population, and all other immigrants. The main patterns can be readily summarized.

The overall rate (0.473) is given at the upper left-hand corner for all men aged 20 to 99. The first row shows the age gradient for the sample. As figure 3.1 revealed, the home ownership rate for those over age 50 is 0.71 and is so relatively high that further age distinctions are not made for this group.[7] The rapid rise in ownership with age plotted in figure 3.1 represents the series of age-specific rates, 0.07, 0.28, 0.47, 0.55, 0.68 and 0.71 for the six age groups 20–24, 25–29 ... 50 and over. To reiterate, it is striking that nearly 30 per cent of men owned some form of home before age 30 and nearly half of all men aged 30 to 34 were already home owners. Despite the general age gradient, did some social groups enjoy clear advantages in attaining homes? In comparing various groups we report age-standardized rates as well as crude rates, since age had such a strong relation to ownership. They are given in the far right-hand column.[8]

The first contrast of note is that between the native and foreign born. The latter were substantially more likely to own homes, just as in chapter 2 we found immigrant farmers were more likely to own land. The precise proportions are 0.401 of the Canadian born and 0.541 of the immigrants. Moreover, the largest immigrant group, the Irish born, were *most* likely to own homes: over 60 per cent in the entire province did so (0.610 in table 3.1). The latter finding corresponds to the results of recent local histories, but we establish here that the drive for home ownership among the Irish was not simply urban or local, but clearly was province wide. Moreover, although there is little difference among the nativity groups in age trends of home acquisition, the Irish were the most confirmed home buyers and builders among the youngest groups and also tended to retain homes in greater proportions after age 50: some 78 per cent of the Irish over age 50 were still owners, compared with about 70 per cent of the other groups.

The far right-hand column of the table reveals that these differences were strongly age dependent. In fact, the age standardization shows that if the groups had the same age composition, the Canadian-born men would have slightly exceeded the foreign-born in ownership of homes (0.487 versus 0.456). Even with hypothetically identical age distributions, however, we

TABLE 3.1
Proportion of home owners among adult males in Ontario, 1871, by age, nativity, occupation, and religion

Group	20–99	20–24	25–29	30–34	35–39	40–49	50–99	Sample size	Standard-ized rates
All	0.473	0.07	0.28	0.47	0.55	0.68	0.71	5,386	0.473
Canadian born	0.401	0.07	0.30	0.51	0.60	0.72	0.71	2,618	0.487
Foreign born	0.541	0.06	0.23	0.43	0.51	0.66	0.72	2,768	0.456
Irish born	0.610	0.07	0.34	0.48	0.58	0.66	0.78	1,026	0.511
Other foreign	0.501	0.05	0.17	0.39	0.46	0.67	0.67	1,742	0.425
Non-farmers	0.303	0.05	0.12	0.27	0.38	0.46	0.51	2,609	0.321
Canadian born	0.242	0.05	0.17	0.32	0.38	0.52	0.47	1,155	0.320
Foreign born	0.351	0.05	0.12	0.27	0.38	0.46	0.51	1,454	0.314
Irish born	0.418	0.02	0.20	0.31	0.45	0.46	0.58	500	0.352
Other foreign	0.316	0.05	0.09	0.25	0.35	0.45	0.45	954	0.294
Farmers	0.633	0.09	0.41	0.65	0.73	0.85	0.86	2,777	0.610
Canadian born	0.527	0.09	0.41	0.63	0.80	0.84	0.85	1,463	0.603
Foreign born	0.752	0.08	0.42	0.68	0.67	0.86	0.87	1,314	0.623
Irish born	0.793	0.15	0.51	0.73	0.70	0.87	0.92	526	0.675
Other foreign	0.724	0.04	0.36	0.65	0.65	0.86	0.83	788	0.586

NOTE: Standardized values have been obtained by applying Ontario male population weights to six age categories.
SOURCE: The film-manuscript sample of size 5,386.

find home ownership by the Irish born would have exceeded that by other groups (0.511).

As remarked above, home ownership was naturally a feature, and part of the continuing attraction, of farm ownership in the last century. We expect large differences between farmers and non-farmers, though we note again that the former include landless adult sons of farmers and the latter many rural non-farm residents.

The results in table 3.1 conform to the expectation. About a third of non-farmers owned homes (0.303) and just less than two-thirds of all farmers were owners (0.633). Below, we shall consider the home ownership rates for those in the province's cities, towns, and villages compared with those for rural residents. The overall non-farm rates given here are of interest, since they indicate a quite considerable capacity on the part of Ontario's nineteenth-century population to purchase or build houses even among those not cultivating the land.

Again the age distributions for the specific groups give us some measure of the probable process of acquisition. The rapidity with which farmers attained homes of their own is reflected in the fact that over four times as many (40 per cent) 25–29-year-old farmers as 20–24-year-olds (9 per cent) were freeholders. Moreover, the proportion of owners increased with every age group to above 85 per cent. Increasing proportions of non-farmers were owners in every age group as well, but only after age 50 did over half own their own homes. Despite the clear and understandable differences, the most striking result is the extent of the ownership for both groups with advancing years.

No doubt there were definite cultural and community variations within the province. We consider the Irish here, given their numerical predominance and the fact that earlier studies have established their unusual penchant for home ownership. Whether farmers or not, once again it is clear that the Irish immigrants distinguished themselves as more intent upon acquiring homes than the rest of the population. Overall, about 40 per cent (0.418) of the non-farming Irish born were home owners, as were a very substantial 80 per cent of all Irish-born farmers (0.793). By contrast about a quarter (0.242) of the Canadian born who were not farmers and just over half of the native-born farmers (0.527) were home owners. It is of note that, although the differences are moderated somewhat, the age standardized rates confirm the Irish immigrant's exceptionality for both farm and non-farm sectors.

URBAN AND RURAL HOME OWNERSHIP

The main studies of nineteenth-century home ownership in North America have been conducted for urban areas.[9] Based on the 1871 census and on tax assessments for other years, the city studies provide a quite consistent picture of home ownership. In nineteenth-century Hamilton, Toronto, and Kingston about a third of the population were owners.

Table 3.2 gives the results of the Ontario sample for adult males, distinguishing villages, towns, and cities among the province's incorporated places.[10] Home ownership opportunities were divided by place of residence. The chance was much greater for the province's rural and village residents than for town and city residents. About half of the rural and small village households owned their residences (0.52 and 0.49), while less than a third of the town and city dwellers were owners in 1871 (0.29 and 0.22).[11]

What would account for the significantly lower chance a person could own a home in towns and cities than in rural villages and in the countryside? Two factors may be immediately cited. First, for the most part, houses were purchased with cash. The most careful study to date reveals that a minority

TABLE 3.2

Proportion of home owners among adult males in Ontario, 1871, by urban-rural residence, type of urban place, and nativity

Group	Actual rates					Age standardized rates				
	All	Rural	Village	Town	City	All	Rural	Village	Town	City
All	0.473	0.52	0.49	0.29	0.22	0.473	0.51	0.49	0.32	0.23
Canadian born	0.401	0.43	0.38	0.23	0.15	0.487	0.51	0.54	0.33	0.20
Foreign born	0.541	0.61	0.57	0.33	0.25	0.456	0.51	0.49	0.30	0.23

NOTE: See table 3.1.
SOURCE: See table 3.1.

of homes were mortgaged in the latter part of the nineteenth century, and these mortgages were for short terms and for a small portion of the purchase price.[12] Small-town and rural homes were even less likely to be financed, since much of the lending was made by the original owners or wealthier residents, not by institutions. Moreover, the main costs were not of material or labour, but of land. Land was simply less available and more expensive in the larger urban areas. Second, and importantly, it appears that many people built their own homes in the nineteenth century. The extent of this 'sweat equity' in housing has only recently been recognized. Given the fewer building restrictions and the greater availability of sites, materials, and, perhaps, neighbourly assistance in building, personal construction would have significantly increased the opportunity for home ownership in villages and in the countryside in comparison with towns and cities.[13]

The relative ease with which homes could be acquired in the countryside and in villages would have been a factor in the continued attraction of rural residence. There is some tendency to exaggerate the relative significance and magnetic force of metropolitan areas in Victorian Ontario, but no doubt they were increasingly places of permanent or prolonged residence, offering a growing range of services and other attractions.[14] In addition, there were those families for whom urban residence was a necessity, as the major site of expanding wage work.

As Katz and his colleagues have emphasized, for the urban working class, as for farming families, no resource afforded greater economic and social security than home ownership. In Hamilton working-class men who stayed in the city over the 1861–71 decade were actually more likely to be home owners than were members of the business class. In 1871 in Peel county's main city, Brampton, Gagan reports that labouring families approximated the city's average rate of home ownership.[15] The provincial evidence in our sample tends to confirm these results. For all urban areas of the province our sample indicates that a quarter of the labourers were home owners. This figure compares with about 30 per cent of all the other urban occupational groups, including skilled workers, master artisans, merchants, manufacturers, and professionals, and with only 16 per cent of rural, agricultural labourers. Given their relative insecurity of employment and the low wages of urban labouring families, the fact that so many owned homes underscores the significance of the *Ontario Workman*'s claim, cited above, that 'there is nothing so important to one's life as to live under one's own roof.'[16]

Table 3.2 also shows the urban-rural differentials between Canadian-born and immigrant men. The immigrant families had an advantage as home owners in all types of urban areas, as well as in the countryside. In fact, their advantage was greatest in the rural and village settings, where 61 and 57 per cent of immigrant men were owners, in contrast to 43 and 38 per cent of the native born. This was the actual experience, but as before, the age-standardized rates indicate that this advantage could be attributed largely to the age differentials of the two groups.

The widespread home ownership among farm families and, relatively, among urban working-class families reinforces the view that it was one of the essential conditions of a viable family economy for both. For the mid-Victorian Ontario women who headed their own households, perhaps no resource could have been so vital.

WOMEN AND HOMES

We have seen that relatively few women headed households or held property in nineteenth-century Ontario. Nevertheless, for our sample of women who were household heads, almost 60 per cent were home owners (0.572). This high rate was first a product of the fact that for widows ownership was a condition of independence, rather than becoming a ward of older sons or other male members of a family. Bruce Elliott notes that over half of the wills of the male Ottawa Valley residents that he traced conferred control of the homestead to their widowed wives for life, even though title reverted to male heirs eventually.[17]

Comparing the sample women with male *heads* of households indicates the women were just 10 per cent less likely to be owners. The rate for male heads was 0.667.[18] An adjustment of the rates for the seven-year average discrepancy in age between women and men heads lowers the 'expected' female ownership rate to 0.52, still a high proportion (the average age of women heads was 50.4 years; of male heads 43.4 years). Closer analysis revealed almost no variation between Canadian-born and foreign-born women. There were significant variations by age, of course. The home ownership proportions by age are given for both female and male heads in table 3.3.

As is the case for men, ownership among women heads rises with age, though even more steeply. Nearly half the male heads aged 20 to 29 were home owners, but only a quarter of the women heads were. Yet over 60 per cent of female heads over age 40 were owners, compared with about 70 per cent of the men. Since about 60 per cent of these young women (twelve of twenty-one in the sample) were already widows, presumably they had inherited the homesteads acquired during their marriages. A few other owners were young married women whose husbands were absent at the time of the census, probably working elsewhere in support of their families. Mainly, however, home ownership implied widowhood for women. Three-quarters of women heads of households aged 30 to 50 were widowed, as were more than 90 per cent of those over 50.

Women heads, even widows, never matched the ownership rates of male heads, but their level of home ownership is significant and indicative of the value of homes for the maintenance of person and family in the last century. Conversely, life must have been especially trying for the other 40 per cent of women solely responsible for families without their own homes as sources of income and security.

Table 3.4 presents more detailed information on the social characteristics of the women home owners in comparison with those of male heads of households. To adjust for the wide age differential between the men and women heads, only age-standardized rates of ownership are presented. Considering urban and rural residence and nativity, women have lower rates in every social group, except one.[19] Canadian-born women and men heads were most likely to be owners of homes, though the women were some 13 per cent less likely than men (57 per cent versus 70 per cent; these samples are of modest size, but the difference is statistically significant[20]). Foreign-born women were very slightly disadvantaged in comparison with foreign-born men, especially the Irish born. The latter finding is intriguing, since it means men benefited more directly than women from the documented Irish immigrants' drive for property ownership, and it perhaps implies there were important variations in inheritance strategies among immigrant groups that have yet to be documented.

The urban-rural comparison between male and female heads shows that in the towns and cities women nearly matched male heads in owning homes, with ownership rates of 39 per cent among women and 44 per cent among

TABLE 3.3

Proportions of female and male heads of households owning homes in Ontario, 1871, by age

Age	Female heads	No. of female heads	Male heads	No. of male heads
20–29	0.24	21	0.46	623
30–39	0.48	56	0.61	1,080
40–49	0.63	71	0.73	888
50–59	0.64	70	0.75	611
60–69	0.58	57	0.85	418
70 and over	0.63	38	0.74	186
Total	0.572	313	0.667	3,806

SOURCE: The film-manuscript sample of 313 females and 5,380 males 20 years old or over. Female heads of households or property owners were included. Only ten of the females were non-heads who possessed or owned acreage or other property.

male heads, a difference that is not statistically significant in these samples. It would be reasonable to suppose that widowed women heads of households tended to move to urban areas, where homes provided a number of sources of income, including boarding. As noted earlier, women heads were more likely to have been urban residents in 1871 than were male heads, when about 34 per cent lived in villages, towns or major cities, in comparison to the urban 19 per cent of men who headed households. In one case, in fact, where almost 60 per cent of non-Irish immigrant women were urban home owners, their home ownership rate considerably exceeded that of urban immigrant male heads (0.59 versus 0.38). We have no basis on which to account for the reversal of the usual male advantage.

In rural areas the contrast between women and men heads was 60 per cent to 72 per cent. Women would have had greater difficulty operating a farm than men, even with the prospect of hiring help, with the assistance of adult children, and with the norms of mutual assistance that prevailed in farming communities. For this reason, the 60 per cent of rural women heads who were home owners is an unexpectedly large proportion. Further, the circumstances of the Canadian- and Irish-born rural women were the reverse of their urban counterparts; they were more likely to be owners than the other foreign-born women. Two-thirds of the Canadian-born women heads owned homes, only 6 per cent less than the male heads in rural areas. For reasons that are not clear, and in direct contrast to those in urban places, non-Irish, foreign-born women were least able to maintain their own homes, falling far behind households headed by foreign-born men (44 per cent

TABLE 3.4
Standardized rates of home ownership for female and male heads of households in Ontario, 1871, by nativity and urban-rural residence

| Group | Home ownership proportion | |
	Females	Males
All	0.52	0.67
Canadian born	0.57	0.70
Foreign born	0.48	0.63
Irish born	0.48	0.69
Other foreign	0.47	0.60
Urban	0.39	0.44
Canadian born	0.38	0.48
Foreign born	0.43	0.41
Irish born	0.36	0.45
Other foreign	0.59	0.38
Rural	0.60	0.72
Canadian born	0.66	0.72
Foreign born	0.51	0.71
Irish born	0.63	0.77
Other foreign	0.44	0.67

NOTES: Standardized values were obtained by applying Ontario population weights of adult male heads for six age categories to the average rates of these categories (weights of 623, 1,080, 888, 611, 418, and 186, totalling 3,806 to rates of age categories from 20–29, 30–39 ... 60–69, 70 and older). Adjustment was necessary, since the average age of the female sample was 50.4 years and the average for males was 43.4 years.
SOURCE: The film-manuscript sample of 313 female and 3,806 male heads; ten of the women were non-head property owners.

versus 67 per cent). A reasonable speculation is that these immigrant families had recently established a precarious toehold on rural small property holding, which gave way when husbands died or were forced to abandon their families.

About half the women who assumed sole responsibility for families, often in widowhood, were able to enlist home ownership as a basis of their family economy. The finding underscores the significance of homes as places in which women anchored their productive activity in the last century. Though fewer of them were owners than were male heads, the relatively large proportion nevertheless reflects the singular importance of homes in maintaining a female-headed family intact in old Ontario.

HOUSING AND REAL ESTATE ACCUMULATION

We have seen that about half of the adult men in Ontario owned their own homes in 1871, and nearly 70 per cent were owners if they were heads of households. Over half the small minority of women who were heads of households were also home owners. The proportions reflect the persistence of the culture of independent family economies and the extent to which people still expected to become home owners by their early middle years. But, as already remarked, for some families the accumulation of houses represented more than the basis of a family economy; they were also investments and sources of wealth, however uncertain. Although many nineteenth-century houses were log or frame constructions, the two-storey brick or stone house was increasingly common by the 1870s and was indeed a substantial investment, especially if more than one was owned.[21] A revealing glimpse of overall property distributions may be given by taking ownership of a second house to be a sign of modest prosperity, and ownership of several houses an indication of substantial real estate wealth in 1871.

Table 3.5 gives the cumulative frequency distributions of men, classified by the number of houses owned. The table also gives the average number owned and the Gini index of inequality, varying from zero to 1, as explained above.[22] The table indicates that only about 9 per cent of the adult male population owned two or more houses. A minuscule number of families owned as many as three or four houses. This evidence of a quite small propertied class is in line with the multiple ownership reported in studies of two Ontario cities for 1871. In Hamilton, 12 per cent of household *heads* owned two or more houses and 13 per cent of Brampton's householders were multiple owners.[23] One would expect the provincial proportions of multiple owners to be smaller than those in the two cities, given the size of the farm economy and the fact most farmers owned only one dwelling. In any case, by this measure, real estate wealth was rather homogeneously distributed in mid-Victorian Ontario.

The equally telling fact is that this small group of men – less than 10 per cent in the province – in fact owned a large portion of Ontario's housing stock, just a fraction less than 40 per cent (39.4 per cent). The top 2.8 per cent of men who held three or more houses, as reported in table 3.5, was found to own 18.8 per cent of all homes in the province. The top 1.3 per cent, with four or more houses, owned 11.7 per cent of the stock. Thus, one needs to consider both the shape of a distribution of housing wealth, in which there was a broadly based 'rough equality' of home ownership among the great majority, who owned just their family residence, and the

TABLE 3.5

Distribution of homes owned by adult males in Ontario, 1871, by farmers and non-farmers

H, number of homes owned	Proportion owning H or more homes		
	All	Farmers	Non-farmers
5	0.007	0.006	0.009
4	0.013	0.013	0.013
3	0.028	0.030	0.026
2	0.093	0.114	0.070
1	0.473	0.633	0.303
	1.000	1.000	1.000
Average, $\overline{H}$	0.628	0.805	0.440
Gini inequality index, G	0.63	0.48	0.78

SOURCE: The film-manuscript sample of 5,386 adult males, including 2,777 farmers and 2,609 non-farmers.

fact that a minority of multiple owners controlled a great deal of wealth in housing stock. The relatively open processes of entry into home ownership and the broadly based structure of inequality in housing parallel those found in access to and inequality in landownership. Presumably, too, like land-ownership the ownership of homes was a very different matter for farm and non-farm sectors of the provincial economy.

Consideration of farmers and non-farmers separately (table 3.5) shows that there was a small minority of substantial property owners in each group; about 3 per cent of the men owned three or more houses in each sector. On the other hand, in the farm sector the dispersion of property was generally much more equal. The small elite group of multiple home owners among farmers would not have been apparent to contemporaries, since there were twice as many farmers as non-farmers owning one home. The Gini indices in table 3.5 reflect this difference in relative inequality. For the farmers the index is 0.48; for the non-farmers it is 0.78. Clearly, inequality in real estate was substantially greater in the non-farm economy. Perhaps this was another sound reason why the ideal of the independent yeoman farmer remained strongly rooted in Ontario after Confederation.

THE SECURELY PROPERTIED AND THE PROPERTYLESS: BEYOND THE HOUSEHOLD ECONOMY

It has been shown that a relatively small group of men, less than 10 per cent of all adult men, owned two or more houses in Ontario in 1871, though a great many more could expect to own a family residence. Male heads of families were far more likely to have been multiple owners than were women heads or single adult men. Chapter 2 also revealed that considerable equality of access to small property for farming men was combined with a steep inequality in the ownership of acreage. As we have argued, broad access to small property holdings and relatively restricted opportunities for even moderate property accumulation are not incompatible social processes. But the land and home ownership patterns raise a larger question of the structure of inequality. Who was able to accumulate more than a family farm or an urban home and who was truly propertyless in nineteenth-century Ontario?

The census of 1871 included a wide variety of questions bearing on ownership and assets. In addition to providing information on land and 'dwelling houses,' the real estate schedule also reported other establishments owned, warehouses, shops, stores, and the like, and the numbers of stables, barns, and vehicles owned. Schedule 4, for agricultural products, also distinguished improved and unimproved acreage and whether one was an owner or an 'occupier' of the land.[24] Taken together, these items of information provide an unusual opportunity to assess the size of Ontario's wholly propertyless class in comparison with the propertied. A central focus of the previous chapter was the extent of propertylessness among farmers. The analysis of this chapter addresses the question more fully by including the non-farming male population.

Consider how one might define a relatively secure propertied class in nineteenth-century Ontario. To this point we have seen that the possession of a family farm or the ownership of a family residence were within the normal expectations of large numbers of quite ordinary Ontarians. Since these resources were so fundamental to making a living and maintaining a family, those who owned them can hardly be considered people of privilege or a propertied elite. We suspect that many who owned small farms and single homes were just making do; we know some would have been routinely in jeopardy of losing their small stake, given the vicissitudes of health, climate, soil, and of local commodity and labour markets. The unusual nineteenth-century diarist, Wilson Benson, reported by Katz, may have been an anomaly, but his travels and travails strike a chord of authenticity. He farmed the same property most of his adult years, but he was subject to one crisis after another and responded by undertaking multiple job and residential changes throughout his lifetime.[25] Among the Tipperary Protestant emigrant families to Ontario, so carefully traced by Elliott, there were many whose fortunes changed dramatically for the worse with the father's early death, or as a result of inheriting plots too small to make do, or with a sudden reversal in their trade or business.[26] For a cross-section of the 1871 census, it is reasonable, then, to distinguish those with a small farm property or a single home from those we may call the 'securely' propertied and, of course, from the truly wealthy.

To define the more privileged groups we examine the distributions for each of the property ownership variables, selecting cut-off points that made substantive sense and included a relatively small percentage of those at the upper tail of each distribution.

Specifically, we define the securely propertied and rich group as follows: those who *occupied* or *owned* 200 or more acres of land or reported over 100 improved acres of farm land. Also qualifying are those who owned two or more houses, or one warehouse, store, shop, or other commercial property, or four or more stables, barns, or carriages, or four or more sleds and wagons, or one or more boats. All such census criteria are more or less arbitrary. We have tried to err on the conservative side; taken individually, these are fairly narrow definitions. In each case less than 6 per cent of the male population is included (5.9 per cent owned 200 or more acres; 4.6 and 5.1 per cent occupied 200 acres or more and 100 acres or more of improved land, respectively. Just 5.1 per cent owned a warehouse, shop, store, or the like). At the other extreme, we consider those who reported no property or real assets of any kind – the literally propertyless.

Taken together, the criteria of secure property reveal that there were, in fact, many ways of establishing some propertied surety in mid-Victorian Ontario. Those with property holdings beyond small farms and single homes made up almost 30 per cent (0.292) of the male heads of households of the province in 1871. This was a diverse group, including a very few, very wealthy men, for example, those who owned large blocks of farm land, large manufactories, or many houses, as well as those who owned a single store, a workshop, or a few wagons. In class terms, we may say they largely represent Ontario's combined bourgeoisie and petite bourgeoisie. The latter especially was a varied assortment of master artisans, shop owners, small merchants, and, quite likely, even the more successful pedlars and hucksters.[27] As we would expect from the preceding analysis, secure holdings were essentially denied to those who were not yet heads of households. Less than 1 per cent of the male non-heads in the province qualified by our criteria as securely propertied.

Those with substantial or secure property holdings formed a quite significant portion of Ontario's population; the virtually propertyless comprised an even larger group. Nearly 40 per cent (0.390) of all adult men fell in to the latter category. Again, as in the case of the analysis of farm

Small commercial establishments were a common form of property ownership in nineteenth-century Ontario towns. Dundas Street, Woodstock, 1865

Small factories and workshops were among Victorian Ontario's many forms of small property. Gardner and Rose Co.: Carriages, Waggons and Sleighs, Vansittart Avenue, Woodstock, c. 1865

land, an understanding of the implications of the numbers who were propertyless depends entirely on also knowing that only slightly more than 14
per cent of the male heads of households were without holdings, compared
with fully 98 per cent of those who were not heads. Clearly, among non-
heads of all ages one could simply not escape being propertyless. Only a
few unusual male dependants aged 50 to 59 had acquired a piece of Ontario's
property pie in 1871, even if it was a small slice (in the sample of 1,580
non-heads fewer than ten men).

We noted earlier that there are two different approaches to the question
of propertyless dependants. The issues bear brief review in the context of
this analysis. First, the life-cycle and family situations of dependants can be
ignored, risking inflating the social and class implications of their lack of
formal ownership. Alternatively, there is a temptation to dismiss these non-
heads as mainly young men whose propertyless state would merely pass in
the fullness of time. In fact, they were mainly young men; in Ontario in
1871, 88 per cent were under age 40, and 75 per cent were under 30. And
as we have seen in the analyses of land and home acquisition, if one survived
through adulthood, the passage of time was rather likely to be accompanied
by property ownership.

However, neither simply including nor simply excluding the adult non-
heads will do. On the one hand, their current lack of property directly
reflected their social status as subordinate members of families and households, although most expected some assistance in establishing themselves
independently, and families were very largely organized around that expectation.[28] On the other hand, the young propertyless in 1871 were as much
a component of the structure of inequality as those in their middle years or
the aged. Moreover, if the young had sensible hopes of modest property
attainment and could readily observe that their immediate elders had fared
well in its acquisition, they nevertheless faced a changing social and economic order. We have argued above that there is good reason to emphasize
the structural continuity of the largely agrarian economy of Ontario through
the third quarter of the century. Nevertheless, the economy had visibly
altered with the explosion of the railway network after 1850 and the uneven,
but visible, spread of manufacturing and wage labour in the urban centres
of south-central Ontario.[29] Even in the relative prosperity of the 1860s and
very early 1870s, there was little room for youthful complacency, as the
depression following 1873 was sure proof.

Though both sides of this interpretive coin need to be considered, the
majority of men were married and headed households by the age of thirty
and most widowers tended to remarry relatively quickly, so far as current

studies indicate.[30] A central fact of nineteenth-century Ontario life was simply that property was almost always attained in the context of family formation and independent household production. And the fact also remains that among heads of households fewer than one man in seven was propertyless in the province just after Confederation, a small proportion by any historical standard.[31]

WOMEN AND PROPERTY

Given the surprisingly high levels of land and home ownership that we found among women heads of households, what numbers held substantial or secure property by our working definition? In fact, despite the social and legal dependence of the great majority of nineteenth-century women, nearly a quarter of female household heads had significant property holdings. The largest proportion was the 16 per cent who owned two or more residences, followed by the 8 per cent who claimed ownership of shops, stores, or warehouses (compared with 13 and 7 per cent of male *heads*). A somewhat larger proportion, 28 per cent, were propertyless. The remainder, less than half of women heads, were owners of modest farms or single homes.

The sample results allow us to estimate the proportion of women who held property in their own names in this era. Slightly less than 8 per cent of the families in the sample were headed by women and almost no single women reported property holding. Given that we find approximately 70 per cent of these women heads held property of some description, then about 5 or 6 per cent (0.08 x 0.7) of all women in nineteenth-century Ontario were probably property holders in their own right. Others may have held some personal estate or financial assets. We find some confirmation in the fact that this small proportion corresponds very closely to the numbers that can be calculated from Soltow's study of the United States census data for 1860.

The rather high proportion in the secure and wealthy category in 1871 reflects in part the relative rarity of women as heads of households. Most were dependants. As we suggested earlier, it was often women with minor children to raise who were principal heirs of their husband's property for their lifetimes. In our sample it is the women in their middle years, aged 40–60, who were most likely to hold secure property, although the sample numbers are too small for much confidence in the estimate. Many were widows.

It has usually been suggested that widows were largely dependent on their older children, just as they had been dependent on their husbands.[32] We note, in contrast, some recent evidence suggesting that widows were fairly often inheritors of family property and were very competent in managing it. Elliott discovered that half of the Ontario Tipperary Protestant widows in this era were direct inheritors of residential property.[33] Our evidence of property holding among widows suggests further that many of them had been intimately involved in managing property throughout their married lives and maintained the farms, shops, and rental properties they inherited.

SOCIAL CHARACTERISTICS OF PROPERTY HOLDERS AND THE PROPERTYLESS IN 1871

What are the social characteristics associated with propertied wealth and propertylessness in nineteenth-century Ontario? Table 3.6 presents the proportions of the securely propertied and of the propertyless among male heads of households in the provincial sample. The proportions are given for rural and urban areas and among the types of urban places. Most household heads were rural residents, of course, and among them, over 30 per cent (0.310) qualified as holding an amount of property that was substantial or sufficient, we judge, to consider them secure in their immediate economic prospects. The largest single group was the 13 per cent owning two or more houses, followed by 8.3 per cent owning 200 or more acres, and 7.2 per cent owning 100 or more improved acres. Another substantial 7.2 per cent, mostly urban men, reported owning at least one store, shop, warehouse, or factory. If we consider all forms of ownership, over 20 per cent (0.218) of urban male heads could be classified as minimally secure in property owning, the variations among villages, towns, and cities being unexpectedly small (0.187, 0.234 and 0.212), as given in table 3.6. We emphasize that any such definition is a matter of judgment. The levels we choose refer, at best, to minimal security in property. After all, ownership of 200 acres hardly assured a farmer of prosperity, and the ownership of a single shop indicates only an often risky and short-lived stake in the commercial world. Nevertheless, these data do give a first historical account of the major divisions in property holding in nineteenth-century Ontario.

Many limitations of the estimates can be cited. If we had a measure of the actual value of land and buildings or of inventories, inequalities probably would be more evident. In chapter 6 several estimates of overall levels of inequality, in dollar terms, are made for the province. In the present context there is the question of the comparability of the criteria of secure and substantial property, especially for urban areas, where the census tabulation makes no distinction between owning a tiny village store or a precarious

TABLE 3.6
Securely propertied and propertyless among male heads of households in Ontario, 1871, by urban-rural residence

	Sample size	Proportion securely propertied		Proportion propertyless	
		A^*	S^*	A	S
Total	3,806	0.292	0.292	0.144	0.144
Rural	3,095	0.310	0.307	0.079	0.080
Urban	711	0.218	0.224	0.406	0.423
Villages	139	0.187	0.187	0.144	0.130
Towns	247	0.234	0.248	0.364	0.337
Cities	325	0.212	0.219	0.588	0.577

$^*A$ = actual rate; S = age standardized rate, as defined in the text.
SOURCE: The film-manuscript sample of 3,806 male heads of households. See the text for definitions of the variables.

shoemaker's shop and owning one of the few factories of Toronto or Hamilton employing fifty or 100 hands.[34] The estimates of secure farm acreage are similarly limited by unknown variations in productivity. Moreover, in the last century even relatively well-established family fortunes were often altered quite abruptly by changed economic circumstances, illness, and death.

Despite the qualifications, there is evidence here to indicate that there was a broad stratum of mid-Victorian Ontario families who had at least attained limited security in property holdings. And though it was notably smaller than in the countryside, the urban stratum was quite marked, forming a fifth of the households.

The picture alters dramatically, however, when one considers the other side of the coin. The table also gives the proportions of male heads who were propertyless. The data reveal that the image of a rough equality of circumstance and modest security in the province was broken by deep urban pockets of propertylessness. Less than 8 per cent of rural male heads were without some form of property, and just 14 per cent of those residing in the villages of the province. In contrast, in the province's forty-or-so towns, over a third (0.364) of the heads of households were without homes, craft shops, stores, manufactories, or any other form of property of their own. And in the five major cities, a huge 59 per cent of the heads owned no property. Moreover, given the general tendency for larger urban places to attract young men and their families, if often temporarily, it is striking that age standardization does not appreciably alter the pattern, as the table indicates.

The province's towns and cities, of course, were the major sites of the politics of class, as a producer ideology gave way and the traditions of craft control were challenged and defended in the emergence of an increasingly deep division between wage labour and capitalist entrepreneurship.[35] If the cities and towns carried a portent of the future in this division of propertied wealth, we may ask what other conditions were most important in determining security in property holdings or propertylessness in Victorian Ontario? Given the nominal census information on a variety of social and demographic characteristics of the population, we can again enlist the analytic power of a multivariate statistical model in addressing the question.

Even considering relatively few social and demographic characteristics yields a complex array of conditions that may have contributed to the likelihood that a head of household would own property. A multivariate regression analysis will assess the relative importance of the several variables. Two models are reported in table 3.7. A brief account can be given. In the first instance, the statistical analysis predicts the chance an individual in the sample would be securely propertied, in the terms given above. The second analysis predicts the chance of being propertyless. The appropriate models are logit regression models in which the dependent variables are the log of the odds that a male head of household is securely propertied and the log odds of being propertyless.[36] As independent variables we use age, nativity, urban or rural residence, ethnicity, and religion. Like the dependent variables, they are also represented as a series of dichotomies; for example, either a person is in a specific age group or not, or a person is an immigrant or not, and so forth.[37]

We are primarily interested here in the relative importance of the main variables, not in the specific categories within them: that is, in the overall effect of age compared with, say, that of religion, rather than in comparisons among various age groups or among religious groups. To assess the rank or relative importance of such a *subset* of variables, a baseline or complete model that includes all variables is contrasted to models *excluding* a specific variable (a subset of categories).[38] The relative importance of an *excluded* variable can be assessed in terms of the summary statistic, the likelihood ratio, reported in the left-hand column of the table. The statistical probability of the difference between the variable in question and the baseline model can also be assessed and is shown for each model in the far right column of the table. There are five comparisons, each showing the effect on the explanatory capacity of the model resulting from the exclusion of one of the five variables.

The results indicate that the chance a male head of household would own

TABLE 3.7
Likelihood ratio assessment of the relative importance of social conditions of secure property and propertylessness among male heads of households in Ontario, 1871

	−2 log likelihood ratio	Degrees of freedom	Difference from baseline model (222.47)	Probability of the difference
	Probability of being securely propertied			
Baseline model	222.47	19		
All variables except age	52.17	14	170.30	<0.001
All except foreign born	197.03	18	25.44	<0.001
All except ethnicity	205.68	14	16.79	<0.005
All except residence	211.12	16	11.35	<0.005
All except religion	216.46	14	6.01	<0.300
	Probability of being propertyless			
Baseline model	709.95	19		
All variables except residence	224.51	16	485.44	<0.001
All except age	574.51	14	135.44	<0.001
All except ethnicity	686.65	14	23.30	<0.001
All except religion	699.71	14	10.24	<0.100
All except foreign born	708.07	18	1.88	<0.200

SOURCE: See table 3.6.

secure property was, above all, conditioned by age, as we have seen in previous analysis. The magnitude of the difference between the test statistics (column 4) shows this life-cycle factor to be by far the most important one contributing to property accumulation. Three of the four other variables had far fewer, but still statistically significant, independent effects (the probability of the differences from the baseline model, shown in column 5, is less than 0.005). They were nativity (the native born were more likely to hold property), ethnicity (the Irish, in particular, were more likely than the English and Welsh to be securely propertied), and residence (specifically being rural rather than urban). The main result is that opportunities for property accumulation were far more strongly affected by a man's stage in the life cycle than by any other factor we can assess with census evidence. This life-cycle process was no guarantee of propertied security or genuine wealth, of course. The analysis establishes only that age was the first condition of their attainment. Once age is taken into account, propertied security was also conditioned by a combination of native birth, Irish origin, and rural residence.

The second model represents the other side of this story: what socio-demographic factors conspired against property ownership in mid-Victorian Ontario? The results confirm the analysis of table 3.6, indicating that it was urban residence above all that increased the chances a man and his family would be without property. It is important to recall that the statistical results take account of the influence of the other variables in the model, such as age. In fact, age was of next-greatest importance: younger heads of households had distinctly less chance of ownership than older men. It is of interest, too, that ethnic origin and religious affiliation also had statistically significant effects on propertylessness, though less than age or residence, as measured by the test statistics. Finally, in this case, whether one was of native or foreign birth was not a factor, given these other conditions.

In sum, modestly large numbers of men and their families attained more than a family home and small plot of land in mid-Victorian Ontario. Nevertheless, this structure of opportunity was quite distinctly broken by the significant numbers of those living in urban areas, especially in the province's major cities, who lacked property of any sort. There were other restrictive factors, but they were of much less importance.

The statistical analysis prompted a still closer look at the relationship among the major variables. One result was especially striking. Although religious affiliation in general was not a major condition of property attainment in the statistical models, comparing specific groups showed that Catholics were rather less likely to be secure property owners overall, about 24 per cent compared with 30 per cent of Protestants.[39] This difference was further traced to the relative impoverishment of a very specific group – Canadian-born Catholics residing in urban areas. A tiny 8 per cent of these native-born urban Catholics held sufficient property to qualify by our criteria as secure, compared with nearly 30 per cent (twenty-nine) of the Protestants who were also native born and living in urban places. A parallel finding is that urban Catholic Canadians were far more likely to be among the propertyless poor than any other identifiable group: a full 59 per cent of the Canadian-born Catholics residing in Ontario's villages, towns, and cities were apparently without any sort of property. This compared with some 36 per cent of urban, Canadian-born Protestants, for example. The identification of this distinctly deprived urban Catholic minority led to a more detailed analysis of ownership among Ontario's denominational groups.

RELIGION AND HOME OWNERSHIP IN MID-VICTORIAN
ONTARIO

As noted in chapter 2, Ontario society after mid-century was a profoundly
and, in some respects, an increasingly religious order. The dominant Protestant culture seemingly gathered institutional strength in the course of its
accommodation to the expansion of the market and the capitalist ethos. Our
main source, the 1871 census, reveals the trend. Whereas, in the mid-century
census, large numbers disclaimed any religious affiliation and many others
were recorded as members of scattered sectarian groups, by 1871 almost
everyone enumerated proclaimed some church affiliation. The four main
Protestant churches had expanded at the expense of the smaller groups.[40]
If religious convictions informed and shaped the relation of church and
state, the nature of education and social reform, they may also have influenced individual expectations and opportunities of material security and
economic aggrandizement. Westfall has perceptively observed that in Ontario's history 'The myth of our creation is a decidedly materialistic one,
with the days of Canada's genesis reckoned in lines of boxcars and acres
of wheat ... But many Victorians argued that secular and material forces
could not adequately explain the character and meaning of reality and that
society and history were also shaped by other powers, quite different from
those associated with materialism.'

Within the limits of our sources, we pursue the implications of this advice
of contemporaries. Despite a general convergence in institutional form in
Victorian Ontario, there were still well-drawn boundaries between the several Protestant congregations and, of course, a deep divide between Protestants and Catholics.[41] Beginning with the observation that Canadian-born
Catholics in towns and cities were severely restricted in access to property,
we take up the more general question of a Catholic-Protestant divide. The
analysis is focused on home ownership alone.

The proportions of home owners among Protestants and Catholics are
given in table 3.8, classified by age, nativity, and economic sector. As in
the general population, the likelihood of home ownership rose quickly with
age for both Protestants and Catholics. The most notable result is that among
Catholics and Protestants in mid-Victorian Ontario in 1871 nearly identical
proportions owned homes (0.475 and 0.465). Although anti-Catholicism
was common in nineteenth-century Ontario, members of the Catholic minority (approximately 17 per cent of the population) were no less able apparently than Protestants to put together the land, materials, and personal

effort to buy or build their own homes. Moreover, the table indicates that the similarity was not just a product of egalitarianism within the farm sector, but it existed among the province's non-farmers, and among the Canadian born as well as among immigrants. It is true that Canadian-born Catholics were least likely to own homes, with about one-fifth (0.21) doing so and only one in ten owners among young men (0.11). But the figures are more or less the same for Protestant men.

A closer inspection of the data does suggest an interesting contrast within the Catholic community. The majority of the native-born Catholics were francophone (specifically, of French nationality in the census), whose limited home ownership was offset by the penchant of Irish-origin immigrants for owning homes. Specifically, as the table indicates, almost 40 (0.39) per cent of immigrant Catholics who were not farming were home owners: the majority were Irish born.

The pattern is essentially duplicated when we consider urban populations rather than non-farming occupational groups. Without presenting a full array of evidence, we can report that although urban rates of home ownership were again about the same for Protestants and Catholics in general (0.29 for the former; 0.31 for the latter), the difference between the urban Catholic Canadian born and the urban Catholic Irish born was even more marked than among non-farmers generally.[42] A paltry 14 per cent of the former were home owners in Ontario's urban places, compared with a remarkable 48 per cent of the latter.

REAL ESTATE ACCUMULATION AMONG CATHOLICS AND PROTESTANTS

The differences in home ownership among Catholics and Protestants raises the further question of their capacity for property accumulation. Again, employing the *numbers* of houses owned as a sensible proxy for nineteenth-century real estate wealth allows us to examine the patterns.

Consider the average number of houses owned, given in table 3.9, for the same categories used above. The variation in the means among the groups reflects their relative tendencies for the accumulation of residential property. The table shows that a rather select group of adult men tended to own more than one house, *on average*. Generally, Protestants over age forty were multiple home owners. Specifically, and interestingly, although both older Catholic and Protestant farmers tended to own more than one house, the Protestant farmers were more likely to have investments in housing. One

TABLE 3.8

Proportion of home owners among adult males in Ontario, 1871, by major religion, economic sector, nativity, and age

	All		Age 20–39		Age 40–99	
	Protestant	Catholic	Protestant	Catholic	Protestant	Catholic
All	0.48	0.47	0.31	0.29	0.70	0.71
Canadian born	0.41	0.38	0.30	0.27	0.73	0.64
Foreign born	0.54	0.54	0.33	0.31	0.69	0.74
Non-farmers	0.30	0.31	0.19	0.16	0.48	0.53
Canadian born	0.25	0.21	0.18	0.11	0.51	0.45
Foreign born	0.34	0.39	0.21	0.21	0.48	0.56
Farmers	0.63	0.64	0.43	0.44	0.85	0.89
Canadian born	0.52	0.54	0.39	0.43	0.85	0.83
Foreign born	0.75	0.74	0.53	0.46	0.86	0.92

SOURCE: Film-manuscript sample of 5,386 males.

wonders if this pattern reflects a family strategy among the more substantial farmers for transferring property to their children.

In contrast to simple ownership, there is a more distinctive Catholic-Protestant discrepancy in residential real estate accumulation. The mean number of houses owned by Protestants is 0.64 while that for Catholics is only 0.55. Although averages can be deceptive in summarizing whole distributions, this difference represents a 20 per cent advantage for Protestants in real estate wealth. The difference is 13 to 14 per cent within both farm and non-farm sectors (0.45–0.40; 0.82–0.72). Among non-farmers, foreign-born Catholics and Protestants were nearly equivalent in numbers of homes owned, but the native-born Catholics owned only half as many homes as immigrant Catholics (averages of 0.26 and 0.52) and were less likely to have real estate investments than Canadian-born Protestants (0.38 versus 0.26). Behind this contrast again lies the disproportionate tendency for Irish-Catholic immigrants to own homes and for the French-origin Canadian born to rent.

Using the mean number of houses to assess patterns of real estate assets includes both the effect of simple ownership and the important effect of the real estate investments of the elite 10 per cent of Ontario residents who owned two or more houses. Table 3.10 provides the distributions of men by *actual numbers* of houses owned, distinguishing Protestants and Catholics. The evidence of a Protestant advantage is clear. A Protestant was half again as likely to be among multiple house owners as a Catholic. The census

TABLE 3.9

Mean number of homes owned among adult males in Ontario, 1871, by major religion, economic sector, nativity, and age

	All		Age 20–39		Age 40–99	
	Protestant	Catholic	Protestant	Catholic	Protestant	Catholic
All	0.64	0.55	0.37	0.32	1.01	0.87
Canadian born	0.55	0.45	0.36	0.32	1.14	0.77
Foreign born	0.73	0.64	0.39	0.32	0.96	0.91
Non-farmers	0.45	0.40	0.25	0.19	0.78	0.71
Canadian born	0.38	0.26	0.24	0.15	0.91	0.52
Foreign born	0.51	0.52	0.27	0.24	0.73	0.80
Farmers	0.82	0.72	0.49	0.47	1.18	1.02
Canadian born	0.69	0.63	0.46	0.48	1.27	1.02
Foreign born	0.97	0.80	0.60	0.46	1.14	1.02

SOURCE: Film-manuscript sample.

sources, of course, do not reveal the processes that engender the Protestant advantage. On the one hand, borrowing from the Weberian legacy, we might speculate that the distributions result primarily from a more active entrepreneurial spirit among Protestants than existed among Catholics. On the other hand, they may mainly reflect the limitations imposed on Catholics by obstacles in the real estate market, perhaps indicating other forms of systemic discrimination. Despite legal equality, anti-Catholicism was a virulent element of nineteenth-century Ontario life. No doubt it had direct material consequences. Of course, both factors may have been at play, with the greater acquisitiveness often attributed to Protestant sectarianism reinforcing prejudice and institutional discrimination.

Again we turn the census enumeration of 1871 directly to the question. Among the various Protestant congregations can we detect a pattern of variations in real estate acquisition that suggests they may be culturally engendered?

PATTERNS OF PROTESTANT HOME OWNERSHIP

A long intellectual tradition asserts the implications of evangelical sectarianism for capitalist enterprise. Although there has been limited subsequent analysis, S.D. Clark's pioneering and perceptive comments on the relation of religious sectarianism to capitalist expansion in Canada suggests that, despite secularization, the more evangelical denominations retained more

TABLE 3.10
Number of homes owned among adult males in Ontario, 1871, by
Protestant and Catholic religion

H, number of homes owned	Proportion owning H or more	
	Protestants	Catholics
Four or more	0.015	0.002
Three	0.030	0.017
Two	0.098	0.065
One	0.473	0.465
Zero	1.000	1.000

SOURCE: Film-manuscript sample.

ascetic and entrepreneurial tendencies in the last century.[43] Documentary
evidence can readily be cited to support the claim. Baptists, in particular,
stressed the value of frugality in their church literature. Thus, an issue of
the *Canadian Baptist* in 1873 intones: 'The spirit of worldliness is gradually
diffusing itself. It brings in its train a fondness for outward display and a
heartless formality, which mar the beauty and paralyse the energies of the
churches of Christ.'[44] The Methodists, too, felt that consumption should
be moderated and remonstrated against conspicuous living: 'Endeavour to
influence those committed to your care against the evils of extravagance in
dress, which is amongst the most dangerous tendencies of the times. Cost-
liness of living is, with its manifold evils, inflicting its legitimate penalties
on many. Be it yours, by frugality and simplicity, to escape its snares your-
selves, and to reprove it in others.'[45] Drinking and gambling particularly
were thought to cut heavily into saving and would eliminate possibilities of
substantial capital accumulation.[46]

  But would the specific variations in moral codes among the Protestant
congregations translate into differences in social and economic conditions?
In chapter 2, we found an orderly pattern of quite modest differences in
landownership among the major Protestant churches. We examine home
ownership patterns here. First, we consider the proportion of homes owned,
and then multiple ownership is again taken to be a proxy for real estate
accumulation.[47]

  Comparing the Church of England with the Presbyterian, Baptist, Methodist, and 'Other' Protestant congregations showed only that the once-
establishment Church of England group had the lowest rates of ownership,
about 42 per cent, compared with some 48 or 49 per cent of the three other
major congregations. The collection of smaller, more sectarian churches in

the 'other' group had the highest home ownership rate, 52 per cent, 10 per cent greater than that of the Anglicans. The modest differences conform to the expected pattern of increasing ownership of property associated with increased evangelicalism.[48]

If the Anglican congregations of nineteenth-century Ontario were relatively limited in home ownership in comparison with other Protestant groups, what about economic accumulation, as reflected in mean numbers of houses owned? The data given in Table 3.11 show there are rather greater differences. The result parallels that found in the case of acreage owned among farmers; that is, increasing sectarianism appears to foster greater real estate wealth. The Baptists were especially likely to have members owning several houses. The Baptist averages are half again as large as the Anglican ones for all the Canadian born and among Canadian-born farmers. Employing a procedure for standardizing the averages simultaneously for age, farm–non-farm occupation, and nativity gives the following rates: 0.58 for Anglicans, 0.64 for Presbyterians, 0.69 for Methodists, and 0.70 for Baptists. That is, though Baptists remain the most likely to have one or more houses, the Baptist advantage would have been slightly reduced if the groups had been identical in age, economic sector, and nativity. Clearly in Ontario as late in the century as 1871, however, membership in the Church of England was least likely to foster real estate wealth and being Baptist strongly encouraged such investments.

The averages for denominations tend to reflect the concentrated property owning of a relatively few members more than of the circumstances of the majority of adherents. The question of inequality within Ontario's nineteenth-century church communities has never been systematically addressed. The evidence on multiple house ownership permits a first assessment. The proportion of men in each denomination who held two or more houses might be taken as an indicator of the size of economically privileged groups within the congregations. Table 3.12 provides this evidence and, in this case, includes the Catholic male population for comparison. We see the familiar pattern; the proportion of Baptists among the well off was about twice that of Anglicans. The Catholic population had the smallest propertied elite: among Catholics, only 6.5 per cent were owners of at least two residences, the lowest proportion of any major church. More strikingly, neither the Anglican nor the Presbyterian communities had much larger elites than the Catholics, with about 9 per cent (0.088 and 0.086) owning two or more houses. In contrast, among Baptists, a remarkable 15 per cent were owners of two or more houses throughout the province in 1871.

These observed systematic differences among the Protestant denomina-

TABLE 3.11

Mean number of homes owned by adult males in Ontario, 1871, by Protestant denomination

	Church of England	Presbyterian	Methodist	Baptist	Other
All	0.57	0.65	0.67	0.74	0.69
Canadian born	0.46	0.46	0.61	0.68	0.65
Foreign born	0.63	0.78	0.76	0.84	0.73
Non-farmers	0.39	0.47	0.48	0.56	0.42
Canadian born	0.32	0.30	0.44	0.47	0.36
Foreign born	0.42	0.57	0.53	0.68	0.46
Farmer	0.80	0.78	0.82	0.90	0.92
Canadian born	0.63	0.54	0.73	0.82	0.87
Foreign born	0.90	0.97	1.02	1.08	0.98

SOURCE: Film-manuscript sample.

tions might be the product of a variety of associated social and economic conditions. We explored this possibility. In appendix A to this chapter we report several multivariate statistical analyses of the effects of religious affiliation on the chance of owning a home and on the numbers of houses owned, controlling for the possible confounding effects of several other variables. We report here only that the observed differences between more and less evangelical churches survive the competition with other variables in these models and the specified differences among denominations are statistically significant. This more complex analysis gives us confidence that the denominational differences among Protestant churches in real estate wealth were neither artefacts nor the result of chance alone.

There could be both social and cultural reasons for the systematic differences among denominational communities in tendencies towards investing in several houses. Taking our measure as a proxy for speculation in real estate, we might follow Clark's argument that the development of capitalist enterprise was hastened not only by the ethos, but by the informal corporate organization of the more evangelical communities. The latter engendered cooperative labour, the use of collective financial resources, and endogamous inheritance. Such community-oriented practices can be understood as integral aspects of a Protestant moral order fostering work discipline and the drive to accumulate. It is not mere coincidence that Scottish and English Baptists were prominent in the business life of Ontario after the middle of the century, and it is indicative of their position that a Scottish Baptist became prime minister in 1874.[49]

TABLE 3.12
Proportion of men with two, three, four or more homes in Ontario, 1871, by denomination

H, number of homes	Catholic	Church of England	Presbyterian	Methodist	Baptist	Other
Four or more	0.002	0.012	0.015	0.017	0.019	0.013
Three	0.017	0.024	0.025	0.036	0.046	0.026
Two	0.065	0.088	0.086	0.104	0.147	0.109

SOURCE: Film-manuscript sample.

Of course, one would like to enlist in this investigation an institutional and cultural analysis of nineteenth-century church communities in order to understand the specific dispositions and behavioural patterns that underlie the statistical ones. Such fine-grained differences in moral codes, identities, and ways of community life have not yet been traced for religious communities in Ontario's social and cultural history, although recent work by Westfall and Grant gives us a new vantage point.[50]

There are a number of indirect indicators of the cultural differences that can be drawn from diverse sources and bear on the apparent statistical patterns reported above. The details of the sources and analysis are discussed in appendix C to this chapter. We sum them here. First, for a later period, the 1880s, unusual data from the Bureau of Industries' budget surveys tend to confirm the expectation that the capacity to save went hand in glove with home ownership. In addition, these data and the 1871 census sample indicate that family sizes are lowest among the most evangelical groups. Other evidence shows that members of the evangelical congregations were much underrepresented among the inmates of nineteenth-century Ontario's gaols and much overrepresented among teachers and among normal school students in comparison with the more orthodox Church of England group. The evidence is consistent: it appears that the groups with the strongest Protestant sectarian roots were most likely to foster middle-class standards of family life, social respectability, and self-discipline. It seems the familiar twentieth-century culture of striving, individualistic liberalism had an auspicious early ally in Ontario's moderated evangelical Protestantism of the 1870s.

This fragmentary, but systematic, evidence takes us well beyond the question of home ownership as the basis of nineteenth-century family economies and wealth accumulation. But home ownership was a cultural phenomenon, not merely an economic strategy.[51] Indeed, we suggest it was very close to the heart of Ontario's mid-Victorian cultural formation. As the Victorian era progressed, the family home was increasingly imbued with symbolic value – it became a protected and private sphere and a sign of moral standing in an increasingly materialistic and competitive society.

We can be informed by the knowledge that for the growing professional and business class of eighteenth- and nineteenth-century England the private dwelling had become much more than a place of residence, but 'also a stage for social ritual and outward manifestation of status in the community'.[52] Beyond mere symbolic value, the privately owned residence was taken to be a bulwark against the amoral social environment of the emerging market economy. 'Anglicans, Congregationalists, Quakers, and Unitarians could all agree that the home must be the basis for a proper moral order in the amoral world of the market, that the new world of political economy necessitated a new sphere of domestic economy, that men could operate in that amoral world only if they would be rescued by women's moral vigilance at home.'[53] Ryan's documentation of the rise by mid-century of an evangelical Protestant, home-centred culture of the 'new' middle classes of Upper New York State brings a similar ethos very close to Victorian Ontario.[54] As much as they were concerned to take advantage of its economic opportunities, Ontario's Protestants were deeply concerned with the secularization of their society. Aiming above all to secure and perpetuate their family economies, they would also have shared a sense of this home-centred moral order and placed a premium on ownership of their moral refuge.

OVERVIEW

Home ownership in the last century was for many a vital resource in maintaining a secure family livelihood. It was a presumption of independent farm families and a deeply held aspiration among immigrants, rural migrants to cities, and the urban working class. Homes were, we suggest, of particular social and symbolic significance to the family-oriented small producers both in cities and on the farms. Accumulating two or more dwellings was also an obvious, readily available, if not assuredly optimal, form of economic investment for those with entrepreneurial intentions and resources.[55]

There has been rather little study of wealth accumulation in Ontario in the last century. The 1871 census tabulation of numbers of houses owned provides a rare chance to assess real estate investments. This chapter offers the first analysis of patterns of home ownership in mid-Victorian Ontario as a whole. Nearly half of adult males in the province owned their homes in 1871 and ownership was strongly associated with age, implying that men expected to and did acquire homes in large numbers up to and throughout

'Goodwood,' built in 1867 by Robert Brown for Mrs Brown, Douro township

their middle years. Farmers were more than twice as likely as non-farmers to own their homes, and although the foreign born were more likely than natives to be owners, this was largely found to be the consequence of age composition, with one important exception: the Irish born were unusually intent on owning homes, as others have found.

Living in villages, like rural residence, fostered home ownership, in contrast to residence in towns and especially in Ontario's five major mid-Victorian cities. About a third of the province's town residents owned homes, but only a fifth of the city residents were home owners. At least half of rural- and village-residing men were owners.

Women *heads* of households had much less chance than male *heads* of being home owners, but widowhood appears to have conferred ownership, especially for women in their middle years, when they would often have been responsible for young children. Urban residence increased the chances that women heads were legal owners.

An examination of real estate wealth in terms of the ownership of two or more dwellings indicated that just less than 10 per cent of men were in this economic minority, but they controlled about 40 per cent of the province's housing stock.

A measure of the 'securely' propertied was developed on the basis of a variety of census questions regarding land, home, barn, shop, and vehicle ownership. A substantial 30 per cent of adult men were in this bourgeois and petit bourgeois group. Over 40 per cent of the male heads of households were so classified, and barely 1 per cent of the adult non-heads. In contrast, 40 per cent of all men were propertyless, but only 14 per cent of male heads of households, reflecting again the peculiar circumstances of adult dependants, sharing in the work and prospects of inheritance of their households, but socially and economically reliant.

Propertyless men were found to be uncommon in rural areas and villages but quite conspicuous in towns and cities. Strikingly, the least likely to have secure property holdings were native-born urban Roman Catholics – nearly 60 per cent were propertyless.

Among the small number of the provinces' women heads, about 24 per cent were secure or significant property owners and 28 per cent propertyless. The propertied again appear largely to be widows responsible for families. The evidence suggests that about 5 per cent of all adult women in nineteenth-century Ontario may have held property in their own right.

A multivariate analysis confirmed that the chances of being among Ontario's propertied male household heads was most strongly affected by age, though native birth, Irish origin, and rural residence significantly contributed. The most important factor contributing to the lack of property among male heads, on the other hand, was simply urban residence, followed by age and ethnic origin.

Pursuing the religious divisions, it was found that Catholics and Protestants in general did not significantly differ in the proportions owning homes. In contrast, Protestants in general enjoyed a very considerable advantage over Catholics in terms of the accumulation of houses. Further, there was a systematic pattern among the main Protestant denominations in which members of the traditionally most orthodox congregation, the Church of England, were least likely to be home owners, and those with the strongest evangelical roots, the Baptists and Methodists, were most likely to be. Among native Canadians, Baptists were a third more likely than Anglicans to be home owners. A similar though even more obvious pattern emerged with respect to tendencies to accumulate several houses. The denominational differences survived several statistical attempts to take into account the effects of other variables on the chance of home owning and on wealth in homes.

A number of unusual, indirect indications of the denominational differences, such as family size, incarceration rates, and teacher training, lent further support to the notion of consistent social and cultural differences, reflecting the continuum from more orthodox to more evangelical congregations. In addition to their importance as the foundation of family economies in Victorian Ontario, home ownership likely reflected the significance of the private home as the basis of a moral order of family-centred life within Ontario's evangelical Protestant culture.

Some people were obviously left out of the nineteenth-century social equation that tended to tie family security to the attainment of small property in land and homes. Their lives are probably the most difficult to reconstruct either through traditional documentary sources or through routinely generated ones, such as the census. One possibility of at least approaching the question is to examine the circumstances of the least visible and articulate of those captured by the census enumerators, the illiterate.

APPENDIX 3A: THE EFFECT OF RELIGIOUS AFFILIATION, AGE, AND NATIVITY ON HOME OWNERSHIP: A MULTIVARIATE ANALYSIS

As we did in the foregoing analysis of landownership and acreage, we can specify a number of multivariate models that assess the effects of religious affiliation on home ownership but take account of the possible confounding effects of other variables. The first model reported here employs multiple regression to consider religious group differences when the important effects of age and nativity on home ownership are also included in the analysis. The dependent variable is the *average* number of houses owned, taken to measure real estate accumulation. Each of the religious groups is treated as a simple dichotomy, representing membership or non-membership in the group. In addition, age is represented as a set of discrete categories and nativity as a dichotomy. For example, when an individual is between age 30 and 39, the value for that variable is one and is otherwise zero. When all explicit variables are zero, we have the home average (H^*) for an individual who is a member of the Church of England, is native born, and is of age 20–29; these serve as the reference categories.
The multiple regression equation is as follows:

$$H^* = 0.132 + 0.172\text{Bapt} + 0.135\text{Meth} + 0.089\text{Pres} \ (0.000\text{CofE})$$
$$\quad\quad (0.059) \quad\quad (0.035) \quad\quad (0.035)$$

$$- \ 0.008\text{Cath} - 0.073\text{Foreignborn} \ (+ \ 0.000\text{age}_{20\text{--}29}) + 0.443\text{age}_{30\text{--}39}$$
$$\quad\quad (0.039) \quad\quad (0.026) \quad\quad\quad\quad\quad\quad\quad\quad (0.032)$$

$$+ \; 0.781 \text{age}_{40-49} + 0.912 \text{age}_{50-59} + 0.935 \text{age}_{60-69} + 0.702 \text{age}_{70-99}$$
$$(0.036) \qquad\quad (0.041) \qquad\quad (0.046) \qquad\quad (0.061)$$

$N = 5,386$ and $R^2 = 0.151$.

Consider the coefficient for the Baptist group of 0.172. It signifies that an adult Baptist man would have an expected number of houses that is 0.172 homes greater than a member of the Church of England *for those of comparable age and nativity*. Recalling that the average number of houses owned was 0.63 for all of Ontario's adult men, this figure represents a quite substantial increment for adherents of the Baptist church, independent of the effects of age and nativity.

In statistical terms, the equation shows that the Baptists, Methodists, and Presbyterians all enjoyed significantly greater home accumulation than the members of the Church of England, even when the effects of age and nativity are taken into account. The Catholics were, in fact, virtually identical to Anglicans in this simple, but important respect, despite the context of the early Anglican slander that Roman Catholicism was a 'jumble of irrational superstitions and a system of religious idolatry and temporal slavery.'[56]

We note again the entirely methodical diminution of coefficients from 0.172, 0.135, 0.089, to -0.008, representing in order, from the greatest advantage to the least, the Baptists, Methodists, Presbyterians, and Catholic groups in comparison with the Church of England congregation. When we separate the farmers and non-farmers, precisely the same pattern is found for each. In sum, it was a fact of economic life in Ontario after Confederation that the class of men who had accumulated significant real estate holdings tended to be members of the once 'enthusiastic' evangelical churches, now well established.

We can also specify a multivariate analysis of the differences in the *chances* of home ownership among religious groups reported above. Although the differences in proportions of home owners were modest, they followed the now familiar pattern, lowest for Anglicans (0.42), but with only minor differences among the Catholic (0.47) and other Protestant groups (0.48 and 0.49). Here we specify a more complex model, including urban or rural residence and ethnicity. Either of the latter variables might account for much of the variation in ownership among religious groups. A logistic regression model is specified in which the probability of owning a home is estimated from a set of independent variables. Each religious group is again treated as a dichotomous independent variable. Age and nativity are included, as well as variables representing village, town, or city residence (with rural location as the reference category), and ethnic origin (as five dichotomies, with English and Welsh origin as a reference category).

The relatively complicated equation is not displayed here, but the results directly confirm the foregoing analysis. In comparison with the case of Anglican men, the probability of owning a home was significantly greater for *each* of the other denominations, even considering the effect of these several other variables. The expected pattern of differentials was replicated: the Baptists had the greatest likelihood of being owners (in comparison with Anglicans) followed in order by the Methodists, the other churches, the Presbyterians, and the Roman Catholics. The results are more interesting, because in comparison with religion, the only contrast between the English and Welsh group and other *ethnic-origin* groups that was statistically significant was for those of Irish origin.[57] The simple ethnic-origin pattern of proportions owning houses was as follows, from lowest to highest: French origin, 0.42; Other, 0.43; English and Welsh, 0.44; Scottish, 0.47; Irish and German, each 0.51.

Other results of interest are the fact that the chances of ownership did *not* vary significantly between natives and the foreign born, although the odds did increase with age, as expected, and both town and city, but *not* village, residents were significantly less likely to be home owners than rural residents, again as expected. A similar logistic regression analysis, including a dichotomous variable to represent gender, specified the extent of the *women household heads'* disadvantage with respect to the odds on owning a home. Being a woman head decreased the probability of owning a home by 53 per cent in comparison with male heads, after the influence of age, religion, ethnic-origin, urban or rural residence, and nativity is considered.

APPENDIX 3B: SHANTIES, HOUSING STOCK, AND THE
RELATIVELY POOR IN ONTARIO IN 1851: A GLANCE FURTHER
BACKWARD

The data of this study derive from the 1871 census, which provides at best an incomplete picture of those with below-average real estate holdings and certainly only a glimpse of the struggling and truly poor. In a previous analysis we considered nine forms of assets tabulated in the census and found 39 per cent of all adult males and 14 per cent of the adult male heads in the sample to be propertyless. Knowing something about the economic circumstances and social characteristics of those in the lower tail of the distribution would be most revealing. The unusual housing data of the 1851-2 census gives us one such glimpse, though of a period two decades earlier than our main focus. Some historical perspective on economic development at least may be obtained by stepping back two decades in the process.

The 1851-2 census form asked several questions about houses, distinguishing log and shanty as well as the more substantial residences; these dwellings were tallied for Upper Canada as a whole, as shown in table 3B.1. The tallies immediately suggest a unimodal curve, with a few stone and brick houses of substantial value and a significant minority of poor houses. A surprising number were still made of log; there were many of even more rudimentary construction classified as shanties. The two major types were frame and log with a preponderance of the latter. The frequencies almost suggest a skewed distribution, perhaps one that is lognormal in shape. Previous studies indicate, in fact, that housing values often tend to follow the lognormal form.[58] Our interest here centres on shanties as a proxy for the poorest families at this time. We do not know the exact definition of a shanty, except that it was considered inferior to a log house. Many of the structures were noted as 'log shanty' as distinguished from 'log.' One enumerator's tally stressed that shanties were 'temporary' structures. Harris and Warkentin suggest that shanties were the first log buildings put up by many settlers, that they could be erected by two skilled men in a few days, and that they often had dirt floors and rudimentary chimneys, if they had the latter at all. The authors do not appear to be aware of the prevalence of shanties in the province as given in the census, but they do suggest that most settlers left them after a few years.[59]

We drew a disproportionate stratified random sample of eighty-three shanties and 156 other houses from the even-numbered microfilm of the 1851-2 census of Upper Canada.[60] The intriguing aspects of the data are those revealing the characteristics of the heads of the households or census families. They are given in table 3B.2.

Those in shanties tended to be younger than those living in more substantial buildings. Specifically, the average age of those living in log houses was a year or two greater than the age of those in shanties and thirteen years less than for those living in frame or better housing. The pattern suggests movement from shanty to log houses in a few years and subsequently to the more substantial housing, as suggested by Cole and Warkentin. As well, labourers and Catholics tended to be overrepresented in shanties.

We also note that the native born were less likely to live in shanties than those born elsewhere. The pattern is provided in more detail in table 3B.3.

The age and nativity results can be specified in a general logistic equation derived from the sample of the probability of *not* living in a shanty =

$$- 0.525 + 0.0215 \text{age} + 0.876 \text{NB}, P(\chi^2 = 12.5) < 0.005,$$
$$(0.0113) \qquad (0.319)$$

TABLE 3B.1
Number and proportion of types of houses in Ontario,
1851–2

Type	Number	Proportion
Stone	4,211	0.029
Brick	5,117	0.035
Frame	53,931	0.370
Log	65,503	0.449
Shanty	17,191	0.118
Number of families	145,953	1.000

SOURCE: *Appendix to the Census of Canada*, no. 15,
431; *Census of the Canadas for 1851–52* (Quebec: John
Lovell 1854), table 1, vol. 1, 179, and vol. 2, 431.

where NB is one if the head is native born and zero if foreign born. If dwelling values are inferred directly from types of housing, the data suggest an interesting pattern for the life cycle of individuals, as shown in figure 3B.1 (see p. 108). That is, the native-born men had a sustained housing advantage over the foreign-born men throughout the life cycle. Similar results are found for the United States in 1870, using wealth in real and personal estate.[61] The Ontario data allow us to consider religion (but not origin) in 1851–2. The logistic equation can be expanded to include a dichotomous variable representing religious denominations. A similar plot for the sample shows Protestants maintaining a life-cycle advantage over Catholics.

APPENDIX 3C: INDICATORS OF SOCIAL AND CULTURAL
DIFFERENCES AMONG PROTESTANT DENOMINATIONS IN
NINETEENTH-CENTURY ONTARIO

First we consider the rare source of historical evidence on savings habits and housing expenditures for cities given by the Bureau of Industries, though it relates to a somewhat later period. We then examine simple, but intriguing, correlations between religious affiliations and family size, incarceration in gaols, and teacher training.

Savings and homes

There is exceedingly limited nineteenth-century evidence on patterns of savings and consumption at the individual or the family level. One unusual source is the annual surveys of *urban* wage earners in Ontario conducted

TABLE 3B.2
Shanties and other residences in Ontario, 1851–2, by age,
occupation, religion, and birthplace

	Shanties	Non-shanties
Number in sample	83	156
Average age of head	39.8	47
Proportion of sample cases		
Occupation		
Labourer	0.204	0.109
Farmer	0.651	0.602
Other	0.145	0.289
Religion		
Catholic	0.361	0.167
Baptist	0.024	0.083
Church of England	0.229	0.173
Methodist	0.084	0.192
Presbyterian	0.253	0.250
Other	0.048	0.134
Birthplace		
Ontario	0.193	0.276
United States	0.217	0.391
Ireland	0.506	0.282
Scotland	0.156	0.167
Other	0.060	0.057

SOURCE: Microfilms C11712 to C11762, National Archives,
Ottawa.

from 1884 to 1889. Employees in 'every' occupation in a city were asked
to make estimates of their annual incomes, expenses, and surplus or deficit.
The representativeness of the samples cannot be confirmed, but the evidence
relating to home ownership is of considerable interest. The surveys report
that wage earners owning houses had average earnings 5 per cent greater
than tenants, overall expenses some 5 per cent less than tenants, and surplus
income (presumably savings) three times as large.[62]

Ownership may imply more stable and renumerative employment and
greater frugality, although there are many attendant unknown factors. It has
been suggested that nineteenth-century urban tenancy was a possible economic strategy among commercial and professional strata, freeing family
capital for more renumerative investments.[63] But the Bureau of Industries'
data indicate, in general, that savings and ownership went hand in hand. In

TABLE 3B.3
Proportion of native- and foreign-born heads in Ontario, 1851–2, by
type of house

	Shanties	Log	Frame or better
Native born	0.216	0.333	0.458
Foreign born	0.784	0.667	0.542
	1.000	1.000	1.000

SOURCE: See table 3B.2.

fact, the evidence provides a surprisingly similar picture of urban home ownership to that of the census sample we have reported. About a third of individuals reported owning their homes to the bureau, precisely the proportion of adult male owners in the urban portion of our sample. Approximately one-half the individuals reported some surplus or savings to the bureau. The Gini inequality coefficient summarizing the distribution of saving was 0.78, which is a figure close to that for the distribution of homes in our sample of 0.74. The correspondence provides initial evidence that the ability to save translated directly into urban home ownership.

Family size

Family size and the numbers of dependants are key factors conditioning income, savings, and consumption. Although in the late nineteenth century the work of older children was still often essential to the economic security of families, especially farm families, dependent children and other dependants were a clear economic drain.[64] The Bureau of Industries' budget studies in the 1880s provide a view of the relationship. Wage earners reported smaller surpluses, or earnings less cost of living, for families with dependants, particularly for those with five or more dependants.[65] The effects might well have been passed from generation to generation, since individual inheritances would normally be smaller among families with large numbers of children.

Further, from the 1871 census manuscripts we can determine the number of persons in each 'census' family (co-residing in a separate household) and calculate the simple association between total household size and religious affiliation. There is a clear relation, with members of the least orthodox denominations, Baptists and Methodists, tending to have the smaller house-

FIGURE 3B.1 Approximate relationship between value of dwellings and age, Ontario, 1851–2, by nativity

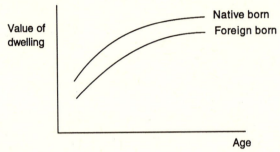

SOURCE: See table 3B.2.

holds as a consequence probably of having fewer children, although the question of variation among other, co-residing members of the households is left open.

To specify the relation between religious affiliation and size of household, the latter was predicted in a multiple regression equation with age, nativity, religion, and economic sector as independent variables. The net regression coefficients were −0.05 persons for the Baptist dichotomy, −0.19 for Methodists, 0.19 for Presbyterians, (0.00 for Anglicans), and 0.48 for Catholics, where the average number of persons in the family was 6.2 for the 5,386 men. Thus, Methodists had the smallest households, followed by Baptists, Anglicans, Presbyterians, and Catholics. The coefficients indicate that the Catholics had an expected household size of 0.48 members *more* than Anglicans, the reference group in this model, and the Methodists had −0.19 fewer residents. For the non-farm sector alone (for 2,609 individuals) an even greater differential between Methodists, Anglicans and Catholics is shown. The coefficients were −0.02 for Baptists, −0.44 for Methodists, 0.04 for Presbyterians, (0.00 for Anglicans), and 0.67 for Catholics, where the average size of households was also 6.2. We might then say that a non-farming Catholic family had four children to every three for a comparable Methodist family. The correspondence between these patterns and the pattern of home ownership and accumulation established above suggests that the differentials in the burden of dependency within households might have been a condition of real estate accumulation among the groups, or, more generally, reduced family and household size was an aspect of the home-centred culture that also fostered accumulation.

Incarceration tendencies

It is particularly difficult to obtain systematic evidence regarding the conduct or deportment of people in the past. One revealing source used in recent social history has been the gaol records. Observers in late nineteenth-century Ontario shared the rising concern that rapid social change, especially the growth of the cities, was fuelling the growth of a veritable 'criminal class.'

The recent literature has argued that even the rhetoric of prison reform of the late 1860s clothed an intent to control by detention the perceived criminal threat to respectable, middle-class community standards and sense of social harmony.[66] For the most part, the inmate population was composed of relatively young, disadvantaged working-class men and women, who were convicted of minor offences against public order and property and, usually, were given brief sentences.

We can employ the same data to ask if this concern with the protection of property and propriety also reflected variations in denominational conformity to codes of personal conduct. Previous studies report little correlation with ethnicity or religion, with the exception of the Irish born and Roman Catholics, who were much overrepresented as a consequence of their relatively disadvantaged class position.[67] Table 3C.1 gives the denominational distribution for the 6,615 offenders in Ontario as a whole in 1871. One-third of them were arrested for being drunken and disorderly.

In line with previous studies, we expect to find that the Roman Catholics are much overrepresented in comparison with their provincial population. It is a good deal more surprising to find that the Church of England group was also significantly overrepresented and was over a third of all inmates, nearly matching the Roman Catholic population. Moreover, by comparison, the underrepresentation of the more evangelical groups is very marked. Particularly noticeable is the fact that Baptists and members of other small denominations and sects were thoroughly underrepresented among inmates. Class and economic position are intertwined with cultural predispositions in these data, but the striking break between the two diocesan and the more evangelical groups remains.

Church involvement in education and the attainment of literacy

Educational debates were at the centre of denominational conflicts in the last century. Within this complicated question, the activities of denominations in organized education are a further manifestation of their cultural

TABLE 3C.1
Jailed persons in Ontario, 1871, by denomination

	Population of males 20 and older (per cent)	Persons committed to gaol (per cent)
Roman Catholic	16.6	37.4
Church of England	20.9	34.0
Presbyterian	22.6	11.4
Methodist	26.6	12.2
Other	13.3	5.1
	100.0	100.0

SOURCE: Gaol Statistics of the Province of Ontario, October, 1871
– September, 1872, *Sessional Papers*, no. 4, Province of Ontario,
1871–2, 21; the film-manuscript sample for male populations.

differences. It is sufficient to note here that there was a long-standing re-
luctance on the part of the more orthodox denominations in Upper Canada
to accept the development of elementary education as it unfolded in the
three decades before 1871. The opposition of Anglicans to the growth of
a public school system expressed their belief that social order and good
government required a social and educational role of the established church
as an arm of the state. It is said there was an 'attitude, unsympathetic, if
not hostile, generally taken by the clergy towards the (school) system.'[68]

By mid-century, a movement towards Protestant compromise was spurred
by common resistance to Catholic separate schools. After 1852 the Catholic
clergy became increasingly wary of the common or public schools. The
active Protestantism within the common schools was decisive, apparently,
in cementing this attitude.[69]

By 1871 just how active was the participation of members of the evangelical or less orthodox denominations in promoting the common school
system? One measure of this involvement is the number of teachers of a
given affiliation in the system. Table 3C.2 compares the church distribution
of the sample population with the distribution of teachers and of male students in teacher training at the Normal School. Once again the data reveal
the expected pattern. There was disproportionate representation from less
orthodox groups among teachers in the school system as a whole. The
pattern held among students at the Normal School. Presbyterians, Methodists, and Baptists had much stronger representation as teachers and student
teachers than would be expected on the basis of their numbers in the population. Presbyterians were especially overrepresented in the number of

TABLE 3C.2
Male population, teachers, and Normal School students in Ontario, 1871, by denomination

	Male population 20 and older in Ontario in 1871	Teachers in public schools and Roman Catholic separate schools, 1871	Male students training at the Normal School, 1871
Roman Catholic	0.166	0.118	0.038
Church of England	0.209	0.173	0.151
Presbyterian	0.226	0.301	0.290
Methodist	0.266	0.316	0.364
Baptist	0.048	0.057	0.076
Other	0.085	0.035	0.080
	1.000	1.000	1.000

SOURCE: Film-manuscript sample of size 5,386 for population data; Annual Report of the Normal, Model, High and Public Schools of Ontario for the Year 1871, *Sessional Papers*, no. 5, vol. V, Part II, 1872, 4, 5 (IV. table D) and unnumbered page (Abstract no. 3).

teachers the community produced; Baptists had an even stronger representation from its population engaged in teacher training.

The consistency of the pattern in these varied indicators suggests that the moral order of the more evangelical Protestant denominations promoted a combination of smaller families, personal rectitude, and greater involvement in formal education that historically has been associated with the economic acquisitiveness of the more sectarian communities. The systematic evidence is circumstantial, of course, but not trivial in strengthening the view that the association between real estate accumulation and Protestant denominations in nineteenth-century Ontario reflects persistent cultural differences.

4

Literacy and Illiteracy in Ontario in 1871: Trends, Social Patterns, and Property Holding

INTRODUCTION

The last twenty years have seen the growth of an impressive body of historical studies of the rise of literacy in the west.[1] Although the routes and rates were very different, nearly universal levels of literacy were attained in western countries after the mid-nineteenth century and in several places well before that time, for example, in Sweden and New England.[2] In Ontario by 1861 about 90 per cent of adults reported to census enumerators that they could read.[3] In Quebec the rates were lower, but they still approximated universal elementary literacy towards the end of the century.[4]

The generally high levels of literacy in nineteenth-century Ontario make the illiterate minority of particular interest: their identification through manuscript census records provides a rare opportunity to study the least articulate people of the past. The social identity of this minority has particular relevance to our understanding of the mid-Victorian social order. The spread of literacy was both source and symbol of the ascendancy of Victorian culture. That emerging culture and its social rhetoric placed overweening emphasis on an equation that linked literacy with respectability, social improvement, and property. To be illiterate was to have been largely left out of this social formula, or so Victorians in Ontario, as elsewhere, thought.[5]

If those known to be illiterate were stigmatized in mid-Victorian Ontario, it is another question whether or not they also suffered material deprivation and limited opportunities. To date Harvey Graff has most pointedly addressed the question.[6] In the present analysis we are interested in the questions of both the social characteristics of illiterates and whether literacy mattered much for individual and family well-being, specifically for property holding.

Despite the considerable recent body of research on literacy many questions are unanswered. We know much more about the broad national or regional trends in the growth of literacy than about the leads and lags among local populations and communities. For Ontario, there is early, important work on urban populations, but it is confined to a few cities.

We first employ aggregate census data to consider Canadian regional illiteracy patterns and historic trends. These are of general comparative interest and also provide a context for a detailed analysis of Ontario in 1871. First, we use the sample of census manuscript data to undertake an analysis that links illiteracy rates to age and urban residence and to social patterns of immigration, ethnicity, and religion. Then we compare the property owning of illiterates with that of the literate population.

REGIONAL ILLITERACY RATES

Recent historical studies document the wide variation among countries and regions in the spread of literacy.[7] We set the context for this analysis by considering differences in Canadian provincial illiteracy trends using aggregate census data. The definitions of *illiteracy* (unable to read / unable to write) from the 1871 and subsequent censuses are used in table 4.1 to show regional differences and historical patterns. There are two striking features of the data: the illiteracy rate was very high for Canada as a whole, though distinctly declining after 1871, and Quebec had a dramatically higher rate than elsewhere in the country. Column 2 of the table shows that in Canada as a whole *one in every four men* aged 21 or older reported that he could not *write* in 1871. The proportions varied greatly by region. In Quebec 47 per cent of adult men could not write. In Nova Scotia and New Brunswick 21 and 20 per cent were illiterate, but only 11 per cent were so in Ontario. Although we have to compare rather differing definitions of illiteracy, the evidence of both panels of table 4.1 suggests that rates declined slowly to 1891, then were substantially lowered by 1911.

There is strong evidence of a general downward trend in illiteracy in many countries in the last half of the nineteenth century. For Canada illiteracy for all persons five and older declined by half, from about 19 per cent in 1891 to 9 per cent in 1921, and declined most dramatically for Quebec (as shown in the table). Using several sources, Greer has shown that the greatest decline in illiteracy occurred somewhat earlier in Quebec, between 1840 and 1860, when rural residents began rapidly to attain basic literacy skills.[8] For Ontario, the rate of illiteracy among those 5 years and older was approximately cut in half in the twenty years between 1891 and 1911;

TABLE 4.1
Illiteracy rates in Canada and selected provinces, 1871–1921

	Proportion of males 21 years old and over			
	1871		1911	
Area	Unable to read	Unable to write	Unable to read	Unable to write
Ontario	0.078	0.113	0.060	0.065
Quebec	0.407	0.468	0.146	0.157
New Brunswick	0.151	0.197	0.128	0.137
Nova Scotia	0.149	0.206	0.078	0.089
The four provinces	0.202	0.249	0.099	0.106
Other provinces			0.113	0.117
Canada	0.202	0.249	0.103	0.109

	Proportion of persons 5 years old and over unable to write			
Area	1891	1901	1911	1921
Ontario	0.113	0.088	0.066	0.064
Quebec	0.307	0.177	0.127	0.103
Canada	0.189	0.144	0.105	0.092

SOURCES: *Census of Canada, 1871*, vol. II, 164–5, 211, tables VII and X. Census and Statistics Office, *Bulletin XV*, Fifth Census of Canada, 'Educational Status of the People of Canada for the Year 1911 as Enumerated Under Date of First June' (Ottawa 1913) 7, 8. See also *Yearbook of Canada*, 1893, 164. There was no census of literacy in 1881. Data for later years are from *Census of Canada*, 1931, vol. I, 1064, table 63.

the rates were 0.113 and .0.064, as given in the lower panel of the table.

National and regional comparisons are complicated by linguistic, cultural, and economic differences. With a settlement history rather like that of Ontario, New Zealand serves as an interesting English-speaking point of comparison. National illiteracy rates for New Zealand, as indicated by marks rather than signatures on marriage licences, appear to have been halved every decade after 1880. The rates were 0.032 in 1881, 0.019 in 1886, 0.016 in 1890, 0.009 in 1895, and 0.005 in 1900.[9] This measure very likely minimizes illiteracy rates, and, of course, there is a question regarding the comparability of the indicators. We may still note the general trends these measures reveal, in which the decline of illiteracy in New Zealand appears to parallel that of Ontario, though it was more rapid. Further, England and Wales, France, Ireland, and Italy have different proportions of those who only 'mark,' rather than sign their names after the middle of the last century, but all experienced more or less similar patterns of illiteracy decline by the turn of the twentieth century.[10]

The rates of literacy for Canada and the United States were also broadly similar in this period. In this case, the ratios of the number able to write to the number able to read in the censuses indicate that the meaning of reported illiteracy was similar in the two countries. Appendix A to this chapter gives the definitions. The comparisons are pursued briefly.

The United States had a high rate of persons unable to write in 1870; approximately 17 per cent of all males 21 and over were illiterate by this definition, although the rate appears to be lower than the overall Canadian rate. The U.S. rate was 0.090 for *white* males 21 and over, a figure rather closer to the Ontario rate in 1871. Moreover, the rate for white males 20 and older was reported to be slightly lower in earlier years, 0.067 in 1860 and 0.079 in 1850. The higher 1870 rate of illiteracy may reflect the deep disruption of the Civil War, but otherwise it remains inexplicable. In general, illiteracy rates in the United States decreased in the last half of the century except for this discontinuity; rates for all males and females 10 and over were 0.20 in 1870, 0.17 in 1880, 0.13 in 1890, 0.11 in 1900, and 0.08 in 1910.[11]

Finally in this context, for reasons of proximity and settlement history, it is interesting to compare Ontario's historical experience with that of Ohio. Ohio's rate of illiteracy among adult men (unable to write) in 1870 was 0.073, notably lower than the 0.113 rate in Ontario in 1871. In examining interstate variations in illiteracy in the United States, Soltow and Stevens found that the northwestern states had experienced marked increases in literacy after 1840 and that they compared quite favourably with those in the northeastern states. They suggest that literacy followed rapidly increasing population densities of areas like Ohio, with population growth stimulating the print industry and the rise of educational institutions, the schools, libraries, and churches.[12]

It is not immediately obvious why there were higher average levels of illiteracy in Ontario than among men of comparable age in the United States especially among those in Ohio or New York, states to which there were a good many Canadian emigrants. New York state had an illiteracy rate almost exactly the same as Ohio's, about 7 per cent of all adults over age 21 were unable to read and write.[13] It seems that the school promoters and the ideology of literacy were well in place in Ontario after mid-century. Possibly the few years' difference in the rise of the formal educational system and in the politics of literacy promotion were sufficient to account for the lag. More independent local government in the United States in the earlier decades may also have contributed to more rapid development in education.

PATTERNS AND RATES OF CHANGE OF ILLITERACY IN NINETEENTH-CENTURY ONTARIO

The published figures from the nineteenth-century censuses of Canada provide a limited perspective on illiteracy patterns.[14] An analysis of illiteracy's social variations and implications clearly requires nominal data, such as those provided by the Ontario-wide sample.

Elementary reading was a more basic skill than writing and was usually acquired first. We take the inability to *write* as the more conservative measure. First, we examine illiteracy among adult men. Women and male heads of households are considered subsequently.

Just less than 11 per cent (0.108) of men age 20 or over in the film-manuscript sample for Ontario were illiterate in 1871.[15] Although obviously the illiterate were a relatively small minority in the province, the average rate masks important variations among social groups.

Table 4.2 presents rates of illiteracy for subgroups defined by the cross-classification of age, nativity, and farm–non-farm sectors. The table provides for a number of related analyses. To reveal the general age pattern, the first two lines of the table have been plotted in figure 4.1, showing the age trends in illiteracy for all males and for the Canadian born.

PATTERNS AND TRENDS IN ILLITERACY IN NINETEENTH-CENTURY ONTARIO

Age patterns and historical trends

Consider the relation of age and illiteracy as represented by the age-specific illiteracy rates in table 4.2. The rates increased more or less linearly with age. The rate for males aged 20–29 was 0.07, consisting of a rate for those 20–24 years of 0.05 and a rate for those aged 25–29 of 0.09. Illiteracy rises slowly, but consistently, to 0.10 for those aged 30–39 and to 0.14 for those 40 and over. The latter was composed of rates of 0.13 for those 40–59, and of 0.19 for those 60 or over. Thus, illiteracy was two to three times as great for the old as for the young in Ontario. A rate of some 14 or 15 per cent is moderately high by international standards in 1871; a rate of 0.19, of course, is high by any standard, indicating that about one in five of the eldest group of men was unable to write.

TABLE 4.2
Illiteracy rates of adult males in Ontario, 1871, by age, nativity, and farm–non-farm sector

	Illiteracy rate				Sample	Standardized
	20–99	20–29	30–39	40–99	size	illiteracy rate*
All	0.108	0.07	0.10	0.14	5,386	0.108
Canadian born	0.110	0.06	0.13	0.18	2,618	0.132
Foreign born	0.105	0.07	0.07	0.13	2,768	0.094
Irish born	0.144	0.10	0.10	0.17	1,026	0.102
Other foreign	0.082	0.06	0.06	0.10	1,742	0.075
Non-farmers	0.106	0.07	0.10	0.15	2,609	0.109
Canadian born	0.134	0.08	0.15	0.24	1,155	0.167
Foreign born	0.084	0.05	0.06	0.11	1,454	0.078
Irish born	0.100	0.07	0.07	0.13	500	0.091
Other foreign	0.077	0.04	0.06	0.11	954	0.073
Farmers	0.109	0.06	0.10	0.14	2,777	0.105
Canadian born	0.092	0.05	0.11	0.15	1,463	0.108
Foreign born	0.128	0.11	0.09	0.14	1,314	0.117
Irish born	0.186	0.15	0.13	0.21	526	0.171
Other foreign	0.089	0.09	0.07	0.10	788	0.086

*Standardized rates are computed using the population of adult males in the province for six age groups, 20–29, 30–39 ... 60–69, 70 and over.
SOURCE: The film-manuscript sample of size 5,386.

With the caveat that social trends are not identical to age patterns, there are persuasive reasons to think that the increasing illiteracy with age for men in Ontario reflects quite directly their historical experience. The near-linear form of the age-illiteracy relation for Ontario males, shown in figure 4.1, parallels that found in Belgium in 1880, in Italy in 1881, and in Austria and the United States in 1890.[16] The age patterns represent the international cultural movement in the spread of basic literacy, with important regional and national variations.

One possible qualification to the assumption that the cross-section for 1871 captures the actual decrease in Ontario's male illiteracy should be noted. It is reasonable to think that some of the elderly in 1871 had actually lost literacy skills they once had mastered. The elementary writing ability they attained in their youth may not have been useful or practised as time wore on. This might be the case, for example, of farmers or craftsmen who were not regularly required by their limited commercial transactions to keep account books. On the other hand, it also is possible that other older persons learned to write later in life. We tend to presume that the acquisition of

FIGURE 4.1 Illiteracy rates for adult males in Ontario, 1871, by age

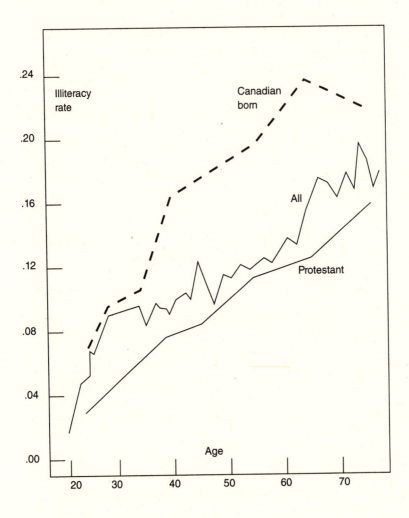

NOTE: The line for all adult men is a five-year moving average to age 48, then a fifteen-year moving average.

SOURCE: The film-manuscript sample of size 5,386.

literacy skills is the preserve of the young, but this was not always so. Graff cites Frederick Philip Grove, the nineteenth-century novelist and commentator, on his Canadian and U.S. experience: 'But – I speak from manifold experience – show me the grown-up who wishes to master the arts of reading and writing and cannot do so in a short time – in one-hundredth the time we waste on them in our schools, incidentally making our children into verbalists and spoiling them for reality – and I will show you a mental laggard.'[17]

Given some balance, then, in the acquisition and loss of literacy with age, we venture to say that the illiteracy rate of those over age 60 (about one in five) represents average illiteracy in Ontario before, say, 1840 (in 1871 the average age of men 20 and older was 39 years and of those 60 and older was 68 years). Greer's estimates for the 1891 census are very similar. Examining age-specific rates, he suggests that some 17 per cent of Ontario men in the 1840s could not read or write.[18]

The estimates indicate that the male illiteracy rate declined in Ontario by half in the generation before 1871. We noted a similar decline indicated by the figures of table 4.1 for the forty years after 1871. These data, however, refer to both native born and immigrant groups; speculation on Ontario's historical trends from age cohort data would be better served by focusing on the native born alone.

Illiteracy among the native and the foreign born in nineteenth-century Ontario

There was a continuous, if erratic, stream of immigrants arriving in Ontario throughout the decades preceding Confederation: slightly more than half of the adult male population in 1871 was foreign born. What was the relation between nativity and illiteracy in Ontario? As in the previous analysis, the nativity classification distinguishes the Canadian born from the foreign born and, within the latter, the large Irish-born group from all other foreign born. A more detailed analysis of illiteracy differentials for Irish-Protestants and Irish-Catholics follows.

First, given the strong relation between age and illiteracy it is useful to be aware of the differences in the age distributions between the immigrant and the native-born groups. The details are provided in the appendix of the book, but it is sufficient to note here that the male, Canadian-born population of 1871 steadily declined in numbers from age 20 in the form of a flattened reverse J; the foreign-born distribution comprised a much smaller proportion in the younger ages, rising to exceed the native-born proportion at about age 34 and decreasing modestly after age 38. In general terms, there were relatively many more native born below age 35 and many more foreign born above age 35 (the average age was about 33 years for native born and 44 years for foreign born).

It has become widely recognized that migrants are an uncommon people, often distinguished as much by their higher levels of education and literacy as by any other social characteristic.[19] Contrary to some conventional images, it is likely that the great majority of immigrants to North America after mid-century were essentially literate.

The second and third lines of table 4.2 provide overall and age-specific comparisons of illiteracy rates for native- and foreign-born men of Ontario in 1871. The comparisons reveal that illiteracy was, indeed, substantially *lower* for the foreign born than for the Canadian born among those above age 30. In fact, the rates for the Canadian born are quite high: for any age group they approximate the rate of the foreign born who are ten to twenty years older. For example, there is about the same proportion of illiterates among 20–29-year-old native-born men as there is among the foreign born aged 30–39 (0.06 and 0.07); there is exactly the same proportion among the 30–39-year-old natives as among immigrants over 40 (0.13).

In terms of minimal lexical education, then, Ontario's immigrants were relatively sophisticated compared with the native born. The difference is underscored in figure 4.1, where the plot of illiteracy by age for the Canadian born rises quite steeply from just over age 30 to over age 60. Although we cannot identify the specific sources, immigrants' relative literacy would have resulted from both the selectivity of migration, and from the spreading literacy of many areas of Europe. We note further that the ten- to twenty-year age advantage in literacy that immigrants enjoyed more than compensates for the fact that on average the foreign born were some eleven years older than natives. On balance, as the first column of the table shows, the *overall* male illiteracy rates for the two groups were nearly identical, 0.110 for Canadian born and 0.105 for foreign born. When the two rates are standardized for age, weighting the age-specific rates by the age composition of *all* men in Ontario, they become 0.132 and 0.094, as shown in the right-hand column of the table. This is to say that, if immigrants and natives had had identical age distributions, about 4 per cent more of the native born would have been illiterate in 1871.

Table 4.2 provides further evidence on the differences between the very large Irish-born immigrant group and the other foreign-born population. It has been commonplace in recent research to note the fact that among all northern European emigrants to North America, the Irish suffered from exceptional illiteracy. The 1841 census for Ireland revealed that less than 30 per cent could read or write, although after mid-century Irish national literacy began to rise significantly. It is relevant, too, that emigration was certainly as selective of the more literate among all Irish immigrants as for any other nationality.[20]

Graff's examination of three Ontario cities in 1861 indicated that the rates of illiteracy of the Irish immigrants (about 20 per cent) exceeded all other nationality groups. Among these, the large Irish-Catholic group far exceeded the illiteracy of the Protestant Irish in the three cities.[21] We pursue the question of the Catholic-Protestant and, specifically Irish, Catholic-Protestant differences for Ontario in a subsequent section of this chapter.

On the whole, the sample data for Ontario substantiate Graff's findings for the cities. Among adult men in Ontario in 1871 the Irish born had an overall rate of illiteracy of 0.144, compared with a rate of just 0.082 for all other foreign born (rows 4 and 5 of the table; the samples are relatively large, and the differences are statistically significant). In fact, there were significant differentials between these two groups of immigrants at every age, with the rate of the Irish born over 40 rivalling the very high illiteracy rate of the Canadian born of that age group (0.17 and 0.18). We note, however, that it was not greater.

Age was a significant factor in the Irish immigrants' illiteracy. Standardizing for age differences (again using the provincial age distributions as the standard) *reduces* the Irish-born rate to 0.102, or by about 10 per cent. This rate of illiteracy is still higher than that of other immigrants (0.075) but is clearly lower than the age-standardized rate (0.132) for the Canadian born. This finding raises the question of the *relative* effects of ethnicity and other social and demographic factors. Given the very high Irish-Catholic illiteracy in the cities he studied, Graff argued that ethnicity was the *first* factor among determinants of illiteracy in nineteenth-century Ontario.[22] Our sample reveals that a further specification is in order for the province as a whole: though in general Irish immigrants were the most illiterate group throughout Ontario, for those over the age of 30 this unenviable status was held by the province's native born. Later in the chapter a statistical analysis helps to unravel the relative effects on illiteracy of age, nativity, and ethnic origin, as well as religion. For the moment the very significant age differences in illiteracy in the last century draw us back to the question of the process of literacy attainment. It is revealing to ask how long it might take to eliminate a differential in rates of illiteracy between two groups, such as the Canadian and the foreign born.

The difference between the age-standardized rates for the nativity groups was given above as a slim 0.038 (0.132–0.094). Although illiteracy increases with age somewhat unevenly, the general pattern may be approximated by a linear least-squares estimate for all adult males from age 20 to 79 (estimating twelve age-specific illiteracy rates for the age groups 20–24, 25–29 ... 74–79). The resulting equation for estimated illiteracy (IL*) is IL* = 0.022 + 0.0022 age, with R^2 = 0.74.[23] The slope of the fitted relation can be interpreted to mean that for every year of age, literacy increases 0.0022 per cent on average. Thus, the apparently slight difference (0.038 or less than 4 per cent) in age-standardized rates of illiteracy between the Canadian and foreign born was equivalent to about 17 years (0.038/0.0022) of average increase in literacy during this era. In other words, it would have taken the Canadian born over a decade and a half to match the average literacy of the foreign born of Ontario.

This estimate again raises the question of the *general* rate of decline of male illiteracy in Ontario during the half-century after 1871. A projection can be based on the cross-sectional relationship between illiteracy and age for the native-born men in 1871 and compared with the rates of change derived from reports of the aggregate census results, available for the somewhat later period, 1891–1931.

Consider the pattern of Ontario illiteracy rates for native-born men classified by age from 20–79 in 1871 (figure 4.1). Plotted as a semi-logarithmic trend, the relation yields a yearly rate of change of 1.8 per cent. The aggregate 1891–1931 census data give a close, though slightly higher, yearly rate of change of 2.0 per cent. The semi-logarithmic trend fitted to age data for *all* men in 1871, rather than for the native born, exactly matches the 2.0 per cent annual rate of change obtained from the 1891–1931 reports. We take a 1.8 to 2.0 per cent figure to stand as a reasonable estimate of the annual rate of decline of male illiteracy in Ontario from 1871 to the point when literacy became virtually universal.

ILLITERACY AND ECONOMIC SECTOR: FARMERS AND NON-FARMERS

It is frequently assumed that the march towards universal literacy was led by the urban, commercial, or, at least, the non-agricultural sector of national or regional economies. Educational facilities, for example, are commonly thought to have been key to literacy gains and spread first through non-farm areas.[24] Beyond schools there were other major, and largely urban institutional developments fostering basic reading skills. There were, for example, the social and mechanics' libraries, local newspapers, and the expansion of the book trade, all actively promoting the 'reading habit.'

The assumption of a clear and persistent farm–non-farm difference for the nineteenth century, however, requires careful consideration. There are few detailed studies. For the United States and for an Ohio case study in particular, Soltow and Stevens show that newspapers, circulating libraries, and book reading spread quite widely through rural areas in the early part of the century. The circulation of newspapers grew rapidly between 1810 and 1850. Their study of the subscriber records of two small-town Ohio newspapers shows that in the 1820s and 1830s a clear majority of subscribers (and presumably readers) were out-of-town residents, spread over a 100-mile radius.[25] Moreover, in Ontario as elsewhere in North America, the influence of the common school system was by no means confined to urban areas. Indeed, the early and quite successful local demand for both schools and their control in *rural* areas has been one of the most important and surprising findings of the social history of education in the province.[26]

Despite the impressive increase in literacy-spreading institutions in many rural areas, Soltow and Stevens present convincing evidence that the growth of the urban, commercial and manufacturing sectors of the United States economy did tend to lead the way in reducing illiteracy in the last century.[27] For Ontario, our sample first allows for a comparison of literacy between the farm and the non-farm sectors. We shall see that with respect to literacy the economic or occupation division must be distinguished from the rural-urban one, though both are of historical interest. The latter is taken up in a subsequent analysis.

We refer once again to the patterns of table 4.2. Rows 6 and 11 of the table give the illiteracy rates for non-farmers and farmers. If we consider the first column for all those over 20, we see there is effectively no difference between non-farmers and farmers in rates of illiteracy (0.106 versus 0.109). Certainly there is no evidence here of a strong literacy advantage in the non-farm sector, as we might expect for an urban population. Of course, a good many non-farmers, especially small craft producers and day-labourers, lived in the countryside and in the province's small, non-incorporated, cross-roads villages. Ontario's farmers were at least as literate as these men, if not, as we shall see, as literate as urban residents.

Consideration of the components of these rates between farmers and non-farmers reveals a more puzzling initial result. Strangely, among non-farmers it was the *Canadian born* who had the highest rates of illiteracy. The Canadian-born rate of 0.134 is well above that of all foreign-born non-farmers (0.084) and even exceeds the rate for the non-farming Irish born (0.100), emigrating from a country with known illiteracy rates among the highest in the western world (these and each of the direct comparisons of the simple rates that follow are statistically significant at the level of 0.05 or better, unless explicitly noted). The relatively low illiteracy rate among non-farmers in 1871 was largely the result of the widespread elementary skills among non-Irish immigrants, whose illiteracy rate was below 8 per cent.

What about Canadian-born farmers? Table 4.2 indicates that fewer than 10 per cent (0.092) were illiterate, a rate considerably lower than that of the non-agricultural Canadian-born men. This statistic appears as a reversal of conventional expectations of farmers' relative illiteracy. A more detailed analysis of labour-force patterns reported below shows that the difference in literacy between common labourers and other non-farm workers is the key to the apparent anomaly. At this point we wish only to emphasize that Canadian-born farmers in mid-Victorian Ontario generally expected to be at least minimally literate. In contrast, nearly two of ten immigrant Irish *farm* men were illiterate (0.186), a rate that is largely responsible for the relatively high illiteracy of the foreign-born farmers as a whole (0.128).

Further, consider the age patterns of illiteracy for each of the nativity groups. Among the youngest men, aged 20–29, the Irish born slightly exceeded others in their illiteracy. But for those 30 to 39 and over 40 years, it is clearly the Canadian born, especially the non-farmers, who were exceptionally illiterate. One in four of the Canadian-born non-farmers over age 40 was unlettered, and those between 30 and 39 had a rate of illiteracy of about 15 per cent, which was double that of any other non-farm group of the same age. Why should these non-farming native-born Canadians have been so relatively illiterate?

Given the considerable differences among groups in the relation of illiteracy to age, it is again informative to standardize the rates for age composition. A complex age standardization procedure applied six population weights for ten-year age groups, (age = 20–29, 30–39 ... 70–79) for Ontario's entire adult-male population to corresponding age-specific illiteracy rates classified by both occupation and nativity. The results are given in the far right-hand column of table 4.2 and can be compared with the crude rates in the first column. These age-standardized rates underscore the curious difference in illiteracy rates between the Canadian born and the foreign born in the non-farm sector. That is, assuming that the native-born and immigrant groups had the same age composition in 1871 gives illiteracy rates of nearly 17 per cent (0.167) for the *Canadian born* and just 8 per cent (0.078) for the foreign born. The result reflects the relative youth of the Canadian born and the fact that the older members were most often illiterate.

We further standardized the crude rates for the farmers and non-farmers

The rudimentary schoolhouse promoted relatively widespread literacy among farmers in nineteenth-century Ontario, Pine Grove Elementary School, Durham county, c. 1870

simultaneously for age and nativity, as if both economic sectors had identical age distributions *and* the same proportions of natives and immigrants. The method is one way of descriptively examining the effect of both variables on illiteracy.[28] In sum, the rates before and after standardization are as follows:

	Not standardized	*Standardized for age*	*Standardized: age and nativity*
Non-farmers	0.106	0.109	0.114
Farmers	0.109	0.105	0.107

Standardization for age augments the age of non-farmers and thus also their illiteracy rate. Although the rates are essentially reversed, they remain similar (0.109 and 0.105). The additional age and nativity standardization increases the difference between the farm and non-farm groups. This result reflects an important interaction between economic sector and nativity: the large numbers of immigrant men among non-farmers tends to reduce the observed rate of illiteracy in this sector. Once these differences are taken into account, it is *farmers* as a whole who appear to have had a slight literacy advantage in 1871 (standardized rates of 0.114 versus 0.107). Again, this result is obviously contrary to the conventional wisdom about the relative 'backwardness' and isolation of farm life. It may reflect the extent of routine market involvement of Ontario's farmers by 1871, although the question remains largely open.

In sum, the evidence suggests there were specific historical conditions that led illiterate Canadian-born men into non-farm work. Among farmers, on the other hand, the age-standardized rates of illiteracy are quite similar for both natives and immigrants. The question of these differences is pursued with respect to urban and rural patterns and then for religious and ethnic groups.

ILLITERACY AND URBAN-RURAL RESIDENCE

With respect to literacy, it is particularly important to distinguish farm and non-farm patterns from rural-urban ones. There is a strong tendency to assume the identity of the two contrasts in linking the rise of literacy with the presumed, unilinear processes of 'modernization', industrialization, and urbanization. Table 4.3 substitutes the rural-urban distinction for that of farm and non-farm used in the previous analysis, without presenting the detailed age patterns. The rates in the top panel are duplicated to make the comparison clear. As before, we adopt the census definition of urban areas as incorporated villages, towns, and cities.

The urban and rural rates of illiteracy for adult men are substantially different. The published census volumes for 1871 report that urban males over age 20 had an illiteracy rate of 0.075, counting only men residing in the *five major cities*. The non-city rate was 0.117. The sample rates, adjusted to match this age and limited-urban group, are 0.067 and 0.111 (again attesting to the sample's representativeness). Taking a wider definition of urban areas to include Ontario's sixty-five village and forty-three town populations gives the rates of table 4.3. This much wider definition does not much alter the rates. Just over 7 per cent (0.072) of the men in urban areas were illiterate in 1871, as were nearly 12 per cent (0.116) of rural men. This result contrasts, of course, with the nearly identical farm and non-farm rates and more closely matches conventional images and specific findings, for example, of Soltow and Stevens for the United States in this period.[29] Standardization for age differences does not alter the rates.

The rural-urban contrast, however, does reveal once more the curiously

The pupils of early rural schools varied widely in age. Elementary school, Oxford county, 1875

high rate of illiteracy of the Canadian born. In urban areas they have the highest rates of all groups compared, matching the urban Irish born (the difference, 0.108 and 0.076, is not statistically significant in our sample). In this case, standardizing the rates for age increases the Canadian-born disadvantage (0.133 versus 0.051 for the foreign born).

Rural residents of the province had notably higher illiteracy, about 12 per cent overall. The rural Irish born were more illiterate than either natives or other immigrants (about 16 per cent), although standardization suggests that if the groups had identical age compositions, the Canadian born would nearly have matched them.

In sum, then, urban rates of illiteracy were lower than those of all non-farmers, and rural rates generally were higher than those for farmers alone. Native-born Canadians, whether urban residents or simply not farmers, were unexpectedly illiterate; indeed, both groups were less literate than Canadian-born farmers.

TABLE 4.3
Actual and standardized illiteracy rates for adult males in Ontario, 1871, by rural-urban residence and nativity

Group	Actual rate	Standardized illiteracy rate*	Sample size
All	0.108	0.108	5,386
Canadian born	0.110	0.132	2,618
Foreign born	0.105	0.095	2,768
Irish born	0.144	0.128	1,026
Other foreign	0.082	0.076	1,742
Urban	0.072	0.076	1,029
Canadian born	0.108	0.133	360
Foreign born	0.052	0.051	669
Irish born	0.076	0.066	224
Other foreign	0.040	0.039	445
Rural	0.116	0.155	4,357
Canadian born	0.111	0.131	2,258
Foreign born	0.122	0.111	2,099
Irish born	0.163	0.149	802
Other foreign	0.096	0.089	1,297

*See table 4.2.
SOURCE: See table 4.2.

We are not aware of other studies that suggest the anomaly of an immigrant population measurably more literate than native Canadians except among farmers. Indeed, quite the opposite is true. There are good reasons to expect that the Canadian born, in contrast to immigrants, would have taken advantage of the expanding school system before 1871. Further, Graff's ground-breaking study of literacy in Hamilton, London, and Kingston does not reveal a Canadian-born disadvantage in comparison with immigrants or suggest their particular illiteracy in urban areas. On the contrary, that study indicates that the Canadian-born adults in these cities were among the most literate (a figure is given only for Hamilton of about 3 per cent Canadian-born illiteracy).[30] We shall pursue a more detailed analysis of the seeming anomaly. For the moment, however, it is enough to note that in the midst of the Ryersonian era in Ontario there were significant pockets of native Canadians who had simply not been affected by the concerted campaign for moral and material improvement through formal education.

Another pattern of interest is the variation in illiteracy among the three types of urban places – cities, towns, and villages – as determined by municipal incorporation status. Table 4.4 gives these data, distinguishing the

TABLE 4.4

Illiteracy rates for adult males in Ontario, 1871, by residence in rural areas, villages, towns, and cities and by nativity

Group	All	Rural	Village	Town	City
All	0.108	0.116	0.090	0.069	0.067
Canadian born	0.110	0.111	0.138	0.089	0.112
Foreign born	0.105	0.122	0.056	0.057	0.048

SOURCE: See table 4.2.

Canadian and foreign born (there are eighty men in the smallest sample for the Canadian born in villages). If we consider the total male population, we see a clear and expected trend: rural residents are the most illiterate, followed by village, town, and city residents in that order. The urban Canadian-born disadvantage in comparison with the foreign born is once more underscored. In fact, it holds in each type of urban setting, and their illiteracy was more than double the rates of the immigrant population in both the province's villages and in its five major cities. The contrasts in illiteracy rates between all farmers and others in the labour force and between urban and rural areas raise the question of other occupational divisions. As we noted earlier, the initial decisions on the size of the sample and on data collection prevent us from undertaking an analysis of very detailed occupational differences. However, we can distinguish between the still large day labouring population and all other non-farmers. This turns out to be a revealing comparison.

LABOURING AND ILLITERACY

Common labouring continued to be a feature of the Ontario economy throughout the last century. Despite the special attraction of 'independent' family farming and the craft economy, as early as the 1820s large numbers of day labourers worked in both the major cities and the countryside, where they were employed in the construction of public works, especially in canal building.[31] By 1871 the sample data indicate that, whereas farmers made up 51.6 per cent of the adult male labour force, common labourers represented 12.3 per cent.

Table 4.5 gives the broad occupational distributions for the province and rural and urban areas separately, as well as for the relevant illiteracy rates for the groups. Among *rural* men over 20, 63.2 per cent were farmers, 11.5 per cent were labourers, and a quarter, 25.4 per cent, were 'other' workers.

TABLE 4.5
Sample distribution and illiteracy rates for adult men in Ontario, 1871, by urban and rural areas and major occupation

Group	Sample size	Proportion of rural and urban male population	Proportion of all adult males	Illiteracy rate
Rural				
Farmers	2,752	0.632	0.511	0.109
Labourers	499	0.115	0.093	0.248
Other	1,106	0.254	0.205	0.074
Urban				
Farmers	25	0.024	0.005	0.080
Labourers	161	0.156	0.030	0.236
Other	843	0.819	0.157	0.040

SOURCE: See table 4.2.

The other occupations include the entire gamut from semi-skilled wage workers to small craft producers, shopkeepers, merchants, and manufacturers. In the urban areas, there were a few 'gentlemen' or absentee farmers (2.4 per cent). Day-labourers comprised 15.6 per cent, and the highly varied, specific occupational groups represented the bulk, 81.9 per cent, of the urban labour force.

Although working conditions of many occupational groups were not altogether different from those of labourers, for example, and all were subject to the same vagaries of unpredictable employment, the illiteracy rates suggest there was a major social divide between labourers and all others. There were very small numbers of illiterates – just 7 and 4 per cent in rural and urban areas, respectively – among all who assumed a non-labouring occupational title. Among common labourers, in contrast, nearly a quarter of the adult men could not write (24.8 in rural areas, 23.6 in urban). In so far as elementary literacy was concerned, the common labourers of Ontario, it appears, lived in a world apart.

One of the features of Ontario in 1871 was the intersection between labouring and particular religious, ethnic, and birthplace groups. As in the case of tracing the social basis of those who lacked property (in chapter 3), unravelling the sources of the high illiteracy among the labouring men reveals two distinct and complex ethno-religious communities. One, the Irish-Catholic immigrant group, was made up mainly of urban residents. The other, the French-Canadian Catholics, laboured mainly in the countryside. The two groups probably shared little but their labouring, their Catholicism, and the large numbers who were wholly dependent upon oral communication and oral traditions. Of the two, the French-Canadians were the most illiterate. In the urban areas, the Catholic labouring men had an illiteracy rate of over 37 per cent, compared with about 14 per cent among Protestant labourers. And of the former, the majority were immigrants, although the few Catholic native born of Irish origin shared the high illiteracy. In the rural areas of the province, the rate of illiteracy among Catholic men was even higher than in villages, towns, and cities – reaching almost 44 per cent. Our sample indicates there were nearly as many native as foreign born among these rural Catholic labourers, but that among natives a quite astonishing 60 per cent (0.596) were illiterate. In the western world in the early 1870s this was a rare deprivation. By comparison, immigrant rural Catholic labourers had an illiteracy rate of about 25 per cent (0.255).

Our sample is large enough to allow a closer view, which reveals the clear division between the Irish-Catholic immigrant and French-Canadian labourers. Among the Irish-origin labourers in Ontario's urban areas, the majority were immigrant and Catholic and over one in three men (0.341) were illiterate, as Graff had indicated in his three-cities study. The comparable rural labouring group had rather lower illiteracy, about 27 per cent. As for the Franco-Ontario community that has escaped previous analysis, there was a tiny group of men working as labourers in cities in 1871 and a large majority concentrated in rural areas. Among these rural labourers illiteracy was the norm: 70 per cent of these men could not write in 1871.

To sum, then, the most illiterate of Ontario's men in 1871 were simple labourers, Catholic in faith, but they were divided into separate worlds of the rural French-Canadians and the urban immigrant Irish. To ask which of these characteristics was most determinative of their social circumstances is to attempt to cut through circles of historical causation and mutual reinforcement. Choosing to focus analytically on the conditions fostering illiteracy, we provide the results of one multivariate statistical analysis after we have examined variations among ethnic and religious groups more generally. It is relevant to report here, however, that even when the major differences between urban and rural areas and differences among labourers, farmers, and other occupational groups are accounted for, both ethnicity and religion are found to have statistically significant and independent effects on illiteracy. The separate cultural communities of the Irish-Catholic immigrants and, to a greater extent, of the French-Canadians have the appearance of a form of passive resistance to the march of formal education in Victorian Ontario.

Our analysis has focused on nineteenth-century Ontario's men. What about illiteracy among the women heads of households and property holders we have previously discussed?

ILLITERACY AMONG WOMEN HEADS OF HOUSEHOLDS IN ONTARIO, 1871

The 1871 published census volumes allow us to calculate a rate of illiteracy for women over age 20. It is 0.145.[32] The rate for men of the same age was given above as 0.113. The illiteracy rate of the generally older female *heads* of households in our sample was only marginally higher at about 16 per cent. Table 4.6 indicates that the age-specific rates vary from about 0.10 for those 20–29 years to 0.18 or 0.19 for those over age 50, with little age variation among the latter. By comparison, the far more numerous male *heads* of households had an overall illiteracy rate of 0.120, and the males who were not heads had a lower rate still of 0.078 (in the statistical sense both were significantly different from the rate for female heads). The oldest male heads were twice as illiterate as the youngest cohort (0.17 or 0.18 versus 0.08). The effects of spreading education were most notable among non-heads, where only about 6 per cent of the youngest group could not write, but 22 and 27 per cent of the oldest groups reported illiteracy to the enumerators.

Comparing age-standardized rates is essential here, since women heads were seven years older than male heads on average. The rates are given in table 4.7 and reveal that, taking account of the age difference, the female illiteracy rate was slightly greater, about 15 per cent, compared with 12 per cent for men.

Table 4.7 also reports illiteracy by nativity and urban-rural residence. The comparison within nativity groups shows that the Canadian-born heads were more alike than were the immigrant heads. Foreign-born males appear to have a gender advantage in literacy skills: about 5 per cent more were able to write than were immigrant women heads of households. In contrast, the Canadian-born women and men heads were virtually identical in literacy levels. The large Irish-born groups of women and men heads also had virtually identical age-standardized rates (0.16 versus 0.15). The non-Irish foreign born had the largest gender differences. The men had the lowest rates of illiteracy among all the groups presented here, while the women heads had only slightly lower rates than Canadian or Irish-born female heads.

The lower portions of the table give the urban and rural patterns. In one respect the pattern is broadly similar for both areas, in that the non-Irish

TABLE 4.6
Illiteracy rates among female and male heads of households in Ontario, 1871

Age	Female heads	Number	Male heads	Number	Male non-heads	Number
20–29	0.10	21	0.08	623	0.06	1,179
30–39	0.16	56	0.10	1,080	0.10	215
40–49	0.13	71	0.12	888	0.13	61
50–59	0.19	70	0.13	611	0.14	36
60–69	0.19	57	0.18	418	0.22	41
70 and over	0.18	38	0.17	186	0.27	48
Total	0.163	313	0.120	3,806	0.078	1,580

SOURCE: Film-manuscript sample of 313 females and 5,386 males 20 years and over; ten women were non-heads who owned property in the Ontario sample.

immigrant men have the lowest illiteracy rates – just 5 per cent of urban male heads and 9 per cent of those in rural areas. And again we witness the fact that Canadian-born men in *urban* areas far exceeded immigrants in illiteracy, with an age-standardized rate twice that of the new arrivals (0.14 versus 0.07). The experience of women heads, it turns out in this case, duplicates that of males. Their illiteracy levels in urban areas are somewhat greater than for males in every case, but it is the Canadian-born women heads who apparently have by far the highest rate, nearly 20 per cent (0.19). Though it is of some interest, this estimate is based on a small sample of just twenty-six individuals and warrants less confidence than other estimates in the table.

The rural patterns for women heads are very similar to those of men. Their illiteracy rates are higher in all cases. The Irish born in the countryside had very high rates, 21 and 17 per cent among women and men heads, followed quite closely by the Canadian born of both sexes, at 16 and 15 per cent.

The distinctive cultural differences in illiteracy identified above lead us to examine cultural patterns of illiteracy more fully. We concentrate on the larger sample of men only.

ILLITERACY, RELIGION, AND ETHNICITY IN 1871

A central focus of the history of literacy has been the identifiable national variations in the rates and timing of its rise, reflecting differences in state policy and in institutional and cultural orientations. These national differences have been relatively amenable to study through state papers and the documents of national educational policy making. Local community and

TABLE 4.7
Standardized illiteracy rates of female and male heads of households in Ontario, 1871, by nativity and rural-urban residence

Group	Females	Number	Males	Number
All	0.15	313	0.12	3,806
Canadian born	0.16	93	0.15	1,583
Foreign born	0.15	220	0.10	2,223
Irish born	0.16	110	0.15	854
Other foreign	0.13	110	0.08	1,369
Urban	0.12	106	0.09	711
Canadian born	0.19	26	0.14	186
Foreign born	0.10	80	0.07	525
Irish born	0.11	47	0.09	188
Other foreign	0.08	33	0.05	337
Rural	0.16	207	0.13	3,095
Canadian born	0.16	67	0.15	1,397
Foreign born	0.18	140	0.12	1,698
Irish born	0.21	63	0.17	666
Other foreign	0.14	77	0.09	1,032

NOTES: Standardized values were obtained by applying Ontario population weights of adult male heads for six age groups (weights of 623, 1,080, 888, 611, 418, and 186, totalling 3,806, to rates for age groups 20–29, 30–39 ... 60–69, 70 and over). The average age of women heads was 50.4 years and of male heads 43.4 years.
SOURCE: See table 4.6.

subcultural variations within national borders are more difficult to trace. The clearest national trajectories in the spread of literacy resulted from relatively homogeneous and long-standing institutional policies, as in the remarkable case of the joint effort of the Lutheran church and the Swedish state from the seventeenth century.[33] In other cases, however, national literacy patterns are statistical artefacts masking deep subcultural, regional, and local community differences. Among the major contributors to those variations were religious differentials. Some account of the larger historical patterns provides a valuable context for those of Ontario.

The growth of literacy in the western world was engendered by Protestantism's mission to spread individual spiritual salvation and, in turn, by literacy's incorporation through Protestantism into the Victorian concept of enlightenment and modernization. In both phases, the attainment of literacy was as much or more a means of conveying moral messages as it was a rational liberating force or a matter of practical necessity in a commercializing world, though in our view the latter two were significant elements of the larger cultural movement.

The tight knot linking literacy, Protestantism, and the moral order of capitalism has received eloquent analysis in some recent historical work.[34] With respect to Protestantism, Lawrence Stone argued in a seminal paper that 'Christianity is a religion of the book, namely the Scriptures, and once this book ceased to be a closely guarded secret fit only to be read by the priests, it generated pressure for the creation of a literate society.' He added, 'The historical record suggests that the critical element has been not so much Christianity as Protestantism.'[35] In one of the major early analyses of patterns of literacy in the west, Carlo Cipolla pointed to the particular regional correlation of Protestantism with literacy for Prussia and Ireland in 1871.[36] The apparently strong relationship between Protestantism and literacy is found also in the Swedish experience, achieving near universal literacy in the wake of the Lutheran Reformation, and in several other regions of intensely pious Protestantism before the end of the eighteenth century, Huguenot France, New England, parts of Scotland, Germany, and Switzerland.[37]

In Canadian studies, particular attention has been given to the relationship between the rise of the school system and heightened concern with social order, which were core elements of the emerging hegemony of Ontario's Protestant, Victorian culture. The promotion of literacy was an aspect of the promotion of a religiously sanctioned ethic of time and work discipline. Ontario's common and separate school systems grew rapidly in a context in which it was taken for granted that education was 'unmistakenly Christian in content, for no one doubted the Christian basis of Upper Canadian society.'[38]

The history of literacy's spread in the western world gives us every reason to expect quite wide variations among nationality and religious groups in nineteenth-century Ontario. As we have already seen, the Catholic-Protestant divide was still a deep gulf in 1871, even if it had been narrowing slowly over time. For Protestants there are again two general hypotheses one can entertain, as we did in the case of housing and property wealth. On the one hand, increasing church unity and a deepening common culture of Victorian capitalism might have largely overcome historic differences among denominational groups. On the other hand, there may still have been significant residual effects of the older institutional and attitudinal variations. The established Anglican church, for example, may have continued to encourage literacy less among its membership than did Methodists and Baptists, whose evangelical roots were closely intertwined with the promotion of the common schools. Our previous finding that evangelical denominations had somewhat greater propertied wealth suggests these communities would also have especially promoted children's education. Again we shall face the question of trying to unravel the effects of several related variables. We first examine the denominational differences in detail, followed by consideration of ethnic differences and, through multivariate analyses, incorporating these and other variables. We begin with the comparison of Protestant and Catholic literacy for the province.

ILLITERACY AMONG OLD ONTARIO'S PROTESTANTS AND CATHOLICS

Table 4.8 gives the rates of illiteracy by age groups, by nativity, and by economic sector, as above, but displayed separately for Protestants and Catholics. Despite some recent qualification of the traditional emphasis on a historic Protestant-Catholic division,[39] there can be no doubt that in Ontario by 1871 Protestantism still much more strongly encouraged literacy, as already remarked. The table gives the provincial rate for Protestants as 0.074 (for all those aged 20–99). The equivalent Catholic rate is 0.279. To facilitate comparison, we have again standardized the rates for age, as in the table, and further standardized them simultaneously for age, nativity, and occupation differences between the two major religious groups. The procedure uses provincial rates for the male population and yields the following standardized rates:

	Rate	Age	Rate standardized for age, nativity, occupation
Protestants	0.074	0.074	0.074
Catholics	0.279	0.277	0.280

With and without standardization, the Catholic illiteracy average is some 20 percentage points above that for Protestants. The fact that adjusting for differences due to age, nativity, and occupation does not affect the gap strongly suggests that the differences are fundamentally religious.[40] We have already shown that a significant portion of the divide can be attributed to the wholesale illiteracy of Ontario's francophone or French-speaking community. Some further detail is relevant.

Expressing the differences in cohort terms provides another perspective on the magnitude of the literacy divide. Table 4.8 shows that illiteracy among

TABLE 4.8
Illiteracy rates of adult males in Ontario, 1871, by age, religion, nativity, and farm–non-farm sectors

	Illiteracy rate				Sample size	Standardized illiteracy rate
	20–99	20–29	30–39	40–99		
Protestant	0.074	0.04	0.07	0.10	4,492	0.074
Canadian born	0.062	0.03	0.08	0.11	2,198	0.076
Foreign born	0.085	0.07	0.07	0.10	2,294	0.079
Irish born	0.098	0.13	0.07	0.10	660	0.101
Other foreign	0.080	0.05	0.07	0.10	1,634	0.072
Non-farmers	0.071	0.04	0.07	0.10	2,140	0.074
Canadian born	0.074	0.04	0.10	0.15	949	0.096
Foreign born	0.068	0.05	0.05	0.09	1,191	0.064
Irish born	0.050	0.06	0.04	0.05	299	0.052
Other foreign	0.075	0.04	0.06	0.10	892	0.072
Farmers	0.076	0.04	0.07	0.10	2,352	0.074
Canadian born	0.053	0.03	0.06	0.09	1,249	0.064
Foreign born	0.102	0.11	0.08	0.11	1,103	0.102
Irish born	0.139	0.20	0.13	0.14	361	0.150
Other foreign	0.085	0.06	0.07	0.09	742	0.076
Catholics	0.279	0.20	0.23	0.37	894	0.277
Canadian born	0.364	0.25	0.37	0.54	420	0.401
Foreign born	0.203	0.09	0.10	0.29	474	0.175
Irish born	0.227	0.07 ⌣	0.13	0.31	366	0.185
Other foreign	0.120	0.08		0.18	108	0.097
Non-farmers	0.269	0.24	0.20	0.34	469	0.270
Canadian born	0.413	0.34	0.38	0.55	206	0.439
Foreign born	0.156	0.07	0.08	0.24	263	0.137
Irish born	0.174	0.08 ⌣	0.10	0.25	201	0.155
Other foreign	0.097	0.03		0.19	62	0.074
Farmers	0.289	0.15	0.27	0.40	425	0.287
Canadian born	0.318	0.16	0.36	0.53	214	0.316
Foreign born	0.261	0.12	0.15	0.34	211	0.227
Irish born	0.291	0.04 ⌣	0.19	0.37	165	0.226
Other foreign	0.152	0.04		0.18	46	0.108

NOTES: Illiteracy is defined as being unable to write. Standardized values have been obtained by applying Ontario population weights to Protestant (and Catholic) illteracy averages for six age cells.
SOURCE: See table 4.2.

young Catholics, say those aged 20–29, was twice the rate for Protestants *over* 40 (0.20 versus 0.10). We might say that in terms of the course of illiteracy's decline, Ontario Catholics were a full *generation or two* behind Protestants in 1871. The table once again distinguishes the native and the foreign born and the Irish born and others among immigrants. Among Protestants, the Irish born have a slightly higher rate of illiteracy (0.098) than other immigrants or the Canadian born. This is a result mainly of the very high relative illiteracy of Irish immigrant farmers (with a rate of 0.139). A comparison of farm and non-farm sectors reveals quite small differences overall, but the table shows that it was the Protestant Canadian-born *farmers* who had attained the highest elementary literacy levels (illiteracy rate of 0.053: the differences are statistically significant, for example, from those of the Protestant foreign-born farmers and clearly from Catholic rates). Once again this hints at the relative commercial involvement of the different farming populations.

The table also gives detailed illiteracy rates standardized for age in the right-hand column. The comparison for the Protestant groups suggests there is very little difference among them once age is considered. In marked contrast, the lower panel of the table, for Catholics, again reveals much higher illiteracy rates overall and very striking differences between native- and foreign-born populations. Reflecting our earlier inquiry into illiteracy among labouring men, we see here that Canadian-born Catholics had an exceedingly high rate in 1871: nearly four in every ten adult *Catholic native-born* men could not write. Foreign-born Catholics had a significantly lower rate than the native born, though the illiteracy rate was still relatively high, about 20 per cent.

Again the probability of being illiterate was higher for non-farmers than for farmers among Catholics, as it was for Protestants. In the case of Catholics, the advantage was a full 10 per cent (0.413 versus 0.318). The age cohort rates are also revealing. Among those not in farming, over a third of even the youngest Canadian-born Catholic men (aged 20–29) were not able to write in 1871. And over half of the same group over 40 years of age were illiterate. By comparison, many more of the foreign born in the same economic sector were literate in this limited sense of reporting they could write. Moreover, it appears that young native-born Catholics who were in farming apparently had been able to take advantage of some schooling, whereas young men in off-farm work inherited and perpetuated the literacy disadvantage of the older members of the Catholic community.

Further, the most striking finding in this context is that the *native-born Catholics* were much more illiterate than native-born Protestants, than the foreign-born in general, and even more illiterate than the Irish-Catholic immigrant population. The latter carried a national legacy of low literacy, and in conventional imagery as well as in recent studies they appear as uniquely unschooled. Yet the provincial patterns indicate there were particularly limiting conditions at work in nineteenth-century Ontario that left Canadian-born Catholics, especially those in rural labouring, still largely illiterate in 1871.

At the outset we noted that urban and rural patterns in illiteracy are related to, but by no means identical to, those of farm and non-farm, since, for example, there were large numbers of non-farm rural workers. However, the urban-rural contrasts in this case are very similar to the farm–non-farm ones just discussed. Whereas literacy was nearly complete among urban Protestants (97 per cent), one in five Catholic males in urban areas was unable to write. About 8 per cent of rural Protestants, but nearly a third (0.305) of rural Catholics were illiterate.[41]

That Catholics were considerably more illiterate than Protestants in late nineteenth-century Ontario follows the history of the religious divisions in educational development. Ontario's Catholics, however, were not a homogeneous group. Even the relatively small francophone group was split between the older Windsor community and the Ottawa valley migrants from Quebec (those of 'French origin' in Ontario made up less than 5 per cent of the total male population but about a quarter of the province's Catholics). In addition, there was another small community of Scottish Catholics, many of Glengarry origin, and some German-Catholics who had settled in Waterloo and Bruce counties. The provincial sample shows these two groups made up just 6 and 4 per cent of all Catholics, respectively. They were swamped by the large numbers of Irish-origin Catholics, both immigrants from the 1840s and 1850s and the native born. The Irish-Catholics represented just over 60 per cent of the province's Catholic population. The variation raises the question of illiteracy patterns among national-origin groups; it will be addressed below. Does the cultural division we reported earlier among labourers hold for the Canadian-born Catholic community as a whole? In a word, yes. Men of French origin represented over 45 per cent of Ontario's adult male Catholic, Canadian-born population. The English-speaking Catholic community was more diverse, but by far the largest number were of Irish origin (40 per cent of all native Catholics). The French-speaking group had an age-standardized illiteracy rate of over 60 per cent; the English-speaking group had one of 20 per cent. The two major linguistic communities among Ontario's Catholics had common interests to defend, not least with respect to public education and the separate school system, but the illiteracy differential attests to the fact that they surely were, as Grant puts it, 'two solitudes that never really understood each other.'[42]

How can we account for the Canadian-born Catholic experience? Recent local studies provide some detailed analysis of the relationships among social and economic conditions, religion, and schooling in the province. For example, Gaffield gives a detailed account of language and education among anglophones and francophones in the Ottawa valley. He argues that attitudes towards education and school enrolments after mid-century reflected the cultural geography and locational preferences of the two communities, as well as the exigencies of family economies and material security. The Catholic church's strong support for the growth of separate schools, to strengthen the Catholic community, was sometimes reinforced and sometimes resisted by the local lay community in their concern for French-language maintenance.[43] But in the end, the relative irrelevance of schooling to economic well-being and the inadequacy of school facilities conspired to produce very limited educational opportunities for francophone Catholic children.

Akenson has documented an entirely different Catholic school experience further south and west, in Leeds and Lansdowne township.[44] Here, he argues, the thorough adoption in Canada West of the Irish national system of education, including Irish texts, had the effect of smoothing the adaptation of both Irish-Catholic and Irish-Protestant migrants. Moreover, the specific attention given in Ireland to a denominationally neutral, though distinctly Christian, curriculum mitigated local concern with religious conflict. Most important, there were too few Catholics to warrant separate schools and, hence, 'Catholics did not sulkily accept the common schools but adhered to them with as much enthusiasm as did any one else.'[45]

Further detailed studies of Catholic and Protestant educational experiences would, no doubt, discover varying constellations of economic, institutional, and cultural forces. Yet for all the subtleties of local and ethnic variation, the depth of the literacy divide between Catholics and Protestants in the province was so pronounced it requires a more general explanation and may serve as a lens clarifying deeper differences.

Commenting on the institutionalization of separate schools in nineteenth-century Ontario, Grant sketches the radical differences between Protestants and Catholics regarding the place of formal schooling within the political culture of the two communities. For the Catholic hierarchy elementary schools were an essential bulwark in maintaining the faith. The hierarchy's perception of the expanding public school system as essentially Protestant, though formally secular, was not misplaced. Rather than serving to attach the public to the emerging national, industrial, and, putatively, secular order, as it was for a Protestant majority, formal education remained suspiciously conspiratorial in the eyes of Catholic clergy. 'Archbishop Lynch,' argues

Grant, 'the one person who might have lobbied successfully for Roman Catholic secondary schools, never overcame a suspicion that too much education was likely to detach Catholics from their faith. He therefore allowed Ryerson to put a single system into place without serious protest.'[46] The larger implication of the remarkable Catholic absence of elementary literacy in 1871 is that this minority, or dual minority of Irish, but especially French-Canadian, Catholics, stood as a counterpoint, and challenge, to the ascendancy of the liberal, individualist, and very Protestant Victorianism in Ontario. We consider illiteracy first among the Protestant denominations and then among ethnic origin groups.

ILLITERACY AMONG THE PROTESTANT DENOMINATIONS

The question of literacy was intertwined with religion and politics in nineteenth-century Ontario, as it was in western Europe and the United States. The attainment of elementary literacy was taken to be a condition of the maintenance of faith as well as of public order and class position. Debates over the direction of formal education reflected these concerns.

In the first place, in response to the Catholic separate school issues of the 1850s, some consensus was emerging regarding public schooling among Ontario's Protestant churches after mid-century, though still hampered by denominational rivalry. Less obvious, but still influential in encouraging common views was the increasing secularism of the age. Protestants of all denominations shared a deep ambivalence towards what they perceived as the anarchic tendencies of unconstrained commercial and capitalist expansion, posing a threat both to the integrity of the social fabric and to religious principles.[47] Despite worries about the potentially intrusive influence of the state, education within a public system was thought capable of tempering these threats by fostering the ideals of social order and social progress.

Once again, however, pressures towards common ground were offset by a long history of denominational divergence. The Protestant churches in Ontario had varied in their emphasis on education for the laity throughout much of the century. The early and middle decades especially witnessed a great variety of forms of elementary schooling, and supporters of denominational, as opposed to common or public, schools were vocal throughout these years and later.[48] Denominational debates were prominent features of the politics of education, especially in the 1820s and 1830s. They were especially evident, since the two most influential school promoters of the century, the Church of England's John Strachan and the Methodist Egerton Ryerson had made the issue a matter of public and personal debate. The debate was further fuelled by the continuing mid-century association of denominational affiliation with putative class position. 'In the nineteenth-century,' Prentice observes, 'the word "class" itself was often used to mean "denominational" or "sect".' In the 1820s Strachan did not hesitate to charge that non-conformists were simply the social inferiors of Anglicans.[49]

Moreover, the Church of England's hesitation about common schools reflected its sense of privileged place in the social hierarchy and its emphasis on moderation, formality, and stability. *Popular* literacy was not likely to be promoted actively in this establishment context, which de-emphasized personal salvation while fostering genteel standards and religious tradition.[50] In contrast, the more evangelical churches, Baptists and Methodists in particular, historically had encouraged literacy attainment. Central elements of this evangelical tradition stressed the relation of individual free will and perfectibility to salvation, tending, thus, to foster elementary literacy at least for the purposes of attaining a personal knowledge of biblical text.[51]

Ontario's residents provided the 1871 census enumerators with a dazzling variety of church and sect identifications.[52] Our sample is only ample enough to distinguish four main denominations among Protestants. For these groups and the Catholic population, illiteracy rates are given by age and nativity in the top panel of table 4.9. The lower portion of the table gives the rates for the province's main ethnic-origin groups, which are examined later.

The Protestant denominational differences in illiteracy are, in fact, modest, but they are sufficiently large to be of substantive and statistical interest. Using the conventional typology distinguishing church from sect, we see they correspond broadly to the expected gradient from the more orthodox-liturgical to the more evangelical-pietistic.[53] The Church of England adherents clearly had the highest *il*literacy rate, about 10 per cent. They were followed in order by the Methodists, 8 per cent of whose male members were illiterate, then by the Presbyterians and Baptists, at less than 5 per cent. The slightly lower illiteracy rate of Methodists compared with that of Anglicans is not statistically significant, though the differences between Methodists and the Presbyterians and Baptists are. Thus both Baptists and Presbyterians had within their congregations about half as many illiterate members as one would have met among Anglicans, although these rates are not high by absolute standards, representing one and two in twenty adult men. Certainly they do not compare to the very much higher Catholic rate.

These rates and their order are not much altered when we take into account the differences among groups in age composition, or the combined differences in several factors, age, native or foreign-born, and farm–non-farm sector. The pattern appears, thus, to reflect persistent denominational

TABLE 4.9
Illiteracy rates of adult males in Ontario, 1871, by religion, country of origin, and nativity

Group	All			Canadian born			Foreign born			Sample size	Standard-ized rate*
	20–99	20–39	40–99	20–99	20–39	40–99	20–99	20–39	40–99		
All religions	0.108	0.08	0.15	0.110	0.08	0.18	0.105	0.07	0.13	5,386	0.108
Baptist	0.046	0.03	0.07	0.037	0.03	0.04	0.063	0.00	0.09	259	0.047
Presbyterian	0.049	0.04	0.06	0.039	0.03	0.07	0.055	0.05	0.06	1,216	0.048
Methodist	0.081	0.06	0.11	0.069	0.06	0.11	0.100	0.09	0.11	1,433	0.084
Church of England	0.097	0.06	0.14	0.076	0.05	0.15	0.110	0.06	0.14	1,124	0.095
Catholic	0.279	0.21	0.37	0.364	0.29	0.54	0.203	0.10	0.29	894	0.277
Other	0.074	0.06	0.09	0.074	0.05	0.12	0.074	0.07	0.07	460	0.072
All origin groups	0.103	0.08	0.15	0.110	0.08	0.18	0.105	0.07	0.13	5,386	0.103
Scotland	0.045	0.04	0.05	0.035	0.03	0.06	0.052	0.05	0.05	1,098	0.044
Germany	0.070	0.04	0.10	0.068	0.05	0.09	0.074	0.03	0.11	512	0.067
England and Wales	0.073	0.05	0.10	0.056	0.05	0.08	0.087	0.06	0.11	1,542	0.074
Ireland	0.114	0.08	0.17	0.075	0.06	0.12	0.144	0.09	0.18	1,808	0.114
France	0.515	0.46	0.59	0.586	0.52	0.68	0.125	0.10	0.16	260	0.514
Other	0.247	0.15	0.36	0.226	0.17	0.33	0.283	0.12	0.41	166	0.239

*Standardized values have been obtained by applying Ontario population weights to the denomination's illiteracy averages for six age cells.
SOURCE: See table 4.2.

differentials. The results, using provincial distributions to standardize the rates, are given in table 4.10.

The previous table (4.9) also indicates that foreign or Canadian birth affected all the Protestant groups. The foreign born were slightly more literate overall, with the striking exception, emphasized above, that the Canadian-born Catholics significantly exceeded the foreign born in illiteracy. Considering only Protestant churches, the differences in illiteracy persist for both the foreign and native born: the force of religious culture on literacy appears, in this respect, to transcend place of birth.

In sum, the evidence of the nominal data shows that after mid-century membership in the Baptist and Presbyterian churches had fostered moderately greater elementary literacy among adult men than did affiliation with the Methodist or Anglican churches. The latter two were surprisingly similar in the size of their illiterate minorities, and the differences cannot be attributed to age composition. The adherents of all of Ontario's Protestant churches had attained far greater literacy, of course, than had Catholics. Perhaps there were ethnic differences that went beyond denominational ones. We can consider table 4.9 for relevant evidence.

ETHNIC ORIGINS AND ILLITERACY

National variations in literacy and educational policy have been more readily documented historically than differences among religious groups, though the effects of ethnic origin and religious persuasion are often closely tied. We have seen that denominational membership affected a man's chances of being illiterate in nineteenth-century Ontario. For a few Ontario cities in the last century, recent studies have documented ethnic origin differences in literacy and education. Graff's emphasis on the Irish-Catholic disadvantage has been noted. Katz, Doucet, and Stern report that those of Scottish heritage and birth in Hamilton had the highest school attendance rates between 1851 and 1871.[54]

Considering the province as a whole, the lower panel of table 4.9 gives the male illiteracy rates for Ontario's six main ethnic origin groups in 1871 by age and by nativity. It is immediately evident that the experience of the Scottish in Hamilton reflects a provincial pattern. Both native- and foreign-born Scottish men had the lowest overall rates of illiteracy among all ethnic groups. The total rate was just 4.5 per cent. Further, Scottish immigrants were also unique in that the illiteracy rate among those age 40 or over was the same as that of the younger group.

The Scottish in Canada, as in the British Isles, were known particularly

TABLE 4.10
Illiteracy rates and standardized illiteracy rates of adult males in Ontario, 1871, by Protestant denomination

| Denomination | Rate | Rate standardized for | |
		Age	Age, nativity, and sector
Church of England	0.097	0.095	0.096
Methodist	0.081	0.084	0.085
Presbyterian	0.049	0.048	0.046
Baptist	0.046	0.047	0.044
Other	0.074	0.072	0.069

NOTES: The standardized rates employ provincial distributions as the standards. Sector refers to farm and non-farm occupations.
SOURCE: See table 4.2.

to value education. Basic literacy was seen as part of the civilizing process needed to accompany industrialization. Adam Smith well represented the Scottish liberal concern with literacy's capacity to soften the social consequences of industrialization. Scottish children's ability to read and write, Smith thought, would cushion the dulling of sensitivities 'when a person's whole attention is bestowed on the seventeenth part of a pin or the eightieth part of a button.'[55] By the nineteenth century this view had become part of a national heritage of elevated levels of literacy and learning and was clearly fostered by the Scottish community in Ontario.

After the Scottish-origin group, the groups, in order of increasing illiteracy, were the German (0.070), the English and Welsh (0.073), the Irish (0.114), those of 'other' origins (0.247), and, finally, those of French origin, with an exceedingly high rate of 0.515.

Like the Scottish in Canada, the low illiteracy among those of German heritage reflected a national European experience. Rapid industrialization in the Kingdom of Prussia made illiteracy disreputable by the second half of the nineteenth century.[56] Indeed, among the German group the native born and immigrants had virtually identical low rates of illiteracy (0.068 and 0.074).

Among the three dominant British-origin groups, the largest, the Irish, did have the highest illiteracy rate of about 11 per cent, as earlier research indicates. The illiteracy among the Irish was significantly greater than among the English and Welsh and far exceeded the illiteracy among those of Scottish origin. Of course, the question raised by the urban studies of Graff and of Katz and his colleagues is the difference between Catholic and Protestant Irish. The question is considered below.

Irish-origin illiteracy was high in nineteenth-century Ontario, but it was only half that of the diverse 'other origin' groups and truly paled in comparison with the illiteracy of the small French-origin group, with a rate of over 50 per cent. As discussed above, this basic limitation to the spread of literacy was primarily a product of the disadvantage of the native born. Table 4.9 shows that although they represented only 5 per cent of the male population, almost six of every ten (0.586) French-Canadian men in Ontario were still illiterate in 1871.[57] Of course, we are seeing here just the 'ethnic' side of the widespread illiteracy of the Catholic francophone community found earlier with respect to religion. The standardization procedure we have used above is one way of asking whether illiteracy differentials among ethnic-origin groups are specifically a product of the cultural communities or if they can be accounted for by the variations in other variables like age or place of birth. Table 4.11 gives several relevant standardized rates.

First, consider the age-standardized rates for the Canadian born and foreign born separately, where the standard is the provincial age distribution for men. They are in the second and third rows of the table. The adjusted rates can be compared directly with those of the lower portion of table 4.9 for the nativity groups. We found that although age differences among the origin groups affect illiteracy somewhat, the order of the rates is little changed by hypothetically equalizing age composition, as shown in table 4.11.

Second, the results of a more elaborate standardization for age, nativity, and the distribution by farm and non-farm occupation reveal only one significant change. Illiteracy of the French-origin group would have been moderated considerably, from over half of the male population's being illiterate to about a third (0.328), if that group had been equivalent to the provincial male population in all three respects, as also shown in table 4.11.

Since, as we have just seen, age standardization alone had little effect, the results reflect the combination of nativity and economic sector participation. Examination of these distributions underscores a previous finding. As table 4.9 shows, by far the greatest contrast in illiteracy rates was between French-Canadians and the small group of French-origin immigrants. The results of the standardization reflect this gap and the fact that the great majority of the French-origin group were native Canadians, about 80 per cent, compared with a provincial average of about 50 per cent Canadian born.

Throughout the analysis we have dealt with the intersection of several variables, farm and non-farm occupations, urban and rural residence, eth-

TABLE 4.11
Standardized illiteracy rates for country of origin groups, Ontario, 1871

Country of origin	Rate standardized for age		Rate standardized for age, nativity, and economic sector
	Canadian born	Foreign born	
Scotland	0.043	0.054	0.043
Germany	0.069	0.058	0.066
England and Wales	0.066	0.075	0.073
Ireland	0.098	0.129	0.114
France	0.583	0.139	0.328
Other	0.250	0.245	0.226

SOURCE: See table 4.8.

nicity, and religion. We now attempt to assess their relative importance for illiteracy in 1871.

ILLITERACY, ETHNIC ORIGIN, AND RELIGION

Ethnicity and religious persuasion are normally experienced as elements of a single cultural heritage: one is a Scots-Presbyterian, an English-Anglican, an Irish- or French-Catholic. Table 4.12 simply presents the cross-classification of the sample data for men showing illiteracy rates by religious group *within* each country of origin category. Following the previous analysis, the rates reported in the table are age standardized to control for that variable's effect on illiteracy. It is also to be noted that the rates for Protestant groups of French origin are subject to large sampling errors, since these groups are especially small.

The lowest illiteracy rate is found among the fifty-five Scottish Baptists in the sample. They had virtually complete literacy. More generally, the Scottish men of all religious persuasions, except Catholic, had very low illiteracy rates, averaging around 4 per cent. Once again, by contrast, we see that the highest male illiteracy rate in Ontario in 1871 was among French-origin Catholics: well over half of that group were illiterate.

The patterns of the table suggest two particularly consistent cultural influences on nineteenth-century illiteracy in Ontario: Scottish national origin and Baptist religious affiliation. Scottish heritage is associated with the lowest rates of illiteracy for each non-Catholic church group, and Baptist adherence is associated with the lowest rates for all origin groups.

Further, and importantly, the results qualify in a specific way the infer-

TABLE 4.12
Standardized illiteracy rates for adult males in Ontario, 1871, by religion and ethnic origin

Country of origin	Roman Catholic	Baptist	Church of England	Methodist	Presbyterian	Other	Protestant	All
England	0.04	0.03	0.10	0.08	0.10	0.08	0.08	0.074
Scotland	0.19	0.01	0.04	0.04	0.04	0.03	0.04	0.044
Ireland	0.20	0.02	0.09	0.07	0.08	0.07	0.08	0.114
Germany	0.04	0.03	0.09	0.09	0.07	0.05	0.07	0.067
France	0.54	–	0.29	0.24	0.12	–	0.35	0.514
Other	0.43	0.12	0.16	0.25	–	0.29	0.24	0.239
All	0.277	0.047	0.095	0.084	0.048	0.072	0.074	0.108

SOURCE: See table 4.2.

ences one can draw from local studies of Ontario cities in which the Irish-Catholics were identified as especially illiterate.[58] In the province as a whole, Irish-Catholics were, in fact, likely to be illiterate – one man in five was unable to write in 1871. But their illiteracy was matched by the Scottish-Catholics in the province and was far exceeded, as we have seen, by Catholics who were of French or other origins. Among the francophone Catholics a majority of 54 per cent and among the other group a huge minority of 43 per cent were still illiterate in 1871. Significantly, however, not all Catholics had high illiteracy rates: it appears from these data that the small Catholic communities of English- and of German-origin men were quite literate (illiteracy at 0.04 in the table).

This first specification of the joint influences of religion and ethnic origin on illiteracy has proved revealing. A further statistical specification can illuminate the several effects.

A MULTIVARIATE ANALYSIS OF ILLITERACY IN 1871

Given the foregoing analysis, we are particularly interested in the *relative* effects of religion and ethnic origin in comparison with other variables. The form of the analysis requires brief comment.

Following the multivariate analysis of the previous chapter, both more familiar ordinary least squares regression and logistic regression analyses were conducted, including in each several variables in addition to origin and religion. Although it is known that ordinary least squares regression normally provides very similar results, logistic regression is the appropriate procedure, since the men in the sample were classified as either literate or illiterate and only a relatively small proportion of the sample was illiterate.[59]

In the logistic regression, the dependent variable is simply the chance that a man is illiterate, represented as the logarithm of the odds (log-odds).

In addition to ethnic origin and religion, the model also includes nativity, age as a set of categories (20–29, 30–39 ... 70 and over), and urban residence. Each is a variable we previously found affected levels of literacy. Entering them into the analysis will reveal whether they largely account for the apparent variation in illiteracy of the origin and religion groups. Another obvious hypothesis is that illiteracy is strongly associated with class or economic position. Specifically, one wonders if the generally deprived economic circumstances of the francophone or Irish-Catholic community in contrast, say, to the Scottish Baptists may not be primarily responsible for their literacy differences. To consider this possibility, the model includes five economic variables. Three represent assets in farm land – land occupancy, ownership, and improvement. Two represent other property holding – home ownership and the ownership of commercial buildings, shops, stores, warehouses, and the like.[60]

Each of the independent or predictor variables is treated as a dichotomy or set of dichotomies. Nativity and all five economic variables are simple dichotomies, native born or foreign born, land occupant or not, and so on. Age, residence (rural, village, town, city), ethnic origin, and religion are treated as sets of categories, where, for example, age *a-b* is 1.0 if an individual's age is between *a and b* and is otherwise zero. The tabular presentation of the variables gives the particular categories selected and presents in parentheses for each variable the reference or implicit category with which all others in the relevant set are compared.

We present two forms of the analysis. Table 4.13 provides the results of the logistic regression including all the variables, which is called the base model. As before, this model provides estimated effects of each category of interest in comparison with the selected reference category of that variable. Table 4.14 extends the analysis by presenting the results of a series of logistic regressions comparing the base model with models in which specific variables are *excluded*. The purpose of the latter analysis is to see whether or not the inclusion of a given independent variable represented as a set of categories, makes a statistically significant difference to the model's capacity to account for the probability that men were illiterate and to assess the relative magnitude of that contribution.[61]

Table 4.13 gives the coefficients estimating the effects of the independent variables, their standard errors, and the probability that these results of the model could be attributed to sampling error alone (model chi-square and statistical significance level).

TABLE 4.13
Logistic regression estimates of illiteracy from five predictor variables for adult males in
Ontario, 1871

Variables	Estimate	Standard error	Model chi-square
Constant	-2.78	0.17	
Age (vs. 20–29)			
30–39	0.58	0.15	14.57***
40–49	1.00	0.17	36.24***
50–59	1.04	0.19	31.94***
60–69	1.48	0.19	61.24***
70 and up	1.39	0.22	40.43***
Religion (vs. Anglican)			
Catholic	0.91	0.15	35.50***
Baptist	-0.92	0.38	7.76**
Methodist	-0.20	0.15	1.81
Presbyterian	-0.44	0.20	4.88*
Other	-0.35	0.22	2.42
Residence (vs. Rural)			
Village	-0.63	0.29	4.79*
Town	-0.79	0.23	11.68***
City	-1.16	0.22	27.45***
Ethnicity (vs. English–Welsh)			
Scottish	-0.45	0.21	4.57*
Irish	0.07	0.14	0.22
German	-0.18	0.21	0.70
French	1.85	0.21	80.52***
Other	1.46	0.22	43.62***
Economic factors (5 dichotomies)			
Farmland owned	0.03	0.17	0.03
Farmland occupied	0.30	0.29	1.09
Farmland improved	0.06	0.29	0.04
Home owned	-0.37	0.16	5.26*
Commercial Property	-0.51	0.14	12.97***
Nativity (vs. native born)			
Foreign born	0.01	0.11	0.01

*Significant at 5 per cent level.
**Significant at 1 per cent level.
***Significant beyond 1 per cent level.
NOTES: The parenthetical entries indicate the comparison category for each variable.
Commercial property refers to warehouses, shops, stores, etc., but not to farm buildings,
barns, stables.
SOURCE: The film-manuscript sample of 5,386 men 20 years and older in Ontario, 1871.

The results indicate generally that the chance of a man's being illiterate
was directly affected by his age, religious affiliation, city residence, and

ethnic origin, when the effects of all the other measured variables are taken into account. One negative result is striking in the light of previous analysis. There is *no* illiteracy difference between native and foreign born, when the effects of other factors are considered statistically. We need to be quite clear here. It remains a fact that illiteracy was slightly greater among all Canadian-born men than among immigrants in mid-Victorian Ontario, and the Canadian born were more visibly disadvantaged among non-farm workers and in urban areas, as the previous analysis indicates. But the model shows that this unexpected disadvantage is not due to place of birth but is wholly the consequence of the play of other factors associated with birthplace. And, as we shall see, ethnic heritage and religion have considerable independent force.

The statistically significant effects are discussed in the order in which they appear in table 4.13. With respect to age, in comparison with those aged 20 to 29 (the reference category), the orderly increase in the magnitude of the coefficients indicates that the probability of illiteracy increased for every group to age 69, then declined very slightly. The results reinforce the previous interpretation, though here the age pattern is seen to survive the effects of all other variables on illiteracy.

As for religion, three contrasts among the religious groups were statistically significant, taking the Anglicans as the reference group. The Methodists were not significantly different from Anglicans in illiteracy; Presbyterians and, to a greater extent, Baptist men were less likely to be illiterate. Catholic men, on the other hand, were clearly much more likely to be illiterate than Anglican men. The pattern of coefficients representing interchurch differences conforms precisely to earlier cross-tabular findings. The statistical analysis serves to show again that, with respect to the chance a man was illiterate, these cultural contrasts were statistically significant and independent of the effect of the other demographic and economic influences.

Also confirming the descriptive analysis, the results indicate that each type of urban residence – village, town, and city – reduced the chances of illiteracy among Ontario's men in comparison with rural residents and independent of other measured factors in the model. The effects increased with size of place.

For the ethnic groups, like religion, there are three statistically significant contrasts when the English-Welsh population is the reference group. Those of Scottish origin are somewhat less likely to be illiterate than the English and Welsh group, and those of French and of 'Other' origins had a far greater chance of being illiterate. One of the cases in which origin is *not* of significance happens to be the Irish. Men of Irish origin did not differ from their English and Welsh neighbours in the likelihood of being illiterate, when the effects of other variables, particularly Catholicism, are taken into account.

Given the independent significance of the two cultural variables, religion and ethnicity, the fact that the several economic variables have very weak effects on illiteracy is also of interest. Specifically, whether a man owned, occupied, or held improved farm land did not alter the chance of being illiterate. Home owners were, however, somewhat less likely to be illiterate than non-owners. Similarly, men who owned other forms of commercial small property had a moderately less, though statistically significant, chance of being illiterate than non-owners.

Clearly, one of the main implications of this baseline model is the fact that the effects of demographic, residential, and economic conditions do *not* reduce or eliminate the strong variations among the specific religious and ethnic groups.[62] One is led to wonder about the relative effects of the cultural variables in comparison with the others in the model. If age and rural residence also contribute significantly to illiteracy, how do they compare with the effect of one's ethnic heritage or religious affiliation? And what is the difference between the effects of the cultural variables themselves? The results of a series of regression analyses presented in table 4.14 bear on these issues.

In this analysis, a number of logistic regressions are compared with the baseline model of table 4.13, which includes all the variables. The analysis is identical in form to that reported in chapter 3, in which we assessed the relative contributions of several variables to the odds both of owning secure property and of being propertyless. As in that case, the magnitude of the difference between the value of the test statistic for the baseline model and for each equation is taken as a measure of the relative importance of the excluded variable. The statistical probability of that difference is assessed and is indicated in the far right column of the table. In this case, there are six such comparisons, each assessing the effect on the explanatory power of the model of the exclusion of a variable (the five economic dichotomies are treated as a single set).

The table indicates that with one exception, nativity, each set of categories significantly contributed to the model's capacity to account for the chance a man was illiterate in Ontario in 1871 (at the 0.001 level or better). Most interesting is the relative order of the contributions. In terms of the magnitude of the differences between the test statistics (the differences in likelihood ratios: column 4 of the table), ethnicity made the greatest contribution, followed by religion. After these two, in diminishing order of importance,

TABLE 4.14

Logistic regression estimates of illiteracy, assessing the relative effects of five predictor variables for adult males in Ontario, 1871

Models	−2 log likelihood ratio model chi-square	Degrees of freedom	Difference from baseline	Probability of difference
Baseline model, all variables	619.18	24		
All variables, except ethnicity	451.54	19	167.64	<0.001
All variables, except religion	533.76	19	85.42	<0.001
All variables, except age	538.37	19	80.81	<0.001
All variables, except residence	576.65	21	42.53	<0.001
All variables, except economic	586.28	19	32.90	<0.001
All variables, except nativity	619.17	23	0.01	<0.900

NOTE: For the definition of the variables see the text.
SOURCE: See table 4.13.

are age, residence, and the five economic variables. In sum, there is persuasive evidence that the likelihood a man would be illiterate in Victorian Ontario was first conditioned by his membership in ethnic-origin and religious communities. These factors actually exceeded in importance a man's age, urban or rural residence, and economic circumstances.[63]

The results are also to some extent a matter of the specific choice of variables. Another model was examined in which the occupational classification (farmer, labourer, other) was added. In this analysis of the ranking of the variables, ethnicity was again assessed to be of greatest importance, followed by occupation, age, religion, residence, and the set of economic variables, in that order. Each had statistically significant effects, independent of the other variables. Occupation, age, and religion had very similar overall effects on the explanatory capacity of the model; ethnicity was of considerably greater importance than any of them. As we have previously seen, there was an especially close relationship between occupation and religion in the sense that, in mid-Victorian Ontario, if a man was Catholic he was much less likely to be a farmer and a good deal more likely to be a labourer than men of the other faiths. Despite this interrelationship and the significance for literacy of one's occupational position, ethnicity and religion were major, independent factors.

Our models are limited to cross-sectional data, of course, and they assess only the main effects of the variables. More complex interactions could be specified, but we did not entertain any particular notions that would lead to such specific extensions of the model. More difficult is the question of how to interpret the historical import of the results. It could be argued that despite their relatively greater effect on nineteenth-century illiteracy, the cultural communities were moulded over time by geographic and economic conditions, such as the timing and places of settlement, access to schools, and the availability of time to invest in education. But this circularity of historical effects holds for virtually all analytic separations of cultural and material conditions. Settlement patterns and occupational and educational choices were also undoubtedly influenced by cultural heritage and experiences. Only an analysis following individuals over a considerable span of time could more fully address the questions of the sequencing and interweaving of effects. At least the cross-sectional results require that in further analysis we consider the particular significance of cultural communities for education and illiteracy in nineteenth-century Ontario.

THE PROPERTY HOLDING OF ILLITERATES

We have argued that illiteracy itself had become a major social stigma in Victorian Ontario, which increasingly viewed schooling as a fundamental qualification for the attainment of property, political rights, and respectability. But in material terms, did illiteracy much matter in Ontario in 1871?

The conventional account of the rise of literacy in the west assumes that it confers direct benefits at two levels, to individuals and to nations. In an industrializing world, being lettered is often presumed to increase individual occupational mobility and economic well-being, if not enrichment. For nations, literacy is taken to contribute to national development, by enhancing the productivity of labour and, more diffusely, by contributing to enlightened citizenship. Revisionist interpretations of the history of education have examined and found wanting these progressive, liberal, and largely uncritical tenets. Harvey Graff labelled them 'The Literacy Myth.'[64]

Graff's study provides an essential point of departure for the present analysis: his trenchant critique was first formulated in the Ontario city study. The core of his argument is that literacy was not the key determinant of economic development and individual mobility as claimed by the prevailing orthodoxies of modernization theory. More recently his thesis has developed in scope to emphasize the contradictions in the historical relation between literacy, individual experience, and national development. In the early work, Graff does acknowledge that illiteracy conditioned to some degree individual economic fortunes in nineteenth-century Ontario.[65] Moreover, he suspected, but was unable to consider fully, the role of literacy in mediating the effects on economic circumstances of contextual variables like ethnicity, religion, or immigrant status. It is just this nexus of relations that we are able to examine closely for nineteenth-century Ontario as a whole.

When comparing the economic circumstances of illiterates with literates, one might wish to have a comprehensive, summary measure of individual wealth, though there is the real danger that composite measures mask as much as they reveal. In any case, as we have indicated, no such measure can be derived from census data. Our main indicators of economic circumstances, home ownership and landholding, were the most widespread and significant conditions of economic security and of social status in nineteenth-century Canada, as we noted in chapter 1.

In the multivariate analysis reported just above, we included the two measures of property holding among the independent variables predicting the chance of illiteracy. If economic disadvantage is related to illiteracy, it could well be both cause and consequence. Here we pursue the alternative implication, treating illiteracy as a possible condition of property ownership. We concentrate on measures of the *accumulation* of real property.

The basic data are given in table 4.15. For literate and illiterate men the average number of houses and average acreage owned and the proportions owning each are reported in the form of rates, *simultaneously standardized for age, nativity (native versus foreign born), and economic sector (farm–non-farm)*.

First, the comparisons show that there is a small difference in the proportion owning homes. Although about half (48 per cent) of literate men reported home ownership to the census enumerators, nearly 44 per cent of the illiterate men did also. Illiterate men apparently were *not* much constrained in their capacity to secure a home in nineteenth-century Ontario. The result, of course, corresponds to Graff's general argument that in these years of economic change and the expansion of formal schooling illiteracy was not a desperate handicap – though it seems to have mattered marginally.

Regarding landownership, the illiterate were also exactly 4 per cent less likely to be owners than literate adult men: about 35 per cent versus 39 per cent. It should be recalled that these are not the actual proportions but are already adjusted for the differences between literates and illiterates in age, nativity, and farm–non-farm composition.

TABLE 4.15

Standardized rates of home and acreage ownership, Ontario, 1871, for literate and illiterate adult men

	Average number of homes owned	Proportion owning homes
Literate	0.654	0.484
Illiterate	0.487	0.440
Ratio	1.34	1.10
	Average acreage owned	Proportion owning acreage
Literate	49.1	0.385
Illiterate	32.1	0.345
Ratio	1.53	1.12

SOURCE: See table 4.2.

Apparently the capabilities and good sense of unlettered men were sufficient to permit them to acquire family homes and farm land in proportions very close to those of literate men in mid-Victorian Ontario. But the accumulation of real wealth was another story. There are much larger gaps between lettered and unlettered men both in *numbers* of houses owned and in *average* acreage. The differences are most readily seen in terms of the *ratios* between the rates for literate and illiterate men, as given in the table. The 4 per cent absolute differences just considered translate into some 10–12 per cent greater chance that a literate man would be a land or home owner than an illiterate one (column 2 of the table: ratios of 1.10 and 1.12). In contrast, the average number of houses and the average amount of acreage owned were 34 and 53 per cent higher for literate persons (ratios of 1.34 and 1.53). The number of houses owned may at least be taken as a sensible proxy for a measure of disposable real wealth, assuming that owning more than one home was in most cases an economic investment beyond the needs of the domestic economy. Clearly, literate men had a very significant advantage in property investments in comparison with the illiterate in the last century, even though they enjoyed a much smaller edge in attaining a single residence.

The advantage of the literate over the illiterate in average landownership is clear, but it is given greater social meaning if we think of its implications for the process of property attainment. If per capita growth in landownership is set at about 1.5 per cent per year, to approximate the rate of economic growth, then we can estimate it would have taken some twenty-seven years to make up the approximately 50 per cent difference (1.53 ratio) in acreage owned between the literate and the illiterate groups. The gap represents about one full generation of individual and family property attainment – obviously no mean hurdle.

Given Graff's warning that the ideology of modernization has often substituted for analysis in assessing the implications of literacy, we reiterate the fact that illiterates fared comparatively well in terms of acquiring family homes and farm land. On the other hand, the threads of Victorian ideology that asserted that the formally lettered had a running start in the economic market rested on a basic reality: literacy conferred a significant competitive advantage in terms of accumulating propertied wealth. We can pursue the analysis further by drawing comparisons between farmers and non-farmers, natives and foreign born, as shown in table 4.16.

It is convenient to present simply the ratios between the holdings of literate and illiterates for each of the four measures of property. The higher the ratio, the greater the advantage of literate men. There are important variations in the ratios, but all are positive, reflecting the consistently unfavourable position of illiterates. Non-farming illiterates were clearly more disadvantaged than those on the land. For example, among non-farmers literate men owned 2.69 times as much land as illiterate men, though the ratio for farmers was just 1.40. This figure reflects once more the very high illiteracy rate of labouring men among non-farmers.

Table 4.16 also shows that literates had a greater advantage over illiterates for each measure of property holding among the Canadian born in comparison with the foreign born. The greatest disparities are among the Canadian-born non-farmers, the unusually disadvantaged group we have previously identified. The ratios for the four measures vary from a low of 1.91 for home ownership to a high of 6.76 for average amount of acreage owned. The first, for home ownership, reflects the fact that just 14 per cent of illiterate non-farming Canadian-born men owned homes; only 4 per cent owned any land (giving the ratio of 2.79 between literates and illiterates).

It is important to be reminded that our analysis has been intentionally focused on an inarticulate minority. Just 13 per cent of the Canadian-born non-farmers were illiterate, and this group represented only 3 per cent of the adult male population of the province in 1871. Dispersed in many communities, they might have been nearly invisible to all but those who knew them well, except for the fact that they were readily identifiable in other terms. As the preceding analysis has shown, it was not native birth that increased the chances of illiteracy, but religious and ethnic affiliation, among

TABLE 4.16
Ratios of homes and acreage between literates and illiterates for adult males in Ontario, 1871

	Average number of homes owned	Proportion owning homes	Average acreage owned	Proportion owning acreage
All	1.34	1.10	1.53	1.12
Non-farmers	1.63	1.27	2.69	1.50
Farmers	1.23	1.03	1.40	1.07
Canadian born	1.55	1.21	1.87	1.16
Non-farmers	2.84	1.91	6.76	2.79
Farmers	1.28	1.05	1.63	1.06
Foreign born	1.22	1.04	1.33	1.07
Non-farmers	1.29	1.07	1.86	1.12
Farmers	1.18	1.02	1.26	1.06

SOURCE: The film-manuscript sample of 5,386 males

which being francophone and Catholic was especially important. Ontario's Catholic francophone minority was undoubtedly marked by limited opportunities for accumulating assets in homes and land.

OVERVIEW

As elsewhere in the English-speaking world, Ontario's mid-Victorian culture of respectability made illiteracy increasingly a symbol of failure. The illiterate minority identified by the census enumeration provides a rare opportunity to consider the least articulate and, thus, often least visible of the people of old Ontario. Only about 10 per cent of adult men in Ontario were still illiterate in 1871, at least in the elementary sense that they were recorded in the census as unable to write. About 8 per cent reported they were unable to read. Ontario's rate was the lowest by half among the four provinces in Confederation. Male illiteracy in Ontario increased systematically with age; the age differences appear to reflect rather faithfully the long-run historical change in illiteracy as it decreased in the half century prior to 1871. Surprisingly, however, illiteracy was higher among the Canadian born than among the foreign born, although about the same proportions were illiterate in the farm and the non-farm labour force.

Illiteracy rates were also found to be quite variable among Ontario's religious communities. More than one in four men among Catholics were illiterate compared with a low proportion of just 7 per cent among Protestants. Among Protestant churches, the illiteracy rates were highest, about 10 per cent, for Anglicans and about half that figure among Presbyterians and Baptists. Though the differences were small, the pattern of Protestant rates broadly matches an expectation that the more individualist and pietistic denominations encouraged basic literacy.

Analysis of ethnic group (country of origin) differences underscored the most surprising results: the small French-origin group had a startling illiteracy rate of over 50 per cent, but the rate for the large Irish-origin population of the province was much lower, although it was somewhat greater than the rates of those with English and Welsh or Scottish origins. The results confirm other historical documentation of the emphasis placed on education in Scottish communities both at home and abroad.[66]

The results of multivariate analyses with a number of independent variables suggest that ethnic and religious affiliations were among the most important factors in accounting for variations in male illiteracy. Specifically, Catholic men in Ontario were at least one full generation or, perhaps, two generations behind the Protestants in the course of the rise of literacy; francophone Catholics were singularly far behind.

To what extent did illiteracy matter for economic security or for the accumulation of property? Employing measures of property ownership for Ontario, we find that illiterate men were only moderately hampered in their acquisition of homes and land in comparison with the lettered population; the literate were some 10 or 12 per cent more likely to have acquired these basic resources. On the other hand, illiterate men were more severely limited in the accumulation of property beyond a single home or farm lot. Literate men had acquired between 35 and 55 per cent more houses and acreage than the illiterate, a handicap equivalent perhaps to one generation in terms of economic growth. With respect to accumulating more than a simple competency at least, Victorian experience matched Victorian rhetoric for the illiterate.

Finally, there were quite visible differences among social and economic subgroups. Among the illiterate, one small minority in particular stood out as having especially tenuous economic circumstances – the francophone Canadians engaged in rural labouring. Ontario's francophone Catholic community, and to a lesser degree the separate Irish-Catholic community, were minorities in which large numbers remained marginal in terms of the elementary literacy so valued by that combination of Protestant Victorian morality and ethic of capitalism emerging in late nineteenth-century Ontario.

APPENDIX: CANADIAN AND U.S. CENSUS INSTRUCTIONS
REGARDING LITERACY

The Canadian instructions to the 1871 enumerators pertaining to schedule 1, column 18, entitled 'over 20 unable to read,' and column 19, entitled 'over 20 unable to write,' were simple and vague, stating only that the entries are 'sufficiently explained by their headings.'[67] The United States instructions were similarly vague, noting that 'If he or she cannot read or cannot write ..., mark (1).' There was, however, an additional paragraph: '*Education*: it will not do to assume that, because a person can read, he can, therefore, write. The inquiries contained in columns 16 and 17 must be made separately. Very many persons who will claim to be able to read, though they really do so in the most defective manner, will frankly admit that they cannot write. These inquiries will not be asked of children under ten years of age. In regard to all persons above that age, children or adults, male or female, the information will be obtained.'[68] We note in the text that the ratio of the number who could not write to the number who could not read was very similar in the two countries. It was 1.249 for males 21 and over in the United States in 1870 and 1.233 for males 20 and over in Canada in 1871.

5

Property Ownership among Emigrants, 1860 and 1870: Canadians in the United States and Americans in Ontario

INTRODUCTION

In a lecture in Liverpool in July of 1869 Ontario's special emigration commissioner to Great Britain was confronted with the following charge: 'Probably all the emigrants sent out to Canada will sooner or later find their way to the United States, and in all likelihood do much better than where they are now.' The commissioner did his best to rebut the claim by indicating that one might find a job in Toronto within hours of arrival and that there were substantial numbers of unemployed in New York and Ohio. He might well have wearied of the debate; for emigration to the United States was an issue faced time and again by Canadian politicians and administrators throughout the last century.[1]

Historians and economists have also had reason to take seriously the emigration commissioner's challenger. Despite high levels of immigration from Europe, emigration to the United States was high and exceeded immigration in every decade after mid-century. Many immigrants landing at Quebec in the early decades simply moved on to the United States. The political events from 1827 to 1837 are also thought to have promoted departures. Spelt reports that a contemporary observer in Montreal estimated 60 per cent of the immigrants arriving in the city in that period crossed the border.[2] Census data indicate that from 1861 through 1901 there were substantial net population losses, ranging from about 2 per cent to nearly 6 per cent of the total Canadian population at the start of each decade: most of the emigration was to the United States, and, interestingly, most emigrants were Canadian born.[3]

If emigration rates were high and contemporaries routinely suggested that opportunities were greater in the United States than in Canada, what in fact was the emigrant Canadians' experience? The issue of relative economic advantage is actually quite complicated, involving questions of the availability of land, differences in the demand for labour and in wage levels, as well as the question of how families and communities fostered and limited opportunities on both sides of the border. Moreover, we know little about how information on social and economic prospects was conveyed or about the differences between actual and perceived opportunities, which seem often to have inflated immigrants' hopes of material improvement. Most of these questions can be answered only in detailed studies tracing migrants and their families. A beginning has recently been made in studies such as those by Hareven, Ramirez, and La Marre and by Widdis.[4] In this chapter we pursue the question of the relative economic fortunes of Canadian migrants to the United States, because this emigration was such a common experience and, presumably, in part was a response to felt limits on opportunities in the province. The analysis is contextual, since we do not trace specific individuals from Ontario to the United States, but employ the U.S. manuscript censuses of 1860 and 1870 to identify Canadians and the value of their personal property and real estate. The census records do not allow us to distinguish emigrants from Ontario from other Canadian emigrants, but state of destination and other evidence are used to approach the question.

At the outset, consider the question of overseas immigration to Canada and the United States. Canadian immigration officials seem to have been aware of generally more inviting attitudes towards and facilities for European immigrants to the United States. A letter received by the British Colonial Office from the Immigration Board in Ontario in June 1870 indicated that public officials 'at Toronto were unanimously of the opinion that the free lands were not as a general rule adapted to the settlement of newly arrived emigrants from an old country.' The document further warned against a scheme whereby emigrants would be required to repay part of their passage and suggested that any legal measures taken in this respect would merely drive them to the United States.[5] Perhaps as important, the report also conceded that the immigration facilities in the United States were generally superior to those in Canada. For example, employers in New York came to immigration counters to meet the newly arrived, and the immigrant's luggage might be conveyed without expense to permanent addresses. In addition, telegraph and post-approved brokers were provided in New York to exchange money and prevent fraud. There was even a suspicion expressed in some of the Ontario correspondence that officials in Quebec hoped immigrants would go to the United States rather than stay in the province. At the least there was a general view that facilities for immigrants could have been much improved at Canadian points of entry.[6]

Hansen's 1940 landmark monograph provides rich documentary detail on the regional patterns of southward population movements.[7] Although we focus largely on Ontario's out-migration, the regional variations are an important context, especially in the absence of adequate statistical data on the provincial origins of the U.S.-bound migrants. We provide an appendix to this book that gives a more general analysis of the main parameters of Ontario's out-migration in the Victorian period based on the 1871 census manuscript sample.

The Atlantic provinces regularly lost sons and daughters to the northeastern states, the flow largely responsive to the wide swings in economic conditions, relative especially to New England. The first major waves of out-migration followed changes in imperial trade policy in the 1840s;[8] the second waves followed the loss of reciprocity agreements with the United States in 1866. Emigration south of the border continued throughout the following decades as a consequence, for example, of the depressed condition of the Nova Scotia fishing fleets and the New Brunswick shipbuilding industry, the loss of much of the coal trade, and the division and sale of Prince Edward Island farm land.[9]

French-Canadian emigration to the United States began early in the century but reached significant proportions only after 1840. Most Quebec outmigrants were pressed out of agriculture by the transformation of the provincial economy and by continued high levels of population growth and limited possibilities of new productive settlement within Quebec.[10] There has been a continuing, lively debate over whether there was a 'crisis' in Quebec agriculture through the first half of the century, of which increased emigration was but one consequence.[11] If there was not a virtual crisis after 1830, there was sufficient 'dislocation and impoverishment,'[12] owing to both population pressure and the incursion of capital, to make at least temporary residence in the United States increasingly inviting. It is worth noting, as McCallum reminds us, that in terms of sheer numbers Quebec emigration was modest in comparison with the westward migration from the northeastern United States for similar economic reasons. For Quebeckers, however, the emigration was a matter of deep political concern, and it took place despite the linguistic and cultural barriers faced in the United States.[13]

As for Ontario, the availability of *new* productive land generally decreased after 1854.[14] Yet the implications for the landed settlement of immigrants or for new generations of the native born have not been so obvious as they first appear, as we have argued in chapter 2. In some agricultural areas of the south after 1860 the best farm land seems to have been concentrated in fewer hands among long-term residents.[15] Our evidence and other local studies indicate, however, that farm land was still accessible to many, and no major structural change can be detected after mid-century, although changes in the processes of inheritance and acquisition were undoubtedly in train.

The question of the effects on emigration of population pressure, agricultural dislocation, and altered access to land in Quebec and Ontario are clearly far from settled. Moreover, there is little historical evidence bearing on the differences between Canada and the United States in the demand for skilled labour and in wages. It is generally thought that real wages were higher in the United States during the latter part of the nineteenth century and that the American demand for skilled labour was a primary reason for Canadian emigration. It is possible that the southward population movement was a consequence largely of these differentials, either because they were sufficient in themselves (the demand-side thesis) or because immigrants from overseas to Canada were prepared to work for lower wages and tended to 'displace' the Canadian born.[16]

One can locate contemporary comment that tends to support the view of a wage differential between Ontario and the United States, but there seem to be as many contradictory views in the local press about the demand for labour and wage levels as voices of certainty. The editor of the *Goderich Signal* lamented in May 1865 that 'Every boat for Saginaw or Chicago now bears away scores of our young, strong and vigorous to seek what Canada cannot just now give: wages for work.' Just three years later the editor frets about the local labour shortage and high wages received: 'Labour in our town is so scarce that some of our shippers haven't been able to get fourth-rate men to load a vessel. Those they got demanded $1.25–$1.50 per day. Four good men ... got instant work at first-rate wages' (7 May 1868). The *Barrie Northern Advance* in September 1869 makes a point of citing the local success of skilled British immigrants – a bakery foreman earning $9.00 per week and a jeweller back in his trade at $1.50 daily. A few months earlier, however, the editors worried that many skilled mechanics and manual labourers were without work: 'They will take anything they can get, so farmers should do well this harvest time' (24 June 1869).

Uncertainty about wages and labour demand and variations among communities may have contributed to the attractiveness of emigration to the United States. Our census sample does not permit a systematic assessment of these patterns in Ontario, but we can employ samples of the U.S. census to ask how Canadians fared in the United States.

In the absence of a comparison of Canadian emigrants to the United States with those who remained at home, we compare the wealth of Canadians in the United States to that of U.S. natives and to emigrants of European origin, specifically those of English, Scottish, and Irish origin. These unique data on the economic standing of Canadian emigrants to the United States also shed light indirectly on the question of their migration decisions.

Our data are derived from the unusual censuses of wealth of people in the United States in 1860 and 1870, just prior to and after the Civil War. In each census, individuals were required to declare the value of real estate, and personal estate. The definition of real estate included all improvements and personal estate, including stock, bonds, mortgages, notes, livestock, plate, jewels, or furniture, but excluded wearing apparel (personal estate in southern states included the value of slaves in 1860 but not in 1870; only non-slave states are included in our analysis). In 1870 only personal estate valued at more than $100 was included. The samples on which the analysis is based are drawn in a manner similar to that used for the Ontario samples. As in the Ontario case, too, the census evidence reflects the fact that normally only men were property holders. The samples were originally selected for studies of U.S. property and wealth holding, as reported by Soltow in previous work.[17] We turn them to our purposes here, with the caution that those of Canadian origin were not oversampled in the original study, and, hence, the current analysis is based on small though representative samples – 153 individuals in 1860 and 106 in 1870. They are of sufficient size to sustain basic comparisons with the U.S.-born and other immigrants to the United States, which is our main focus, but caution is required in interpretations drawn from small subsamples, as we note in the course of the analysis.

The wealth distributions are considered in terms of other socio-demographic variables: age, birthplace, and occupation. The census question concerning place of birth unfortunately does not specify province for the Canadian born, nor do we know if the foreign born had ever lived in Canada before emigrating to the United States. The wealth distributions of those from the British Isles, England, Wales, and Scotland, however, provide a particularly useful point of comparison, since the foreign born in Canada were overwhelmingly from the British Isles.

THE CANADIAN BORN IN THE UNITED STATES

The 1870 distribution of the Canadian born, by wealth class, is given in table 5.1 for men living in the northern part of the United States. The first result of note is that just less than half (0.462 in column 1) of the 106 men in the sample reported $100 or more in 1870. This is telling evidence of

TABLE 5.1

Distribution of total estate among men 20 and older born in Canada and the United Kingdom who were living in the northern part of the United States, 1870 and 1860

| Lower class limit | U.S. residence in 1870 | | | | U.S. residence in 1860 | | | |
| | Birth in Canada | | Birth in United Kingdom | | Birth in Canada | | Birth in United Kingdom | |
X	N_X	A_X	N_X	A_X	N_X	A_X	N_X	A_X
$20,000–	0.019	0.50	0.017	0.44	0.007	0.34	0.008	0.36
10,000–	0.019	0.50	0.042	0.61	0.020	0.47	0.016	0.46
5,000–	0.057	0.70	0.080	0.73	0.052	0.63	0.044	0.62
2,000–	0.104	0.79	0.183	0.90	0.124	0.81	0.113	0.81
1,000–	0.217	0.92	0.271	0.96	0.209	0.90	0.201	0.91
500–	0.350	0.98	0.350	0.99	0.320	0.97	0.302	0.96
200–	0.443	0.99	0.429	0.99	0.418	0.99	0.397	0.99
100–	0.462	0.99	0.482	0.99	0.497	0.99	0.471	0.99
1–	0.472	1.00	0.484	1.00	0.596	1.00	0.552	1.00
0–	1.000	1.00	1.000	1.00	1.000	1.00	1.000	1.00

NOTES: N_X is the proportion of men above the lower class limit; A_X is the proportion of total estate above this limit. The northern part of the United States includes those areas that did not have slavery. Values for personal estate less than $100 were generally not recorded in 1870. Summary measures of the distributions are given in tables 5.2 and 5.3.
SOURCE: A partial sample of size 5,726 from the U.S. manuscripts of the 1870 census, including sample sizes of 106 for those born in Canada and 665 for those born in the United Kingdom; a sample of size 13,696 from the U.S. manuscripts of the 1860 census, including sample sizes of 153 for Canadian born and 1,526 for those born in the United Kingdom.

the extreme inequality of wealth in the United States in the last century, as Soltow has reported in detail.[18] The second revealing statistic is the distribution of total estate (A_X, column 2). It shows the proportion of total estate above the specified limit. The proportion of aggregate wealth held by Canadian emigrants having $100–$500, for example, was just 1 per cent (0.99–0.98) and for those having $100–$1,000 it was barely more, 7 per cent (0.99–0.92). The sample suggests that propertied wealth was highly concentrated: those with estates of $1,000 or more held about 90 per cent of *all* this wealth among the Canadian born. Fully 50 per cent of all wealth of this group appears to have been held by those with estates over $20,000.

Table 5.1 also gives the distribution of real-estate wealth among the Canadian born ten years earlier (1860) for the sample of 153 men. The results are almost identical, except that 10 per cent reported estate totals between $1 and $100 in 1860 (0.596–0.497), since there was no reporting minimum in that year. We may generalize the figures by saying that about 60 per cent (0.596) of the emigrant Canadians in the United States in 1860 reported no estate at all, and that effectively 20 per cent held almost all estate wealth. A comparison of the two columns for the Canadian born in 1860 shows that the top 20 per cent held 90 per cent of all reported wealth and the top 10 per cent held about 80 per cent.

The data carry the further possible implication that the position of the Canadian born in the United States deteriorated from 1860 to 1870. This was a decade of rapid price increases; some estimates put the increase at 50 to 60 per cent.[19] But mean wealth and indeed the relative distribution of estate wealth, by deciles, remained roughly constant in money terms over the decade, as shown by the sample distributions of table 5.1. We turn to estimates of average wealth below (tables 5.2 and 5.3), but it is relevant here that mean estate wealth for the Canadian-born samples was $1,240 in 1860 and just $1,320 in 1870.

The census reports that there were twice as many Canadian-born men in the United States in 1870 as in 1860.[20] This represents a truly massive movement south of the forty-ninth parallel, amounting to an *average annual* increase in the Canadian emigrant population of 7 per cent. It is very probable that many of the Canadians emigrating after 1860 had very little propertied wealth on arrival in the United States, and, perhaps, new arrivals in the decade had less than those already settled, thus depressing the average estate wealth of the entire emigrant population. Nevertheless, taken as a whole, the Canadian born did not benefit from the southward migration so rapidly that they compared favourably with other U.S. immigrants, nor were economic gains of the earlier migrants able to compensate for the relative poverty of the new arrivals.

The data on estate wealth distributions obviously cannot address many of the questions regarding conditions and motives fostering high rates of emigration. They do indicate clearly that the move south did not immediately bequeath the pot of gold at the end of the rainbow. On the contrary, though there was a tiny Canadian-born economic elite, the majority of the aspiring migrants had attained virtually *no* estate in either 1860 or 1870, and the economic position of Canadians deteriorated in that decade. If the American Dream exerted a powerful magnetic force on Canadians, as both contemporaries and historians have thought, it is surprising that so few of the emigrants appear to have prospered. The puzzle is more curious in the light of our evidence that many immigrants to Ontario in the same period did modestly well in terms of establishing farms and in other estate holdings. We do not have sufficient comparative evidence on estate wealth and well-being among either those who stayed or those who left to do more than point to the seeming contradiction. But the evidence does open questions that have not been central to the routine historical references in Ontario history to southward migration.

IMMIGRANTS IN THE NORTHERN STATES FROM THE UNITED KINGDOM

Although we are unable to compare directly the relative position of the Canadian born in the United States with that of those in Canada, further purchase on the question of the Canadians' relative economic position may be gained by comparison with other immigrant groups, especially immigrants from the British Isles. Table 5.1 also provides the real-estate wealth distributions for the latter in 1860 and 1870.

Distributions for Canadians and U.K. immigrants seem very similar in 1860, but the proportion of the latter with estates above $1,000 in 1870 is about 27 per cent (0.271), compared with 20 per cent of the Canadian born (0.217). The proportion of U.K. immigrants with estates greater than $2,000 is 18 per cent compared with just 10 per cent for the Canadian born. We note that these subcategories of the samples are quite small. Nevertheless, depending on the exact comparison drawn, we find such differences in proportions are statistically significant at conventional, minimal levels of confidence (0.05). The summary information on average estate given in tables 5.2 and 5.3 adds evidence of the relative deterioration of the position of Canadian immigrants. Most significant, the mean wealth for British Isles' immigrants increased in the decade more than enough to match price increases, but this was *not* the case for Canadian born. Table 5.2 gives summary measures for the wealth and selected socio-demographic characteristics for 1860; table 5.3 gives them for 1870.

Considering only the mean estate wealth reported (men aged 20–99 years), we find that whereas the overseas immigrants averaged $1,140 in 1860 and $1,970 in 1870, the Canadian born averaged $1,240 in 1860 and only $1,320 a decade later, as noted above. Given that land was the major form of wealth, it might be that for lack of capital the Canadian born had greater difficulty entering farming than the European immigrants, though less likely for lack of relevant farm experience. The next section of the analysis addresses this question.

The bulk of the European immigrants were British and Irish born. The tables indicate that their numbers increased much less rapidly in the decade than did those of the Canadian-born immigrants. The latter were about

TABLE 5.2

Socio-economic characteristics of adult males born in Canada, Great Britain, and Ireland, living in the northern United States, 1860

Birth and age group	Population (proportion of number in north)	Mean age	Per cent not farmers	Per cent with $100 or more in estate	Average estate			Gini inequality ratio
					Median	Third quartile	Mean	
Canada								
20–99	0.016	35	67	50	$ 80	$ 800	$1,240	0.86
20–34	0.009	26	74	39	0	350	490	0.85
35–99	0.007	48	57	65	300	1,450	2,300	0.83
United Kingdom								
20–99	0.160	37	68	47	50	600	1,140	0.87
20–34	0.080	27	70	37	0	300	790	0.92
35–99	0.080	47	66	57	150	1,100	1,470	0.82
Great Britain								
20–99	0.046	39	56	59	250	1,200	1,550	0.82
20–34	0.021	27	56	48	50	600	1,020	0.88
35–99	0.025	48	56	68	540	1,800	1,990	0.76
Ireland								
20–99	0.114	36	73	42	25	500	970	0.89
20–34	0.059	27	76	33	0	200	715	0.93
35–99	0.055	47	71	52	100	800	1,240	0.85

NOTE: Results are tentative, since the sample sizes are 153 for Canadian born and 1,526 (including 23 above $100,000) for those born in the United Kingdom, and 1,085 (including 14 above $100,000) for Irish born.

SOURCE: A sample of size 13,696 adult males from the U.S. manuscripts of the 1860 census.

10 per cent of the population of those born in the British Isles in 1860 but 16 per cent in 1870. Again, it is clear that despite the evident decline in their economic circumstances in comparison with other immigrants in the decade, native Canadians continued to cross the border in large numbers, presumably seeking greater economic security or enrichment.

THE IRISH AND BRITISH BORN

Once again it may be revealing to distinguish the Irish born from the British born in making comparisons with Canadians in the northern United States. The summary measures for the two British Isle groups are given in table 5.2 for 1860 and in table 5.3 for 1870. Since age has been shown to be a

TABLE 5.3
Socio-economic characteristics of adult males born in Canada, Great Britain, and Ireland, living in the northern United States, 1870

Birth and age group	Population (proportion of number in north)	Mean age	Per cent not farmers	Per cent with $100 or more in estate	Average estate Median	Third quartile	Mean	Gini inequality ratio
Canada								
20–99	0.028	37	82	48	$ 0	$ 700	$1,320	0.82
20–34	0.014	26	87	31	0	260	660	0.87
35–99	0.014	47	79	61	300	1,500	1,930	0.79
United Kingdom								
20–99	0.177	38	83	48	0	1,000	1,970	0.88
20–34	0.075	27	87	31	0	200	460	0.88
35–99	0.102	47	61	61	0	2,000	3,090	0.61
Great Britain								
20–99	0.060	39	76	52	100	1,500	2,920	0.88
20–34	0.025	27	82	37	0	420	600	0.85
35–99	0.035	47	72	64	50	2,550	4,590	0.72
Ireland								
20–99	0.117	38	87	46	0	860	1,480	0.87
20–34	0.050	27	90	28	0	150	390	0.89
35–99	0.067	47	83	59	200	1,950	2,300	0.82

NOTES: Results are tentative, since the sample sizes are 106, 665, and 438, respectively, for those born in Canada, the United Kingdom, and Ireland. The Gini ratio is the Gini coefficient of estate inequality.
SOURCE: A partial sample of size 5,726 from the U.S. manuscripts of the 1870 census.

significant factor in wealth accumulation, the data are broken down by age groups, defined as those of ages 20–34 and of ages 35–99.[21] The tables also show the proportions of each group who were not farmers and provide the standard measure of inequality of wealth (Gini index) within the nativity and age groups.

The tables establish that differences in propertied wealth among the nativity groups cannot be attributed mainly to differences in age, although the Canadian born did have somewhat higher proportions under age 35 than the European immigrants (nearly 60 per cent in 1860 and 50 per cent in 1870, compared with about 50 per cent and 43 per cent for the U.K. immigrants). More surprising, the estate differences between the Canadian born and the U.K. immigrants as a whole do not appear to be attributable to the proportions who were on the land, as we had first guessed: the proportions who were not farmers was about the same for each immigrant group, about two-thirds in 1860 and over 80 per cent in 1870. Clearly, the bulk of the new arrivals in the United States, including the Canadian born, were constrained to locating non-farm, presumably urban, work, if they were not actually seeking it.

Considering Irish and British immigrants separately, however, we find some tendency in 1860 for estate wealth to be associated with larger numbers in farming: 56 per cent of those born in Britain were not farmers, while 67 and 73 per cent of the Canadian born and Irish born worked off the land. The British reported the largest estates, due mainly to the relative wealth of those under 35 years of age, among whom there was an especially large proportion of farmers. These relatively young British migrants seem to have been able to move swiftly into farm proprietorship in the United States by 1860. We expect they could do so because of modest capital accumulation from wages or land sales prior to emigration. In contrast, the relation between proportions farming and estate values does not hold among the three groups in 1870, although the British immigrants remained the most wealthy overall, now primarily owing to the estate wealth of the older group (mean estate of $4,590), again probably the effect of their early entry into farming.

Regarding the general relation of age and wealth, the tables show that mean and third-quartile estate wealth were much greater for those aged 35–99 than for those 20–34, as one would expect. The averages for the older groups were two to six times as large as those for the younger. Once again there is persuasive evidence that men were able to accumulate estates as they aged and at rather handsome annual rates of increase. There is also a hint in the data that for both the British and Irish immigrants the growth of the estates was largely a product of their experience in the United States, since the differences between older and younger immigrants grew considerably in the decade. In stark contrast, this was not the case for the Canadian born; indeed, for them, the age differential shrank alarmingly between 1860 and 1870. Although once again our relatively small samples warrant caution, the results suggest that Canadian-born migrants to the States faced unusual hardship, even among the older group who may have resided there for some years. The evidence suggests that the relatively deprived economic circumstances of the Canadians in the United States were not merely a consequence of continuing emigration of the young and poor, as we hinted above. The contrast with other immigrant groups underscores the apparent differences in experience.

Comparing the estate data for the two census years emphasizes the extent to which the position of Canadians in the United States deteriorated significantly. Between 1860 and 1870 the Canadians fell from a level midway between that of the British and Irish to about the same level as that of the Irish. Specifically, in 1860 the Canadian born had a distinct advantage over Irish immigrants with mean and third-quartile wealth some 30 to 50 per cent larger. In turn, the British born held similar real-estate wealth advantages over the Canadian born in 1860. By 1870 both the British and Irish had improved their estate holdings significantly, but the Canadian-born community had increased their mean wealth by only $100, while the third-quartile measure of the Canadians' wealth in property actually dropped by $100. In sum, by 1870 the Canadian born had become, on average, the *least* prosperous of the immigrant groups. The share of the fabled American pie that Canadian emigrants to the United States had accumulated by 1870 was little to write home about.

INEQUALITY IN ESTATE WEALTH AMONG IMMIGRANTS AND NATIVE AMERICANS

Despite the apparent deterioration of the immigrant Canadians' relative position, the Gini indices of tables 5.2 and 5.3 indicate that the inequality in estate wealth distributions was very similar among immigrant groups in both years. All the indices are high, reflecting the steep gradients of wealth within each group, although this level of inequality is familiar to students of historical wealth distributions (though in the context of the previous analysis, we should note that this is the inequality among samples of all adult males, not only farmers). It may also be noted that there is somewhat greater estate inequality among younger men; age and time modify wealth inequities, but only slightly. The extent of the inequality and the similarity among immigrant groups can be displayed more directly. Cumulating estate values from those at the top of the heap gives the following results:

Per cent of estate wealth of group held by the top group

Per cent of men, 100 N_X	Canada 1870	United Kingdom 1870	Canada 1860	United Kingdom 1860
10	78	78	77	78
20	91	92	90	91
50	100	100	99	99

The groups are virtually identical in their internal inequality: in both 1860 and 1870 the top 50 per cent of men held all estate wealth among Canadian born and the European immigrants alike, while the wealthiest 10 per cent held 77 or 78 per cent. It is interesting to note further that, despite the decline in their position relative to others, *among* Canadian immigrants the inequality in propertied wealth remained the *same* in 1860 and 1870. The point is further made by the data of tables 5.2 and 5.3 that report the proportions with estate values of $100 or more. The proportion of Canadians in this minimal propertied category was 50 per cent in 1860 and again 48 per cent in 1870.

Although we have noted the relative stability of the average estate wealth of the Canadian immigrants in the northern states and the steep gradient of inequality for all adult men, a substantial proportion still held minimal estates, especially those above the median age. As reported for the residents of Ontario, a deep structure of inequality with respect to all propertied wealth rests on a relatively broad base of smallholding. The tables report the proportions with an estate of $100 or more. Those born in Great Britain led the way throughout the decade, 59 and 52 per cent holding petty property; the proportions rose to 68 and 64 per cent for those over 35 years of age. The Canadian born were also well represented. Half of all male immigrants in each year and almost two of every three of those over age 35 were smallholders. Although it is reasonable to refer to these holdings as petty estates, in fact a $100 estate in 1870 was worth about $1,000 in 1980 prices and would buy eighty acres at $1.25 per acre in the last century.

We turn next to the question of the differences between immigrants and native-born Americans and to the question of the differences between those from Quebec and those from Ontario. It would surely be most surprising if the economic fate of immigrants in the northern states was indistinguishable from that of the native born. The Ontario-Quebec distinction bears on the question of the sources of the Canadian immigrants' relative economic position.

Consider the shares of total estate wealth held by *all* men living in the northern part of the United States:

Per cent of men	Per cent of wealth of all men	
	1870	*1860*
10	68	67
20	84	84
50	99	99

These figures indicate that inequality among immigrants was more sharply defined than it was in the male population as a whole. The most prosperous 10 per cent of the entire population held rather less of total estate wealth than did the top 10 per cent of the British, or even Canadian, immigrants among their respective groups (67 or 68 per cent compared with about 78 per cent). The differences are not dramatic and probably were not sufficient to be recognized beyond the bounds of specific communities. In any case, most of this wealth was owned by the top fourth or fifth of men, irrespective of nativity. At the same time, it might have been more obvious to those struggling simply to secure a foothold on the land that there was a larger proportion of men with little or no estate wealth among the immigrant groups. The proportion of men with less than $100 was 40 per cent among all men in the north in both 1860 and 1870, but, as reported above, the figure was closer to 50 per cent among emigrants from Canada and Britain.

There is some reason to think that the overall deterioration in the economic position of the Canadian born might be accounted for by reference to increasing numbers of migrants originating in Quebec as opposed to Ontario. Language barriers, less initial capital, and less familiarity with economic institutions or sheer discrimination might have conspired to reduce the prospects of economic gains for the Quebec born. As we have commented, however, the census fails to identify the Canadian born by province of origin. Unfortunately, too, our samples of migrants are not sufficiently large to sustain an analysis of the differences between those living in the northwest states and those living in the northeast, which might serve as a rough proxy for the Ontario-Quebec distinction. When we attempt to make such a distinction with the small samples, the mean and third-quartile wealth values in both 1860 and 1870 hint that those migrating to the northwest enjoyed a slight advantage relative to those in the northeast.

In the absence of other evidence, some inferences may be drawn from other quite indirect, but intriguing, data. We can begin with the evidence reported in this study and elsewhere that literacy and wealth *accumulation* are directly related.[22] Rhode Island was one of the major destinations of Quebec migrants, and, as it happens, there are data on illiteracy for Rhode Island giving the proportion of persons 15 and older unable to read or write in any language classified by birthplace of parents.[23] With obvious caveats, we present them as a possible surrogate measure of relative wealth and well-being. The illiteracy rates are: French Canadian, 37 per cent; British American, 4 per cent; American, 2 per cent. Clearly, any presumption of even a moderate positive correlation between literacy and wealth accumulation would place those of French-Canadian origin well behind the other groups with respect to total estate. We might argue further that if the Ontario born were comparable in literacy to the British born living in Rhode Island in 1870, the gap in literacy and average wealth between Quebec and Ontario migrants could have been quite substantial. The evidence, of course, is circumstantial.

A more direct comparison of the estate wealth distributions of the Canadian born and other nationalities is available for one other state, Wisconsin. The data are taken from previous work by Soltow and refer only to 40-year-olds in the state in 1860. Table 5.4 provides the distributions of total estate for five national-origin groups. The comparisons are restricted to those age 40 in order to control for age effects on accumulation.

Given the general migration patterns of the last century, we assume that the great majority of the Canadian born in Wisconsin would have been from Ontario. In this case, however, the data do not conform to a simple assumption, employed just above, that the Ontario born match the English or Scottish born. Conforming to our earlier analysis, the average estate wealth of the Canadian born is closer to that of the Irish born than to the English and Scottish born or to the Welsh born, for that matter. The *median* wealth of the Canadian born, only $350, was the lowest of all groups. It is interesting, too, that the mean estate wealth of the Canadian born in Wisconsin was virtually the same as the mean for the group in the entire northern United States, reported in table 5.2 ($1,240), but inequality was substantially less in this more recently settled region. In Wisconsin, nearly 70 per cent (0.69) of the Canadian born held $100 or more in estate wealth compared with about 50 per cent in the northern States as a whole (table 5.1). Nevertheless, this was the lowest proportion among the five immigrant groups reported for the state, and inequality among the Canadian born was the greatest of any group (Gini ratio of 0.76).

If the evidence we marshal here regarding the relative positions of the Ontario and Quebec born in the United States is limited and ambiguous, the Wisconsin data add support to the view that the Ontario born did not fare as well as many European immigrants and were most like the relatively poor Irish. This fact is striking, since the state was an agricultural frontier not far removed in geographic or cultural conditions from Ontario. As an extension of these questions, we next attempt to compare the fortunes of men residing in Ontario with those of men in the northern states. This comparison may help to address the larger question of the relative economic conditions faced by families in the two countries in 1870.

TABLE 5.4
Distribution of total estate of males 40 and over living in Wisconsin in 1860 who were
born in Canada, Ireland, Scotland, England, or Wales

	Wisconsin residence in 1860				
Lower class limit	Birth in Canada	Birth in Ireland	Birth in Scotland	Birth in England	Birth in Wales
	Proportion of men above the lower class limit				
$20,000–	0.01		0.02	0.01	
10,000–	0.01	0.01	0.02	0.03	0.02
5,000–	0.05	0.02	0.08	0.07	0.07
2,000–	0.11	0.04	0.30	0.26	0.30
1,000–	0.24	0.32	0.51	0.46	0.51
500–	0.46	0.52	0.67	0.57	0.63
200–	0.62	0.67	0.77	0.74	0.70
100–	0.69	0.73	0.79	0.80	0.76
1–	0.75	0.80	0.81	0.84	0.81
0–	1.00	1.00	1.00	1.00	1.00
Mean	$1,202	1,009	2,154	2,112	1,685
Median	$ 350	500	1,000	700	1,050
Gini ratio	0.76	0.66	0.67	0.73	0.62

NOTE: Sample sizes for the countries of birth were 93, 894, 92, 322, and 84, respectively,
for Canada, Ireland, Scotland, England, and Wales.
SOURCE: Lee Soltow, *Patterns of Wealthholding in Wisconsin Since 1850*, (Madison: University of Wisconsin Press 1971) 102, 103.

LAND AND HOME OWNERSHIP IN CANADA AND THE UNITED
STATES

The ownership of land and homes can be directly compared for Ontario
and the northern states using the Ontario census sample for 1871 and a
similar random sample of men collected by Soltow for earlier studies of
wealth inequality in the United States.[24] The samples are of males 20 years
of age and over and are of size 5,386 for Ontario in 1871 and 6,558 for
the northern states in 1870.

The proportion of adult male farmers owning land was 0.626 in Ontario,
as reported in chapter 2. The proportion was 0.607 in the northern states
and 0.599 in the states west of Pennsylvania. We find it remarkable that
the rates of ownership were *virtually the same* in Ontario and in the northern
United States in 1871 and 1870. The Ontario rate is based on acres owned;
rates for the United States are based on real estate of $100 or more. The
U.S. proportions, in fact, would have been slightly greater and, hence, even

more similar to the Ontario rate if the limit of reported estate had been less than $100. Thus, the institutions and processes of property acquisition appear to have been duplicated on each side of the border, despite important differences in geographic conditions, settlement histories, political forms, and the timing of commercial and industrial development.

Landowner proportions are given for various age groups in Ontario and the United States in table 5.5. This evidence further underscores the close match in the figures for the two areas. The institutions governing land acquisition surely must have operated – or yielded to demand – in almost exactly the same fashion in each country in generating such age-specific profiles. The geographic mobility between the regions would have been one factor contributing to the equalization of ownership rates. But the web of political, social, and economic institutions that affected land acquisition was complex, including the land market and credit facilities, the size of farm families, the market for farm products, and tenancy and inheritance practices. Hence we may speculate that it was the common aspirations for family farms and a landed family patrimony that generated enough demand simply to override these institutional differences between the two countries. Although those who crossed the border would have noted cultural, political, and economic differences, clearly they would also have experienced fundamental similarities in agrarian ways of life between the two regions.

We can also consider home ownership in both countries. Again we find striking parallels. The proportion of farmers owning homes was 0.633 in Ontario and 0.607 in the northern United States; the proportion for non-farmers was 0.303 in Ontario and 0.307 in the United States. The rates for specific age groups are given in table 5.6. As in the case of landownership estimates for the United States, the proportions would have been even closer if real estate values of less than $100 had been tabulated as estate by the U.S. census. We indicated in chapter 3 that the demand for homes might have been nearly constant throughout the last century, given their value as sites for the pooling of family income and sources of security and status in times of hardship, illness, and old age. The almost identical rates of ownership in Ontario and the northern states suggest that the supply too was substantially free of institutional idiosyncrasies – like the ownership of land, home ownership appears to have been more in the hands of those who were intent on it, rather than in the grip of national or local market factors. This view corresponds with Richard Harris's documentation of the widespread tendency for non-farm families to build their own homes in the nineteenth century and up to the First World War, especially among the working class.[25]

TABLE 5.5
Proportion of adult male farmers owning land in Ontario, 1871, and
in the northern United States, 1870

| | | United States | |
Age	Ontario	North	Northwest
20–29	0.249	0.269	0.255
30–39	0.670	0.650	0.672
40–49	0.851	0.762	0.786
50–59	0.838	0.833	0.828
60–69	0.882	0.807	0.806
70–99	0.773	0.741	0.706
All	0.626	0.607	0.599

NOTES: The Ontario figures are obtained from declarations of
acreage owned. The United States figures are obtained from dollar
declarations of the value of real estate owned. Those having $100 or
more in value are considered as landowners for purposes of this
table. The north includes states that had not had slavery. The northwest includes those northern states west of Pennsylvania.
SOURCE: The Ontario spin sample of size 5,386 drawn from the
Ontario census of 1871 and the random sample drawn from United
States manuscripts of size 9,823 of which 6,558 are from the north
and 3,190 are from the northwest.

A GLANCE FORWARD: CANADIAN AND FRENCH-CANADIAN
ILLITERACY RATES AND HOME OWNERSHIP IN 1900

Earlier we attempted to bring some circumstantial evidence to bear on the
question of the difference in economic circumstances between French-Canadian and other Canadian immigrants to the United States. As it happens,
the United States census of 1900 does distinguish the two groups and provides evidence regarding both illiteracy and home-ownership, though not
regarding other measures of estate. The relevant data are arrayed by age and
sex categories and for males 35 and older by farm and non-farm occupation.
The two Canadian-born groups can be compared with the U.S. born and
with those born elsewhere.

These are comparisons for groups a full generation after the mid-Victorian
period on which we have concentrated. They reveal that there was a considerable and apparently persisting gap in attainment of literacy and in home
ownership between the French-Canadian immigrants and each of the other
groups. The Quebec-born immigrants' illiteracy rate for those over age 35
is particularly relevant, since these were people whose average age was 48

TABLE 5.6
Home ownership among adult males in Ontario, 1871, and real estate ownership in the northern United States, 1870

| | Proportion of men owning homes or having real estate value | | | | | |
| | All Men | | Farmers | | Non-farmers | |
Age	Ontario	U.S. North	Ontario	U.S. North	Ontario	U.S. North
20–29	0.160	0.171	0.241	0.269	0.090	0.112
30–39	0.507	0.446	0.686	0.650	0.333	0.328
40–49	0.683	0.563	0.854	0.762	0.479	0.433
50–59	0.714	0.655	0.843	0.833	0.504	0.492
60–69	0.776	0.675	0.914	0.807	0.577	0.516
70–99	0.594	0.621	0.807	0.741	0.374	0.485
All	0.473	0.428	0.633	0.607	0.303	0.307

NOTE: In the case of U.S. data, an individual was considered an owner if he had real estate of $100.00 or more.
SOURCE: See table 5.5.

in 1900 and whose average year of entry to the United States was 1873.[26] The first panel of the table indicates that among the older male, Quebec-born immigrants, 36 or 37 per cent were still unable to write in 1900. This rate is markedly higher than the rates reported for the other native or foreign-born males, including non-francophone immigrants from Canada. In fact, the latter were recorded as having an admirably low rate of illiteracy (0.047 overall, and 0.052 among older men). The rates for each age group among non-francophone Canadian immigrants were lower than those for the U.S. native born or immigrants from elsewhere. Canadian women emigrating from places other than Quebec had especially low illiteracy rates.

It is more difficult to generalize regarding home ownership patterns in 1900. Still, the census sample indicates that the French Canadians tended to have the lowest rates of all groups. Non-French-Canadian immigrants over age 35 had achieved a quite respectable level of home ownership – about 50 per cent for both men and women. The rates for men nearly matched those of the native born in the United States and were well above rates of the other foreign born, although non-French-Canadian-born women lagged behind other female foreign born.

The rates of both illiteracy and home ownership are shown to vary by farm and non-farm sector in relatively predictable ways. Proportionately there were more French-Canadians and other foreign born who were farmers. Among the non-farmers, where the samples are large enough to make

TABLE 5.7

Illiteracy and home ownership among those enumerated in the United States census of 1900: adults 20 and older born in Canada, French Canada, the United States, or other foreign countries (C, FC, US, OF), by sex and age

Age	Proportion unable to write				Proportion owning homes				Number in sample			
	C	FC	US	OF	C	FC	US	OF	C	FC	US	OF
Males												
20–34	0.038	0.156	0.083	0.133	0.265	0.141	0.360	0.206	185	64	10,577	2,152
35–99	0.052	0.365	0.123	0.110	0.502	0.325	0.509	0.449	309	126	11,043	4,021
All	0.047	0.294	0.103	0.118	0.413	0.263	0.436	0.365	494	190	21,620	6,173
Females												
20–34	0.000	0.174	0.085	0.129	0.289	0.222	0.407	0.307	201	63	10,627	1,782
35–99	0.038	0.339	0.161	0.177	0.488	0.322	0.553	0.510	287	121	10,439	3,249
All	0.023	0.283	0.123	0.160	0.406	0.388	0.479	0.438	488	184	21,066	5,037
Males 35 and older												
Farm	0.044	0.429	0.164	0.098	0.838	0.786	0.703	0.806	68	14	4,509	876
Non-farm	0.054	0.357	0.095	0.113	0.407	0.268	0.375	0.350	241	112	6,534	3,145

SOURCE: *United States Census Data, 1900: Public Use Sample*, Center for Studies in Demography and Ecology, University of Washington, Inter-university Consortium for Political and Social Research, ICPSR 7825.

comparisons, the francophone immigrants greatly exceeded all others in illiteracy rates and substantially lower proportions owned homes.[27]

MEN OF U.S. BIRTH LIVING IN CANADA

We have found that the average estate of the Canadian born in the northern states did not compare favourably with that of the native-born Americans and, indeed, was less than that of other immigrant groups. There were many fewer migrants who moved north of the forty-ninth parallel, but there were always some with reasons to enter Ontario – reasons ranging from 'ske-daddling' to avoid military service in the Civil War to the simple seizing of commercial opportunity.[28]

In 1871 in Ontario only four of every 100 men were U.S. born. Their record of economic accumulation matched or may have been slightly above average for all Ontario residents. About 63 per cent owned land, exactly the provincial average (table 5.5), but the number who owned homes was greater. Among farmers, some 69 per cent were home-owners, compared with the provincial average of 63 per cent; among non-farmers the rates were nearly identical, 33 per cent were owners compared with 30 per cent for the province (table 5.6).

Table 5.8 makes a further comparison of interest, between the American born in Ontario and those born in the province and still residing in Ontario. In this case, the comparisons are less favourable for the Ontario born than for Ontario residents as a whole. The table gives both proportions and averages for land and home ownership by farmers and non-farmers and by younger and older groups (20–39 years and 40–99 years). Just over half (0.52) of Ontario-born farmers, for example, owned land, whereas over 60 per cent (0.63) of the U.S.-born farmers did, a statistically significant difference (at 0.05). The average acreage owned also significantly favoured the American emigrants (eighty-four versus sixty-three acres). The patterns vary little by age and economic sector, but there was a clear general tendency for the younger Ontario born *not* to have accumulated small property as readily as their American counterparts, while the older Ontario born tended to exceed the American migrants in holdings. Since there were larger proportions of younger Ontario-born males, on average, the Americans were the larger estate owners. Of course, we should be reminded again that these *average* estates were petty property – in this case considerably less than 100 acres per farmer and less than one home owned per person. Differences in home ownership reveal similar, statistically significant advantages for the U.S. born.

In marked contrast to the experience of the Canadian born in the United States, American emigrants to Ontario seem to have acquired homes and land rather more readily than the Ontario-born residents of the province in 1871.[29] Specifically, for men living in the northern part of the United States in 1870, the proportion owning $100 or more of total estate was 0.46 for the Canadian born and 0.65 for the U.S. born. Average total estate for these men was about $1,320 for the Canadian born and $3,500 for the United States born. The comparison needs to be qualified by the fact that the Canadian born in the United States were much more likely to be non-farmers and probably were living in urban areas with more restricted estate accumulating opportunities. Among non-farming men of U.S. birth residing in the United States in 1870, however, 55 per cent owned $100 or more of estate wealth and they had an average wealth of $3,250, still exceeding the Canadian emigrants. Even for non-farmers in the northwest (Ohio and westward), the comparison does not favour the Canadian born; the proportion owning $100 or more was 0.62 and their average estate was $2,500.

TABLE 5.8
Land and home ownership among adult males in Ontario, 1871, by Ontario birth and U.S. birth

Occupation and age	Ontario residence in 1871			
	Ontario born	U.S. born	Ontario born	U.S. born
	Proportion owning land		*Average acreage owned*	
Farmers				
20–39	0.40	0.50	43	38
40–99	0.84	0.71	117	112
20–99	0.52	0.63	63	84
	Proportion owning homes		*Average number of homes owned*	
All men				
20–39	0.29	0.30	0.35	0.32
40–99	0.72	0.62	1.11	1.08
20–99	0.40	0.47	0.53	0.72
Farmers				
20–39	0.40	0.47	0.46	0.50
40–99	0.85	0.83	1.25	1.40
20–99	0.52	0.69	0.67	1.06
Non-farmers				
20–39	0.16	0.22	0.21	0.24
40–99	0.49	0.45	0.84	0.81
20–99	0.22	0.33	0.33	0.50

SOURCE: The spin sample of 5,386 men drawn from the census manuscripts of 1871. The sample size was 2,371 for Ontario born and 218 for U.S. born.

OVERVIEW

A comparison of estate values and rates of ownership of land and homes in the northern (non-slave) states and in Ontario indicates that conditions were surprisingly similar on both sides of the border about 1870. The majority of owners were petty proprietors. It seems that the continued drive for small property and the institutions that facilitated its transfer, purchase, and accumulation were nearly identical in their consequences for ownership, if not in their operation. The dollar value of wealth, however, appears to have been higher in the United States than in Ontario.

A systematic comparison of estate values for the Canadian born and other immigrant groups in the northern states revealed that the former had average estate wealth that was significantly less than the wealth of immigrants from Great Britain in 1870 and very similar to that of the Irish immigrants.

Moreover, the evidence for 1860 and 1870 indicates that the position of the Canadian immigrant population in the States actually deteriorated in this decade. This was a decade of especially heavy emigration from Canada to the United States. Perhaps the relative youth and poverty of the emigrants significantly depressed the estate wealth average, but some evidence for older emigrants suggests otherwise. Indirect evidence bearing on the relative wealth in property of those from Quebec and Ontario was too limited to draw firm conclusions, but it also hinted that the deterioration cannot be attributed primarily to the influx of the Quebec born, although the 1900 U.S. sample indicates that the Quebec born in the United States were persistently more illiterate and less able to acquire homes than other migrants from Canada.

If Canadians contemplating migration to the northern states in 1870 recognized that their prospects for U.S. land and home acquisition were limited, they might still have been motivated to move by the markedly greater relative wealth of the U.S. born. The census record in the United States in 1870 indicates that the average estate wealth of Canadians was about $1,300, while that for the U.S. born was two and one-half times as large. The fewer American born who ventured north also did comparatively well by Ontario standards. On average, their ability to acquire homes and land matched or exceeded all Ontario residents and clearly exceeded that of the Ontario born.

Perhaps these palpable material differences were reason enough for Canadian emigrants to stretch the ties that bound them to families and communities in order to try their luck south of the border. More likely, the southward migration was risked less for the sake of the potential prosperity of the immigrants themselves than in the hope they could enhance the prospects of their children. Commenting on the French-Canadian community in New England, Hansen caught the nub of the matter some years ago: 'Children were the roots that struck deep into the social and economic soil of the American community and planted the transient worker as a permanent immigrant.'[30] Recent research strengthens his point.[31] For Ontario, Quebec, and Maritimes migrants alike, initial relative material deprivation in the United States was probably recognized and tolerated as a stage in the longer-term family strategies of trying to ensure the future security of their children.

6

Estimating the Distribution of Propertied Wealth in Victorian Ontario: Provincial Patterns and Comparisons

ESTIMATES OF THE DISTRIBUTION OF REAL ESTATE WEALTH IN ONTARIO IN 1871

In this chapter we undertake a series of estimates of the overall pattern of Ontario's wealth inequality in property in 1871. The estimates are based on our knowledge of the patterns of ownership of land, homes, and other forms of property. Of course, this tally excludes non-propertied wealth, but as we have explained previously, property constituted the most widespread form and the greatest proportion of wealth in the last century in Ontario.

Only occasionally in the foregoing have we been able to assess patterns of inequality in dollar terms.[1] In the absence of common, dollar assessments of the census tabulations of property, we here employ subdistrict tax assessment data to make several different estimates.

First estimates, regional inequality

A direct approach to an overall measure of propertied wealth inequality for the province might employ the nominal assessment rolls of real and personal estate. The analysis would require collating properties owned by individuals both within subdistricts of residence and across subdistricts for properties owned elsewhere. Of course, it also requires tracing members of the Ontario sample to the nominal records of the rolls. Although large numbers of these manuscript records are available, many on microfilm, all are not in one place, and the task of tracing and collating properties for the full sample is daunting.[2] Our alternative is to resort to a published detailed table of the summation of dollar values for each subdistrict in 1870. The table allows us to attach average dollar values to the distributions of acres and homes owned as given for our 1871 sample of adult males. Thus, we have both subdistrict distributions and an imprecise estimate of the dollar values of the wealth of individuals. The estimates provide rough, but useful, portrayals of the magnitude of overall inequality. We are also able to derive several related estimates that permit some tentative international and historical comparisons. We argue that the measurement error introduced by the method does not preclude reasonable assessment of the relative level of structured inequality of real estate wealth in nineteenth-century Ontario.

The aggregates for the number of acres, taxpayers, real estate, and personal estate (which we label NAC, NTP, RE, PE) were reported for districts and most subdistricts in 1870. These totals allow an assignment of an average value per acre (RE_NAC) or, alternatively, per taxpayer (RE_NTP) to each of the subdistricts in our sample for 1871. In about 4 per cent of the cases it was necessary to assign district rather than subdistrict averages to the assets of sample individuals.[3]

First, consider the overall aggregates for 1870 as they were published for rural and urban areas coupled with their population counts in 1871, as best as they could be determined.[4] They are given in table 6.1. Given the relatively widespread ownership of rural land and homes, we find it surprising that per capita real estate wealth was larger in cities than in rural areas; in fact, it appears to be as almost twice as great, some $1,150 versus $630, as shown in row 5. Moreover, this rural-urban differential contrasts sharply with that of the northern United States in the same period, as we shall note later. The contrast is qualified, first, by the fact that there were a relatively small number of major Ontario cities and towns considered in these data in which wealth may have been especially concentrated. Second, and more important, settlement in Ontario spread largely from south to north, with the latter offering much more marginal land. Acreage was generally less productive and valuable in the mid-north than in the south. In contrast, the United States was settled from east to west, with the most productive land (from the standpoint of potential for cultivation and the proportion of acres ploughed) located in Illinois and Iowa. The relative wealth of these lands tended to balance that of the eastern urban areas, in contrast to the Ontario north-south pattern.

The real estate values per acre, given in row 8, also reflect a number of problems with the data. First, the low average of $11.25 per acre for rural areas most likely underestimates actual market values, given the vague relation of assessments to the market, and also probably reflects the relatively low value of the mid-northern farms. Despite this distortion, the variation among subdistricts will still provide an indication of *regional* inequality of

TABLE 6.1

Population and aggregate assessment values of real and personal estate, Ontario, 1870, by counties and cities

	Thirty-six counties	Twelve cities and towns	Total
1. RE, Aggregate real estate, 1870	$220,960,601	47,175,058	268,135,659
2. PE, Aggregate personal estate, 1870	23,298,970	10,326,210	33,825,180
3. TE, Aggregate total estate, 1870	244,459,571	57,501,268	301,960,268
4. Number of males 20 and older in 1871	351,000	41,000	391,493
5. RE per adult male = (1) / (4)	630	1,150	715
6. NTP, Number of taxpayers assessed in 1871	276,901	42,880	319,781
7. NAC, Number of acres assessed in 1871	19,637,630	21,245	19,658,875
8. RE_NAC, = (1) / (7)	11.25	2,220.53	13.64

SOURCES: *Sessional Papers of Canada, No. 1*, First Session of the Second Parliament, Session 1873, *Miscellaneous Statistics of Canada for the Year 1870*, Part II, Municipal Returns, Ontario (Ottawa 1873) 2–18. *Census of Canada, 1871*, vol. V, table F-I, 36–9.

real estate wealth. Second, the extraordinary per-acre value of real estate in the selected urban areas actually reflects large variations among the twelve cities and towns and hence much measurement error, since some urban areas listed very little or no acreage in their assessment reports.

A further curious aspect of the data is the large number of taxpayers reported, with a particular discrepancy for the urban areas. In the latter case there were more taxpayers reported than adult males given in the 1871 census (lines 6 and 4). The discrepancy may reflect non-resident urban owners and taxpayers, but there is no way we can be sure. It proved impossible to develop a fully consistent combined list from the 1870 tax assessment and 1871 census providing the aggregate real estate and population counts of either adult males or of property owners. We resort, therefore, to a less precise measure of real estate per tax payer, RE_NTP (rows 1 and 6) in our estimates.

To employ the sample data, we need separate estimates of land and of house values. Again, the data permit only very indirect estimates. We infer both from the aggregate data, where real estate values per acre for subdistricts are the closest approximation to land values and real estate values per tax payer are taken as an estimate of the values of homes.[5] Obviously the two estimates are not independent and, if summed, attribute too much total value to each individual. To adjust the total value, weighting factors were applied within rural and urban areas, so that overall averages matched the values of total real estate per adult male (row 5, above).

If we bear in mind these limitations, a number of interesting and not unreasonable patterns emerge from an examination of the data. One can first ask what was the inequality among subdistricts in the province in 1871, if there was no difference among taxpayers within a given subdistrict? Assigning the aggregate real estate per taxpayer, RE_NTP, for the subdistricts to each of the 5,386 men in the sample in those areas yields the following distribution and corresponding Gini index of inequality.

RE_NTP	*Number of males*
$1,000 and up	1,629
500–999	2,461
200–499	1,176
500–199	120
	5,386
Mean	$800.00
Inequality, G	0.257

A level of inequality at least of this magnitude might well be expected in a region with wide geographic differences in land productivity and value.

The Gini coefficient, G, introduced in chapter 2, summarizes the distribution of these total dollar values. The coefficient of 0.257 can be assessed only against some ideal or actual standard. Though the value is far from the complete and impossible limit of inequality, where $G = 1.0$, which implies that only one person owns all wealth, it is actually quite large relative to that in the United States derived from comparable data and the same procedures. Employing assessed values by county, weighted by population size, for the northern states of the United States in 1870 yields an inequality coefficient 0.19. Further, the coefficient for the eighty-nine counties in Ohio, which was a comparable agricultural region in the northern states, gives evidence of even less subregional inequality ($G = 0.13$).[6] Thus, interregional inequality in Ontario in 1871 appears to have been quite significant, and comparisons with the U.S. data indicate that it represented a relatively unequal distribution of dollar values of real estate.

A further sense of the geographic distribution of real estate wealth is obtained from an equation in which real estate per tax payer is regressed on the latitude and longitude of subdistricts and on the rural-urban distinction:

$$RE\_NTP = 12,994 - 216\text{latitude} - 34.6\text{longitude} + 140\text{urban},$$
$$(1.0) \qquad (\ 0.3) \qquad\qquad (\ 12.0)$$
$$N = 5,386, R^2 = 0.19,$$

where the latitude varies between 42.2N, and 47.0N, the longitude varies between 84.0W and 74.6W, and *urban* is a dichotomous variable (urban or rural subdistrict). The latitude and longitude were assigned on the basis of the ninety districts in Ontario as portrayed on the map of the census report, shown in chapter 1.[7] A literal interpretation of the equation would be that average real estate wealth declined $216.00 per degree, or about $1,000 overall, on the *south to north* axis and declined $34.60 per degree, or about $300, in moving from *east to west*. The average real estate holding per tax payer was $799.00. The results of the linear equation imply smooth, incremental geographic differences, when no doubt they were quite uneven from subdistrict to subdistrict. Still, the very considerable inequality on the north-south axis confirms our earlier speculation regarding this source of the general urban-rural differences.

Proportions owning property (POP)

The gross pattern of inequality among counties and cities is of some interest, but since some individuals were not property owners, clearly we can derive a more refined assessment by assigning the values of our subdistrict measure, RE_NTP, solely to persons who reported acreage owned or a home owned. The estimates again are based on the aggregate values assigned to the sample data. Just less than half of all adult men, 49 per cent, reported real estate holdings overall. The Gini coefficient derived from distributions taking account of propertylessness rises very considerably from the previous estimate to 0.64. The relevant distributions are given in table 6.2.

We note, first, that urban propertied wealth, which was greater than rural wealth, was accompanied by greater urban inequality: the respective Gini indices are 0.753 and 0.641. Yet, given that the proportion of urban property owners (POP) was dramatically smaller, about 21 per cent in comparison with over 53 per cent in rural areas, the difference in overall inequality seems moderate. In this context, it is relevant to reiterate our earlier findings that the proportions of adult men in Ontario in 1871 owning land and homes were little short of spectacular by the international standards of the last century. For comparison, the estimates for adult males owning real estate in the United States in 1789 and 1870 are as follows:[8]

	All	*Rural*	*Urban*
POP, U.S., 1789	0.494	0.507	0.359
POP, U.S., 1870	0.39	0.50	0.29

TABLE 6.2
Estimated real estate distributions, Ontario, 1870, by rural and urban subdistricts

RE_NTP	Number of men		
	All	Rural	Urban
$1,000 and up	690	569	121
500–999	1,226	1,077	149
200–499	633	589	47
50–99	84	84	0
0	2,753	2,094	715
	5,386	4,357	1,029
Mean	$ 372	396	271
Inequality (G)	0.642	0.614	0.753
Proportion owning property (POP)	0.489	0.532	0.205

SOURCE: See table 6.1.

Whereas almost half of adult men were owners in Ontario in 1871, this condition was approximated in the United States about six decades, or over two generations, earlier. Though we know that large numbers of men migrated across the border from Ontario, the relatively greater opportunity to own small property in the province must surely have tempered the temptation of many others to leave. Perhaps this historically exceptional access to petty property was also a reason that many in Ontario did not envisage a union with the northern states as a plausible political alternative.

Though the comparisons with the United States are based on equivalent data, the estimates of inequality refer only to persons owning homes or land. What is the effect on inequality if one includes those who reported some asset other than land owned or homes owned, as we did in chapter 3? The extreme case may be estimated by including all persons who were not literally propertyless, that is, who reported any asset to the census, and assigning to each the average portion of aggregate real estate, RE_NTP. Estimates of the maximum proportions with property of any kind and, hence, of minimum inequality are as follows:

Ontario in 1871	All	Rural	Urban
Maximum POP	0.61	0.66	0.40
Minimum inequality (G)	0.55	0.52	0.68

These estimates are extreme in not distinguishing ownership from land in use, that is, treating tenants and renters of land as equivalent to owners. In any case, the result is a substantial reduction of overall inequality from a Gini index of 0.64, reported in table 6.2 to the index of 0.55, based on all those reporting use or ownership of property. An interesting feature of the comparison is that the maximum proportion reporting use or ownership of property in urban areas (0.40) is twice the proportion of owners (0.21), whereas in rural areas the difference is between two-thirds of men (0.66) who have access to property and just over half (0.53) who are owners.

Distribution of wealth in real estate (W_{RE})

We can further incorporate into this analysis a knowledge of the acreage owned (AC) and the number of homes owned (HO), which have been examined in detail in previous chapters. To this point, our computations do not take account of variations *within* districts in acreage owned or in numbers of homes owned. Some proxy for these variations in wealth among owners needs to be attempted to approximate levels of inequality among individuals and families. We combine our sample information on home and land accumulation for individual men with the aggregate assessment roll counts. The procedures, though somewhat tenuous, are still informative.

For the rural sector, considering home and land owners only, wealth in real estate will be measured for the male sample from the equation W_{RE} = RE_NAC × AC + RE_NTP × HO. The relation means, for example, that a person living in a fertile, rural subdistrict might have real estate wealth, W_{RE} = \$16.50 × 100 + \$700 × 2 = \$17,900, representing relatively secure holdings of 100 acres and two houses. Alternatively, we might have W_{RE} = \$1 × 200 + \$300 × 1 = \$500 for a still relatively well-off person in a more marginal subdistrict and so on.

In the case of urban dwellers, we face a more difficult assignment of values as a result of the clear underreporting of acreage in the urban sector in some subdistricts.[9] After some exploration of the data, our more-or-less arbitrary solution was to consider thirty acres of land as equivalent to a single home.

Taking account in this way of both subdistrict variation in aggregate values and the estimated within-area inequality in ownership actually yields quite intriguing results, as shown in table 6.3. The overall level of inequality is given as about 0.80 by the Gini coefficient of relative inequality. This is a level much closer to the known inequality levels for the United States. Thus, once we take into account the unevenness of home and land accumulation,

TABLE 6.3
Rough estimate of the distribution of wealth in real estate among adult males in Ontario, 1871, and in the United States, 1870

N_{RE}, the top proportion of men in the wealth category	ARE, the proportion of total wealth of the N_{RE} group					
	Ontario, 1871			United States, 1870		
	All	Rural	Urban	All	Farmers	Non-farmers
0.01 (richest 1 per cent)	0.24	0.14	0.39	0.25	0.16	0.36
0.02	0.31	0.21	0.50	0.36	0.25	0.49
0.05	0.45	0.35	0.66	0.55	0.43	0.69
0.10	0.60	0.51	0.79	0.73	0.62	0.84
0.20	0.78	0.71	0.93	0.91	0.83	0.97
0.50	1.00	0.99	1.00	1.00	1.00	1.00
No. in sample	5,386	4,357	1,029	9,824	4,736	5,088
Mean	$ 729	630	1,150	2,399	2,494	2,311
Inequality, G	0.777	0.719	0.890	0.83	0.77	0.89
Proportion with wealth, POP	0.49	0.53	0.31	0.39	0.50	0.29

NOTES: Average wealth in the rural and urban sectors has been adjusted to the measured real estate per adult male 20 and older. U.S. distributions are determined from the data described in Soltow, *Men and Wealth*, 108, as applied to real estate.
SOURCE: The sample of 5,386 males 20 and older drawn from the census of Ontario in 1871 coupled RE_NAC and RE_NTP averages for subdistricts in 1870 as stated in *Sessional Papers of Canada, No. 1*, First Session of the Second Parliament, Session 1873, *Miscellaneous Statistics of Canada for the Year 1870–71*, Part I, Municipal Returns, Ontario (Ottawa 1872) 3–21 and *Miscellaneous Statistics of Canada for the Year 1870*, Part II, Municipal Returns, Ontario (Ottawa 1873)

the diversity in asset values within the province approximates that existing within the much wider expanse of the United States in the last century.

Classifications for the rural and urban sectors of Ontario are not strictly comparable with those of farmer (including farm labourer) and non-farmer for the United States. Yet, when the comparisons are drawn, the similarities of shares, inequality coefficients, and proportions of wealthholding, are quite remarkable, as shown in the table. The only notable deviation is among the richest 10 to 20 per cent of rural males. The most wealthy 20 per cent of Ontario men owned, by these estimates, about 80 per cent (0.78) of all real estate wealth. In the United States as a whole in 1870 the top 20 per cent owned over 90 per cent of all assets. Still, we might attribute the difference largely to measurement error arising from our indirect computations.[10] If anything, the method probably underestimates the concentration of Ontario landed wealth. Given the expansion of individual holdings and general improvement of land over several generations in some cases, the average value of *an acre* of land owned by a wealthy family might often have been higher than that of a family of moderate or limited holdings, even within the same subdistrict. Only further studies of holdings within specific tax districts would, of course, reveal these intricacies.

In any case, the wealth averages are best interpreted with respect to their implications within each country. For example, we note that the average estate wealth in urban areas in Ontario was nearly twice the rural average ($1,150 versus $630). On the other hand, the extent of inequality in urban areas was considerably greater ($G = 0.890$) than in the countryside ($G = 0.719$), reflecting the fact that smaller proportions of the population owned wealth in real estate in towns and cities.

Acreage and value

The earlier analysis of the proportions of the Ontario male population owning and occupying land strongly suggested that there was considerable access to farm land in Ontario in 1871 (chapter 2). Moreover, the structure of inequality in total acreage possessed among owners and occupiers also appeared relatively modest by international standards. How, then, can these findings be squared with the foregoing comparison showing only slightly less relative inequality of *dollar* wealth in real estate than existed in the United States at about the same time?

The answer must lie in the distribution of the *values* of the land, acre against acre. Most obvious is the fact that in Ontario an acre in the south was worth much more than one further north, as we have repeatedly remarked. The disparities in terrain and in land fertility along a broad north-south axis may have been less visible and well known in the late nineteenth century than they are today, but they were far from hidden. The editor of the *St Thomas Dispatch* put it bluntly in 1868, averring that 'They must be poor, miserable creatures who would go and bury themselves in the woods for many years of their lives, to cultivate poor lands under an inhospitable climate, when one year's wages, two at the most, would enable an industrious man in the settled parts of Canada to buy 100 acres and settle himself somewhere within reach of civilization and beyond the reach of starvation.'[11]

The Lorenz curves of figure 6.1 illustrate the wide geographic discrepancy. The distribution of acreage owned shows an inequality level about 70 per cent of the (estimated) *value* for the 1,963 owners in the rural sector of our sample (0.380 versus 0.551). The results are similar for land occupied

FIGURE 6.1 Lorenz curves of the acreage and estimated value of land occupied and owned by occupiers and owners in rural Ontario, 1871

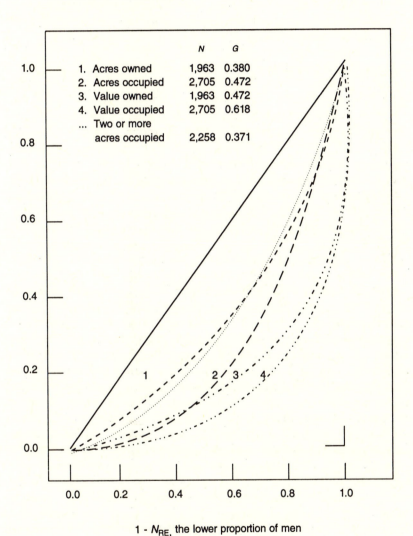

1 - A_{RE}, the proportion of real estate of the 1 - N_{RE} group

		N	G
1.	Acres owned	1,963	0.380
2.	Acres occupied	2,705	0.472
3.	Value owned	1,963	0.472
4.	Value occupied	2,705	0.618
...	Two or more acres occupied	2,258	0.371

1 - N_{RE}, the lower proportion of men

among the 2,705 occupiers in the rural sector. The level of inequality is least for the 2,258 men occupying two or more acres (the curve plotted as dots in figure 6.1), with a Gini coefficient of only 0.371. Although it is not reported, the coefficient for the dollar value of this distribution is again significantly larger than that for acreage. In sum, in late nineteenth-century Ontario there were still comparatively wide opportunities to gain land occupancy or ownership, although the assessed values and, presumably, market values of the land were much more steeply distributed than was the initial opportunity to acquire a family plot.

Comparisons with the British Isles

We have frequently drawn comparisons between Ontario's nineteenth-century pattern of property inequality and that of the northern United States, since there is directly comparable evidence. Another relevant comparison is with the European countries of origin of so many of the province's residents in the last century. We have pointedly argued that despite a fairly steep gradient of inequality, the property ownership rates of the province were high, and a person could obtain a workable plot of land with rare ease. Perhaps the massive migration to the province in the era is evidence enough of this openness relative to Europe, but a more systematic comparison is possible.[12]

There is little difficulty understanding why many British men and women, if they were able, sought opportunities in Ontario. From the early sixteenth to the middle of the nineteenth century the English proletariat grew enormously. David Levine provides rough estimates indicating that in the former century, perhaps a quarter of the adult male population was propertyless. By the mid-nineteenth century, fully four of five members of the labour force were 'employees' or domestic servants.[13] More directly relevant to nineteenth-century Ontario are the distributions among the rural population. The censuses of 1841–71 in England and Wales, Scotland, and Ireland convey the strong impression that the number of farm labourers surpassed, and perhaps exceeded very greatly, the number of farm operators, tenants, and owners. Moreover, the number of farm operators was far larger than the number of farm owners.

In order to draw relevant comparisons to the census data of the nineteenth-century British Isles, we need to recategorize the Ontario data. The strong British image of the 'independent yeoman' informs the British census categories distinguishing landed proprietors, farmers, and farm labourers and servants. The Ontario census data allow for three more or less comparable categories – landowners, farmers, and labourers. The comparability is seriously compromised, however, by the fact that the Ontario owner and farmer categories overlap (they are drawn from different manuscript schedules).

It is possible to make the Ontario census data more or less match the categories of the British census. First, we want to identify landowners. Second, there are tenant farmers – occupiers but not owners.[14] Third, there is farm labour. There is also a fourth group, the poor and truly destitute, that should be considered, though their numbers are nearly impossible to estimate, since this population was not explicitly enumerated by census officials. If enumerated at all, the poor were most likely caught in the farm labourer category, but for the sake of our estimates we also include the 'other occupations' category in the following tabulations.

Unfortunately no direct reclassification of the previously presented occupational and ownership groups will serve for the comparisons with the British classification. Of those classified, for example, as landowners in Ontario obviously all need not be owner occupiers: some, possibly quite a few, may have been retired or have had non-farm occupations, such as blacksmiths or rural doctors. Individuals not owning land could also be tenants, of course, reporting acreage occupied but simply classified as farmers by occupation. Moreover, a number of individuals reported more than one occupation, such as 'blacksmith and farmer.' In this analysis only the first occupation was considered.

There were 4,357 men in rural areas in the Ontario sample. Among them 3,251 were in the 'agricultural sector' in the sense that they were classified by occupation as either farmers or farm labourers. From another census schedule, we find 1,963 of the 4,357 reporting acreage owned and 2,245 reporting acreage occupied. Casting the classifications in a form closest to the British categories leads to the complex array of table 6.4.

There are three groups of interest in the rural agricultural sector. First, the sample shows 1,760 owners of land, most (1,719), but not all, of whom were owners and occupiers. A very small number (forty-one) owned, but did not occupy their land. The second group consists of 1,019 farmers who were tenants or others, such as farmer's sons, classified as farmers but who did not own land. Finally we have 499 farm labourers, a few of whom reported they owned some land (twenty-seven). The data for the three groups can be compared with those for England and Wales and for Scotland.

The British evidence for earlier decades is obviously more directly relevant to the experience of those who migrated from Europe to Ontario before 1871. As it happens, the data for England and Wales and for Scotland do not differ appreciably in relative terms over these years. We choose to

TABLE 6.4

Distribution of acreage owned and occupied, Ontario, 1871, by ownership and occupational categories approximating British census classifications

	Number of cases	Number reporting		Number reporting	
		Acreage owned	No acreage owned	Acreage occupied	No acreage occupied
Rural agriculture	3,251				
Owners		1,760		1,719	41
Farmers	2,752	1,733	1,019	2,014	738
Owners		1,733		1,697	36
Non-owners			1,019	317	702
Farm labourers	499	27	472	173	326
Owners		27		22	5
Non-owners			472	151	321
Rural non-agriculture	1,106				
Other occupations	1,106	203	903	518	588
Owners		203		179	24
Non-owners			903	339	564

SOURCE: The film-manuscript sample of size 5,386.

report the 1851 census figures. Fortuitously for our comparisons, these counts are available for males 20 and older in the agricultural sector; they are given below.[15]

	England and Wales 1851	Scotland 1851	Ontario 1871
Landed proprietors	16,934	1,964	(1,760) (owners)
Farmers	223,318	47,957	2,752 (farmers)
Farm labourers	724,839	107,734	499 (labourers)
	965,091	157,655	3,251

Simply inspecting the relative magnitudes for each area reveals, once again, that in this historical context the relative proportion owning some plot of land in rural areas of Ontario was remarkable. There were qualifications and limits to this landownership, of course, in terms of the land's capacity to support a family, the potential for marketable surpluses, and the troublesome prospects of division or incumbrance upon inheritance. Nevertheless, the British-Ontario contrast is stark.

A sizeable minority of persons in rural Ontario were not specifically in the agricultural sector at all but were engaged in a multitude of related occupations: blacksmiths, coopers, shoemakers, professionals, and merchants. One census classification of occupations in Ontario placed only about five or six in every eight persons in the agricultural portion of the rural sector.[16] As the table shows, in our Ontario sample 3,251, or about three-quarters of rural men, were in agriculture of whom 499, or 12 per cent, were farm labourers.

For the sake of the European comparisons, we could consider 2,752, or 85 per cent of the 3,251 men in agriculture to be 'farmers' – owners and tenants – in the English tradition and the other 499, or 15 per cent, to be farm labourers. To approximate the distinction between landed proprietors and others, we can consider only the 1,760 men in the overlapping category of owners in Ontario (indicated by parentheses in the table).

What are the main features of the comparisons? Given the previous note taken of the relative size of the Ontario population of owners, the comparisons underscore its historical importance. The great majority of those called farmers in Great Britain were, of course, tenants. They apparently had shared broadly in the concentration of landholding and of rising landed income over several centuries.[17] Some of them would have employed significant farm labour. Undoubtedly, some also owned farm land. Including the more substantial tenants might magnify quite considerably the numbers considered as landed proprietors in the British census tabulations. There is clearer evidence for Scotland in this regard. The Scottish data suggest there were as many as 6,000 to 8,000 owners of land in the agricultural sector, rather than the 1,964 reported in the census. It is unlikely there were more; one report gives the number in 1854 as 7,273, which would be only 4–5 per cent of adult males in the agricultural sector. Moreover, there is no good reason to think that the owner proportion could be inflated any more than this in the case of England and Wales.[18] Whatever a definitive determination might be, the comparisons give us a strong sense of what it means to say that the opportunity to own land in Ontario was much greater than in England, Wales, and Scotland in this era of the great migration. Based on census occupational counts, the same may be said in the case of Ireland.[19]

The still more striking feature of the British rural class structure, and more accurately estimated, was the literally huge numbers of farm labourers relative to farmers at mid-century. The ratio for England and Wales was three to one and that for Scotland over two to one. About two of every three adult males working in the rural sector were labourers in Britain, in contrast to Ontario, where they were but one in six. Given these bare data it is no feat of historical imagination to recognize the attraction of westward migration. Unlike the British experience, a large number of immigrant families must have felt some sense that the proverbial independence and competency of the yeoman ideal had been grasped in Ontario.

The contrast between Ontario and Scotland can be refined somewhat by estimating the inequality of holdings among those with property in the old country. From the data of table 6.3 we calculate inequality coefficients for Ontario residents with wealth in property. The Gini coefficient is 0.61, tallying both rural and urban wealthholders, and 0.56 if only rural residents are assessed. In contrast, another recent study gives an equivalently computed Gini coefficient of 0.80 for landholders in Scotland in 1854. A heritage of wealth transmission, heavily influenced by a tradition of large entailed estates, had deeply concentrated landholding wealth in Scotland by the middle of the century.[20]

It is difficult to recover the ways in which images of opportunity and equality in the late nineteenth century were fashioned and were spread internationally.[21] We can be sure, at least, that the links formed by chain migration and by letter writing among relatives and friends transmitted some mixture of fact and fiction across the Atlantic, simultaneously celebrating and rationalizing the migrant's wrenching decision. The vast differences between Ontario and Europe that we have documented in the concentration of landed wealth and in the prospects of family smallholding must have been conspicuous in these images. By European standards, mid-Victorian Ontario would still have appeared, as it had earlier, as a land of nearly unmatched opportunity.[22]

APPENDIX: A MULTIVARIATE REGRESSION ANALYSIS OF
PROPERTIED WEALTHHOLDING IN ONTARIO, 1871

Throughout the study we have attempted to assess the relative effects on property ownership of cultural factors, as well as of social and economic variables. Although we recognize a high level of measurement error associated with our estimate of wealth derived from the subdistrict assessment data, following previous analysis, the results of one multivariate model are given. The specification of the model follows those presented earlier. The results allow interpretation of the relative effects of the main variables, although some of the features make the interpretations very tentative. The basic equation is as follows:

Wealth in real estate = $-267 + 421$age30–39 + 1,026age4049
                                          (118) (133)
    $+ 1,513$age5059 + 1,160age6069 + 876age7099 – 86Catholic
       (153) (250) (228) (159)
    $+ 148$Baptist + 130Methodist + 355Presbyterian + 228Otherreligion
       (224) (130) (156) (186)
    $+ 124$Village + 539Town + 991City + 425Englishori
       (237) (159) (159) (262)
    $+ 163$Scottishori + 319Irishori + 383Germanori – 89Frenchori
       (281) (265) (287) (489)
    $- 299$Foreignborn,
       (144)
$N = 5,386, R^2 = 0.036.$

The first difficulty is that the model has a very low coefficient of determination. The overall variance explained in real estate wealth by the combined set of variables is just 3.6 per cent. No doubt, the fact that the wealth attributed to the sample individuals is derived from the averages of their subdistricts accounts for the low explanatory capacity of the model. We pursue an interpretation on the grounds that the individual coefficients may still provide a first indication of relative effects.

A number of the coefficients of the dummy variables in the equation are statistically significant, as indicated by their computed standard errors (in parentheses). Specifically, each of the coefficients of the selected age categories is substantively and statistically significant, as are the positive coefficients distinguishing town and city from rural residence (though the effect of village residence on propertied wealth is not different from rural residence). The negative coefficient for the foreign born is statistically significant. None of the differences in ethnic and religious affiliations appears to affect estimated overall assessed real-estate wealth, although we found such effects for *specific* forms of property ownership in previous chapters.

For the sample of 5,386 men in Ontario, whose average real-estate wealth is estimated to be $729.00 (table 6.1), we find that wealth rises systematically with age to a peak at about age 60, then tends to decline. The greatest gain appears to be between ages 35 and 45. The wealth in property represented by the coefficient of $1,513.00 at age 50–59 is the largest coefficient in the equation and indicates that this group had about a $1,500.00 advantage in real-estate wealth over those aged 20–29, taking account of the effects of all the other factors represented in the model. The result, of course, underscores the huge significance of life cycle for nineteenth-century wealth and property accumulation in every analysis previously presented.

The coefficients also suggest that propertied wealth in rural areas (and villages) was significantly lower than that in towns and cities and that the city residents of Ontario in 1871 expected a quite substantial advantage of $991.00 over the rural residents. The coefficient, of course, represents the average, not the distribution, of urban property assets, which, as we have seen, was a good deal more steeply inclined than it was among rural residents of the province (table 6.1). The towns and cities were islands of wealth accumulation and inequality in a wider sea of relative rural equality. Other factors considered, the equation also indicates that immigrants had some $299.00 less, on average, than the native-born Canadians of the province.

7

Property, Families, and Class in Victorian Ontario: Some Conclusions

In a reassessment of the economic and social history of Victorian English Canada, only a few years ago, David Gagan could bluntly say, 'In any event, we know virtually nothing about the nature of wealth and the process of acquiring it and keeping it and, hence, about the nature and extent of social mobility in nineteenth-century Canada.'[1] In beginning to fill the void, this study has examined the patterns of property holding and inequality in Ontario in the mid-Victorian period. It is based mainly on a large sample of census manuscript records. These are unusually rich historical sources, as others have acknowledged and demonstrated, despite the limitations of census underenumeration and of the particular biases of the state-sponsored data collection. Most important in this context, they provide a unique opportunity to examine the extent and patterns of property holding in an era still dominated by the ethos and the reality of landed small property.

Although the sample data are cross-sectional, they yield information both on the patterns of property ownership and on the processes of property attainment, accumulation, and exclusion. The historical processes largely must be inferred from age patterns, but these are often so clear, we believe, that considerable confidence can be placed in the inferences drawn from them. The processes are also considered in the context of broad trends indicated by aggregate data over time.

The study examines inequality in three main ways: in terms of the process of acquiring farm land and the inequality in farm acreage owned; in terms of the ownership of homes; and in an analysis of a composite assessment of property holding, adding to land and home acquisition the ownership of shops, warehouses, barns, boats, carriages, and the like, as declared on the manuscript census. In each case, when age patterns were considered, the structures of real-estate wealth inequality appear to have considerable historical stability. At the same time, there is strong evidence that this structural stability did not preclude quite widespread access to ownership of family homes and of modest tracts of farm land. As a consequence, at least to the early 1870s, Ontario would have been recognized as a land in which ordinary men and women could still secure an 'independent' living, mostly on the land, and fulfil their hope of providing minimally secure beginnings for their children. Moreover, we argued that the persistent structural divide and comparative ease of property attainment were integrally linked, aspects of the same historical and demographic processes. Socially reproduced structures of inequality and processes of property acquisition are two sides of the same social coin.

Access to land, above all, held the key to the independence and security promised in the very widely held images of an Ontario society of 'free yeomen.' The ownership of homes was a less often noted, but none the less widely coveted, piece of the foundation of the relative independence and security of the nineteenth-century household economy. Gagan's survey of literary reflections on individual experience and social structure in the last half of the century documents the pervasiveness of the image of Ontario as a society of opportunity and 'altered circumstances.' It was apparently widely believed by articulate observers that 'material success waited every immigrant to Ontario in contradistinction to a life of servitude, or at least the absence of opportunities for individual advancement in the old world.' Despite some commentators' predilection for the dramatic, and the 'egalitarian poses' of others,[2] our systematic analyses demonstrate that their impressions were well founded.

Over 60 per cent of Ontario's farming men owned land in 1871 and about half of all adult males owned some land. These figures also mean, of course, that over a third of farmers, including their adult sons at home, were landless at the time of the census. Over 45 per cent of all men over 20 years of age owned less than one acre of land. Estimated tenancy rates were quite low, involving, perhaps, 10 or 11 per cent of adult men. In these respects, the structural divide between landed and landless in the province was distinct and deep. Further, our estimates from age patterns and aggregate data over time indicate that this structure of landowning was very nearly constant over several decades. It was argued, however, that the impression of a relatively abrupt division must be tempered by recognizing the suspended landed status of many sons of farmers living at home.

Looking beyond the cross-sectional pattern of inequality to the process of land acquisition required a further modification of our understanding of structured inequality in nineteenth-century Ontario. The essential evidence was that landownership rose dramatically with age, especially in the early adult years. At age 50, over 85 per cent of farm men were owners of their own land; a model constructed from these data suggests that about 3 per cent of the landless in *any year* would have become landowners. Young native-born men and immigrants would surely not have failed to notice the age pattern of ownership nor the process of rapid land acquisition among those only a few years their senior.

An examination of the acreage of farms suggested, too, that the size inequality in acreage had been more or less constant over several decades before 1871. A trend towards the local concentration of land, such as that reported by Gagan for Peel county, is not incompatible with the provincial pattern. The age patterns of size of farms indicated that young men entering farming had every reason to be optimistic about the prospects of modest, but steady, expansion of their holdings over the life cycle. Here again the ideology of a leavened and open society had at least some clear foundation in the observations and experience of ordinary men and women in nineteenth-century Ontario.

With respect to home ownership, the structural divide between owners and non-owners appears to be strongly mediated by the life-cycle pattern of home acquisition: over half of all adult males did not own their homes in 1871, but over 85 per cent of farmers were owners at age 50, as were over 50 per cent of the non-farmers.

A further analysis combining land and home ownership with other census indicators of property attempted to distinguish those who held sufficient property to ensure their family's security from those who were marginal owners, just maintaining a single home or small farm, and from the literally propertyless. Just less than a third of all Ontario's men owned several forms of property that might have conferred some minimal prospect of economic security for their families and further accumulation. More important, over 40 per cent of the male heads of households were in this category, although adult men who still lived at home were virtually excluded from the status.

One should not minimize the risks of the nineteenth-century economy, where modest 'family fortunes' might be lost or fragmented by any number of chance events – a loss of health, crops, or credit rating. Still, in sum, these data reveal that in 1871, although 40 per cent of *all* adult men were propertyless and another 30 per cent were truly petty owners, among male heads of households just 14 per cent were without some form of property of their own. Age and family formation strongly conditioned the probability of attaining at least a foothold into the world of the small owner in mid-Victorian Ontario.

Despite initial appearances, it is no contradiction that nineteenth-century Ontario was characterized by both a quite steep structure of inequality in ownership and property accumulation and, in historical perspective, by a marked degree of opportunity for small-property acquisition. In terms of social process, the divide reflected a very orderly pattern of life-cycle acquisition. In terms of the cross-sectional structure of propertied wealth, a broad base of small owners narrowed quite rapidly with the magnitude of ownership. The institutions of the market and of inheritance that fostered modest acquisition of petty property for many also sustained the sharply sloping pattern of inequalities. Systematic comparisons of the Ontario pattern of wealth inequality with the United States and Great Britain suggest that Ontario was rather similar to the northern states and dramatically less divided than were England and Wales, Scotland, or Ireland.

The relation between economic structures and individual and family experiences is at the core of the larger questions of class formation and social mobility.[3] Conventionally the question of mobility is treated as one of occupational change. The more relevant processes for nineteenth-century Ontario residents were those of land and home acquisition and the accumulation of real property. In the travel and immigration tracts of this society, land-ownership was portrayed as the principal symbol of independence; moreover, the amount of land owned was, apparently, taken to be synonymous with the degree of independence.[4] In this respect our evidence strongly suggests there was a palpable, if qualified, reality to the concept of Victorian Ontario as an open, competitive society of independent family economies. It was a society in which many still could avoid the spectre of sole dependence on wage labouring by recourse to family farming and modest landed inheritance.

It merits note in this context that the findings raise a question about the connection between the continuing drive and opportunities for attaining a measure of security and independence through family farming and the urban forms of accommodation and resistance to an emerging order of industrial capitalism, which have been documented in the new working-class history of the province in the same period.[5] They were surely not separate spheres, as they have generally been treated, either in terms of individual life-cycle experiences or with respect to family strategies of pooling sources of income and sustenance. Minimally, the expectation and reality of relatively widespread landed small property as late as 1871 would have helped to maintain what Kealey and Palmer argue was the relatively high cost of urban labour.[6] We expect that men and women often opted to stay on the land or to try to acquire it rather than deal with the work-discipline and uncertainty of relying entirely on wages for a living. At the same time, this continued landed alternative would probably have attenuated a sense of common class experience in these years of nascent industrial development, though this connection remains to be examined.

If the relative access to family farming and home ownership made Ontario one of the most open societies of the last century in comparative international terms, it was still a far from egalitarian environment. Only a very few men accumulated much land or other real estate, and even fewer women owned property of any description. In terms of the estimates of property holding, the richest 1 per cent of men owned about a quarter of all real-estate wealth and the richest 10 per cent owned about 60 per cent. Moreover, our estimates indicate that women made up less than 8 per cent of all household heads, and among this group, a third owned land. It is likely that just 5 per cent of Ontario's adult women owned property in their own right in 1871. Further, by 1871 farms had to be increasingly sought on the much less valuable land of the northern districts, and a gap between rural and urban areas in the likelihood of being propertyless had begun to widen: whereas half of rural and village men owned at least their own home, only one-third of those in towns and one-fifth of the men in Ontario's five major cities were home owners in 1871.

We also pursued a detailed analysis of the illiterate in Victorian Ontario, in the expectation that their circumstances would shed further light on the nature and implications of inequality. They made up a relatively small minority of about 11 per cent of all adult men (defined as unable to write on the census). Women heads of households were slightly more likely to be illiterate than male heads, about 15 per cent compared with 12 per cent.

Among the minority of men who were illiterate we found surprisingly large numbers of native-born Canadians. To a large extent this nativity pattern resulted from differences in illiteracy rates among Ontario's religious communities, especially between Protestants and Catholics. Only about 7 per cent of Protestant men were illiterate, but a quarter of all Catholics were. Anglicans were the most illiterate among Protestants; Presbyterians and Baptists were the least illiterate. A multivariate analysis revealed that the chances of a man's being illiterate were deeply affected by ethnicity, as well as by religion and age. Scottish immigrants were the least illiterate, followed by the English and Welsh. In contrast, there was a striking absence of elementary literacy within Victorian Ontario's dual francophone- and Irish-Catholic minority. Catholic men in general were one or two generations behind Protestants in literacy acquisition, and Canadian-born, French-origin Catholics were singularly marked by their illiteracy. Over 50 per cent of Ontario's French-origin population were still illiterate in 1871. In this sense, at least, they represented a resistant counterpoint to the ascendancy of Protestant Victorianism in nineteenth-century Ontario.

With regard to property, we found that illiterate men were little hampered in their acquisition of homes or smallholdings in comparison with the literate, but a significant difference emerged in terms of the likelihood of accumulating propertied wealth, where the opportunities for literate men considerably exceeded those for the illiterate.

The questions of property attainment and structured inequality in old Ontario led us to consider the economic circumstances of the large numbers of Canadian migrants to the United States through the decades after mid-century. Although we cannot establish the conditions prompting the migration, an examination of the estates of Canadians in the United States (as recorded in the U.S. censuses of 1860 and 1870) revealed a surprising lack of wealth in comparison with other immigrant groups and with the U.S. native born. A tiny Canadian-born minority had prospered, but less than half of all the Canadian born reported estates of even $100 in the northern states in 1870. Despite the small size of the samples, there was still intriguing evidence that the Canadian migrants' circumstances deteriorated between 1860 and 1870, although those of immigrants from the United Kingdom did not. Indeed, the Canadian born appear to have become the least prosperous immigrants, falling behind the Irish born in the northern states by 1870. Even older Canadian immigrants seem to have prospered little. The indirect evidence of illiteracy rates in Rhode Island suggested that French-Canadians in the United States were distinctly deprived, but Wisconsin evidence hinted that English-Canadians also had only quite modest property accumulation. The census of 1900, which gives both illiteracy and home ownership rates, does show, however, that there was a deep and persisting gap between the attainments of French-Canadians and others in the United States.

The marked similarity in property acquisition in Ontario and the northern states suggests further that the demand for farm and home ownership simply overrode institutional differences between the two regions. In contrast to the Canadian experience in the United States, the small numbers of the U.S. born in Ontario significantly exceeded the property accumulation of native-born Ontario residents.

The predominance of a landed smallholding way of life was beginning to be challenged by the emergence of the early form of the now familiar institutional order of the wage labour market and industrial factory production. These changes were accompanied by the rapid growth of the state and the spread of public institutions – schools, hospitals, gaols, and asylums.[7] The emergent economic and political formation rested on a foundation of capital and property accumulation both by those few who amassed substantial wealth in the Victorian era and, more significantly, by the many household economies which simultaneously underwrote family livelihoods and the expansion of the home market.

The founding of Ontario in 1867 as a province within the uncertain federation that was to be the Canadian nation and the development of a coherent regional society have still most frequently been stories told in terms of political and intellectual history, largely leaving aside their social and economic dimensions.[8] In the last two decades, these narratives have been enriched by diverse forms of social history, recovering aspects of the lives of ordinary men and women in the last century at work, at school, in their communities and local politics, and increasingly even in the intimacy of their families and households. For the most part, however, the latter have been local studies of specific cities, townships, towns, and counties.

This study has sought to contribute to the understanding of the formative mid-Victorian years in Ontario by presenting a systematic study of nominal historical sources that reveals the basic structures and patterns of access to property holding and accumulation for the region as a whole. This society was characterized by a combination of clearly etched and only slowly shifting structures of inequality in property and wealthholding, and in historical context, unusual openness to the acquisition of small property. Fluid processes of life-cycle property acquisition reproduced stable structures of inequality. Moreover, if an emerging industrial order represented the face of the future, the actions of a great many mid-Victorians in Ontario indicate that ownership of small acreages and homes was still the reward for hard labour that they believed would best secure their own futures and that of their children. These are legacies that the Victorian era in Ontario bequeathed to the twentieth century.

Appendix: Demographic and Social Patterns among Adult Males and Female Heads of Households, Ontario 1871: A Census Re-analysis

INTRODUCTION

'Human numbers, the Procrustean bed of social history, are rarely dramatic but often determinative.'[1] So writes Donald Akenson in an impressive local history of a nineteenth-century rural Ontario community. Despite a number of recent, valuable studies, however, the historical demography of Ontario remains in its infancy. In this appendix we employ the census manuscript sample to set out the socio-demographic substructure of mid-Victorian Ontario. Although designed for the specific purposes of the study, the film-manuscript sample affords a unique opportunity to undertake detailed analyses of the 1871 census based on individual returns for adult males and for female heads of households. This appendix first provides a general context for the foregoing analyses. In the absence of more general-purpose samples of provincial nominal returns, we hope it will also serve others in pursuing the social and economic history of Ontario.

Those who lived in Ontario from 1840 to 1870 experienced a transformation from a relatively thinly settled, wheat-exporting, agrarian society to one in which there were distinctly urban, commercial, and industrial features on the social landscape.

We begin with an age-specific analysis of Ontario's adult male population in 1871. The characteristics of this population in part reflect the social changes that occurred in the half-century preceding 1871. Those who were ages 50–59 in 1871 had a decade more of adult experience than those 40–49 and a generation more than those 20–29.

Specifically, we set out six related patterns: the age profile of the Ontario adult male population; age-specific native- and foreign-born distributions; age-specific occupational patterns; the ethnic and religious composition of the nativity groups and of farmers and non-farmers and trends in out-migration from Ontario to the United States. The latter provides specific background for the analysis of the economic circumstances of the Canadian born in the United States presented in chapter 5. Finally, a socio-demographic profile of the women in the sample is presented, comparing them with male household heads.

POPULATION GROWTH AND AGE COMPOSITION

The 1871 census gave Ontario's population as 1,620,851.[2] In that year the province represented just less than half, or 46.5 per cent, of the population of the four provinces of Canada at Confederation (Ontario, Quebec, Nova Scotia, and New Brunswick). The province's non-aboriginal population had grown from, perhaps, 20,000 loyalists in the late eighteenth century to still fewer than 100,000 before the end of the Napoleonic wars. Natural increase was very high, though declining. Total population grew rapidly in the post-war period, especially from 1820 to 1835, to over 370,000 and grew quickly again during the period after Great Britain established free trade in grains in 1846. Although the first waves of European immigrants were largely attracted by the economic prospects of British North America, many of those who migrated in the 1846–55 period were likely fleeing economic troubles as much as seeking their fortunes.[3]

Consider the population-age profile of Ontario's adult males 1871 (defined as those age 20 and over). The manuscript-sample data are plotted by five-year age groups as a series of *points* in the two top panels of figure A.1. The other data plotted there are discussed below.

The number of persons in different age groups reflects, in part, past population growth. The plots show that there is a methodical and relatively rapid decrease of the population with age. For the sake of context, table A.1 compares the age distribution reported in the census for all adult men with equivalent distributions for England and Wales, Scotland, and Ireland.

There were few men over age 60 in Ontario in 1871, about 11.5 per cent, compared with some 14 per cent in England and Wales and in Scotland. Nearly half of all adult men in Ontario, 48 per cent, were under 34 years, compared with 43, 44, and 40 per cent for England and Wales, Scotland, and Ireland. Clearly, Ontario had a quite youthful population by historical standards. The mean age of the men over 20 in Ontario was 38.9 years.[4]

Employing the population-by-age profiles, we give some rough calculations illustrating population growth before 1870 in table A.2. These figures are inexact because of the seriously confounding influence of emigration.

FIGURE A.1 Distributions of adult males in Ontario, 1871, by age, native and foreign born (NB, FB), and farmers and non-farmers (*A, nA*).

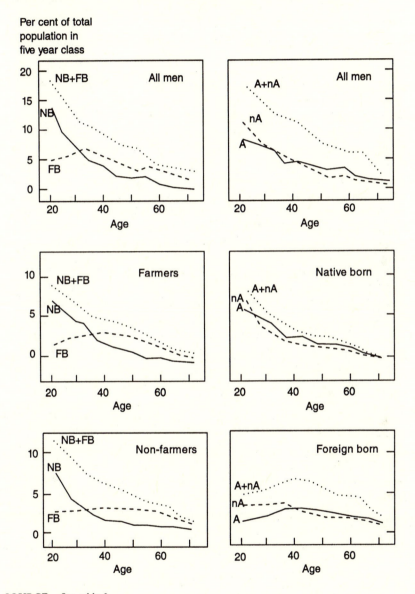

TABLE A.1
Age distributions of adult males in Ontario, England and Wales, Scotland, and Ireland, 1871

		Proportion of males 20 and older			
Age class	Number in Ontario	Ontario	England and Wales	Scotland	Ireland
20–24	74,723	0.191	0.163	0.170	0.152
25–29	60,810	0.155	0.144	0.143 ⎫	0.244
30–34	50,949	0.130	0.127	0.123 ⎬	
35–39	42,224	0.108	0.109	0.104 ⎫	
40–49	69,310	0.177	0.187	0.181 ⎪	
50–59	48,310	0.123	0.137	0.134 ⎬	0.604
60–69	28,650	0.073	0.085	0.089 ⎪	
70 and up	16,518	0.042	0.049	0.054 ⎭	
	391,493	1.000	1.000	1.000	1.000
Number in thousands		391	5,855	811	1,406

SOURCE: *Census of Canada, 1871*, vol. V, table F-I; B.R. Mitchell, *European Historical Statistics, 1750–1975*, (New York: Facts on File 1980) 51, 62–3.

Adjusted for mortality, however, they provide a baseline estimate of the growth of the province's adult male population. The estimate is of particular interest in this study, since inequality of wealth is responsive to rates of population growth and settlement, as well as to changing age distributions.

The relative size of the population given in column (1) can be adjusted upward by an inflator to indicate population size if there had been *no deaths* after age 20. The hypothetical adjusted figures are shown in column (3). Although there have been recent refinements to nineteenth-century mortality estimates, the Massachusetts age-specific death rates have been found to be largely accurate to 1870 and will serve as estimates for Ontario.[5]

The death-inflated population for ages 20–69 is an estimate of population growth from 1821 to 1871, on the assumption that there was no immigration or emigration in those years. A trend line fitted to these data indicates a growth rate of 2 per cent per year. From the aggregate censuses we can calculate that the annual rate of increase of adult males was 2.7 per cent per year from 1851 to 1871.[6] If we ignore net immigration, the population-by-age profile gives a reasonable, though low, estimate of the growth of the adult male population with time.

Obviously immigration and emigration were major factors in the growth of nineteenth-century Ontario's population. The 1850s especially were known to have been a decade of rapid growth resulting from a combination of relatively high rates of natural increase and overseas immigration.[7] Also

TABLE A.2
Age distribution of adult males in Ontario, 1871, by nativity and adjusted for mortality

Age	All males			Native-born males		Foreign-born males	
	Population size (age 20–29 = 100)	Death inflator*	Death-inflated population	Population size (age 20–29 = 100)	Death-inflated population	Population size (age 20–29 = 100)	Death-inflated population
	(1)	(2)	(3)=(1)x(2)	(4)	(5)=(4)x(2)	(6)	(7)=(6)x(2)
20–29	100.0	1.065	106.5	100.0	106.5	100.0	106.5
30–39	71.9	1.204	86.5	50.9	61.3	124.6	150.0
40–49	52.7	1.356	71.4	26.8	36.3	117.7	159.6
50–59	35.9	1.572	56.4	13.8	21.7	91.4	143.6
60–69	25.5	2.030	51.7	8.5	17.2	68.2	138.4
Implied yearly growth**	0.036	−0.016	0.020	0.066	0.049	0.010	−0.005

* The inflator is the reciprocal of the probability of living from age 20 to the mean age of the class as estimated from Massachusetts death rates for 1865.

** The rate is the average annual per cent of change. Rates for Ontario born are 0.071 and 0.054. Foreign born rates for ages 30–69 are 0.021 and 0.004.

SOURCE: The sample of size 5,386 and U.S. Department of Commerce, *Historical Statistics of the United States, Colonial Times to 1957*, Series B, 163–75. Alternative tables of life expectancy in Canada for 1871, based presumably on the 1871 Canadian census and provincial mortality data, are referred to in Dominion Bureau of Statistics, *Canadian Vital Statistics Trends*, Reference Paper No. 70, table 32 (Ottawa 1956).

during this decade, the significant movement of Ontario residents to the United States began. Chapter 5 of this study focused on the economic fate of Ontario migrants to the United States. To consider the effect of migration on population growth in the present case, we can use the manuscript sample to examine the differentials between the Canadian-born and foreign-born populations.

NATIVITY AND POPULATION GROWTH IN NINETEENTH-CENTURY ONTARIO

The census manuscript data give the birthplaces of individuals. If adequate adjustment can be made for deaths and emigration, a quite accurate picture of population changes for the native born could be drawn from the population-by-age profiles. Trends for the foreign born of the province are obviously more difficult to establish using age as a substitute for time, since not all those arriving in any year were the same age. Exact patterns of change for adult males could be established only if each male immigrant had arrived neatly at age 20, had remained in Ontario, and had not died before 1871. Despite the difficulties of estimation, an assessment of the age-specific population data for 1871 tells the general story of the tapering of immigration by 1860 and the net loss between 1861 and 1871.[8]

The classification of the age-specific populations into native and foreign born is quite revealing. If we return to the first panel of figure A.1, we see that the native-born population has a distribution with a reverse-J shape. The distribution is largely dominated by high rates of natural increase as new births, entering our distribution at age 20, appear each year. Although the total population of adult males was quite young (mean age 39), the Canadian-born males in the province were a good deal younger, with an average age of just 33.4 years for those over age 20. The Ontario born were younger still: the mean age of those over 20 was merely 32.8 years.

The youthfulness of this native-born population is underscored when we consider that the number of adult males between ages 20 and 29 was twice that between 30 and 39 and fully four times the number between 40 and 49. The comparison also suggests very rapid growth before 1850. There is a possible qualification. The apparent growth rate would be reduced by the numbers of older Ontario-born persons missing from the columns of table A.2 because they had migrated to the United States. That such an outflow was likely offset by the out-migration of younger men, however, suggests that the high estimated growth rate is not far off the mark.

The foreign-born distribution is substantially different in shape; it rises to a modal age of 35–39 and then tapers off, never falling below the gradient for the native born after age 35. Relatively, this is a quite old population. Certainly it is old in comparison with that of the native born, with an average age of 44.5 years. Consider, for example, the difference between the average age and age of entry into adulthood. For the foreign born it was 24.5 years (44.5 − 20), almost twice that for the native born, 13.4 years (33.4 − 20).

Demographic patterns have subtle social implications. In our data, the striking age differential between native and foreign born implies that a generation gap corresponded closely to one form of 'ethnic' division, as shown by the following percentages.

	20–99	20–39	40–99
Native born	49	63	29
Foreign born	51	37	71
	100 per cent	100 per cent	100 per cent

Whereas there were almost equal proportions of native- and foreign-born men, for example, the foreign born were hugely overrepresented among those aged 40 and over: 71 per cent vs. 29 per cent. A historical study of the Canadian male labour force in the last century suggests that the foreign born did not generally dominate any occupational sector, perhaps as a consequence of the numbers who were from Great Britain, sharing language and institutional heritage with the native born.[9] To the extent that there was occupational specialization in Ontario, our data suggest it would have been strongly reinforced by the marked age differential of the two groups. It also seems possible that seniority might have dictated a strong selection of the foreign born for social and political leadership, although there was a considerable fall-off in immigration in the 1861–71 decade.[10]

THE MOVEMENT FROM FARM TO NON-FARM OCCUPATIONS

Most social and economic theorizing assumes an ineluctable historical movement of population from farm to non-farm employment. Though clearly this assumption is true in the very long term, in fact the transition has often been more prolonged and uneven than theory normally allows. In Ontario, agricultural production continued to engage between 40 and 50 per cent of the labour force until the turn of the century. And nearly a fifth of the labour force was in agricultural employment until after the Second World War.[11]

Assuming that the forces beneath the long-term movement were in place by 1871, the contours of the transition for the province should be revealed by age patterns, specifically in the tendency for greater proportions of younger than older men to be non-farmers. At least this should be the case among the Canadian born or Ontario born.

The upper-right panel of figure A.1 also gives the distribution of Ontario's farmers and non-farmers by age group. Again we consider how age patterns might represent historical trends. As expected, there are more farmers among the prime aged and older males and more non-farmers among the young, with an equal proportion at just about 30 years of age. Semi-logarithmic lines fit closely to the ten age-specific groups, $N_{20-24}, N_{25-29} \ldots N_{65-69}$ for Ontario in 1871, with an implication of growth as follows: for all men the implied gross rate of growth per year of age was 3.6 per cent; for farming men 2.8 per cent; and for non-farmers, 4.5 per cent. These are gross rates in the sense that they do not take account of mortality and migration. As we have noted, the actual number of adult males in Ontario increased 2.7 per cent per year from 1851–71 as contrasted to 3.6 per cent implied by the age distribution of 1871. We can translate the differences into a crude adjustment factor of $0.027 - 0.036 = -0.009$. Employing the adjusted rate gives an estimated rate of increase for *farmers* of about 0.019, or 2 per cent per year, and a rate of growth for *non-farmers* of 0.036, or 3.6 per cent per year. Thus, *both* major sectors of the male labour force appeared to be growing substantially with time, but the non-farm population was increasing at a rate almost twice that of the farm population. Similar occupational transition rates have been found for the United States in 1860 and 1870 (for farmers and non-farmers, 0.022 and 0.044 for 1860 and 0.015 and 0.034 for 1870 for free males over age 20).[12]

No doubt there were significant regional and short-term temporal variations, but for Ontario as a whole these rates indicate that the non-farm population would rise about 1.7 per cent (0.036 − 0.019) per year relative to the farm population. This rate might also be taken to represent the course of the long-run transition away from a predominately agrarian economy in Ontario. Clearly, and importantly, the rate represents a slow, structural change. As in the case of earlier, comparable U.S. estimates, 'The fundamental point of all these calculations is that the rural-urban movement was governed by long-run, slowly changing forces.'[13] Specifically, the differential rates of growth between farm and non-farm populations for Ontario predict a rather slowly shrinking agricultural class from about 52 per cent farmers in 1870 to 40 per cent in 1901 and to 17 per cent in 1971. The actual figure was 40.1 per cent farmers and farm workers in 1901 but less than 10 per cent in 1971.[14] In fact, the most rapid change came only after 1940, as noted above. Agrarian life was a dominant feature of Ontario society for nearly a century after its pioneer stage had passed.

A further refinement using the manuscript sample provides for an analysis of nativity and farm–non-farm sector. The patterns are presented in the four lower panels of figure A.1. Comparing the panels on the left side, it can be seen that the nativity configuration for all male adults, given at the top and discussed above, holds among both farmers and non-farmers. Whereas among all men there were more foreign born above age 35, among farmers the foreign born become more numerous above age 37 and among non-farmers above age 31. Further, the age patterns show that there were decreasing numbers of farmers at every age among the native born, but the numbers of foreign born in farming increased with age to about age 50, declining thereafter. In 1871 the native born in Ontario were still a majority among farmers (0.527), and the foreign born were clearly overrepresented off the farm (0.557).

Considering the age-by-occupation patterns among the native and foreign born, the lower panels on the right side of the figure indicate that farmers were slightly more numerous than non-farmers at virtually every age above

23 for the native born (the middle panel). In contrast, there were greater numbers of farmers among the foreign born only after age 45 (the lower panel). These data strongly suggest that after 1851 immigrants to Ontario tended increasingly to enter the non-farm sector of the economy, with the implication that they increasingly resided in urban areas. Especially in the last century, however, there was a significant rural non-farm economy. We now consider the rural-urban pattern more directly.

URBANIZATION IN ONTARIO, 1871

The main patterns of rural-urban residence by age and nativity for the province's adult men are given in table A.3. In order to provide a baseline, the first section of the table simply shows the age distribution of all men by nativity as computed from our Ontario sample. These proportions by age are quite close to those reported above, taken from the aggregate census. Although only a third of Ontario's male population was between 20 and 29 years of age, the table indicates the divergence between native and immigrant populations, with nearly half the former but only 19 per cent of the foreign born under age 29.

If we turn to the urban-rural distribution, we see from the sample proportions given on the right side of the second section of the table that just 19.1 per cent of all Ontario men resided in urban areas at the time of the census. The figures immediately below indicate that this total was composed of 6.7 per cent natives and 12.4 per cent immigrants.[15] Moreover, the age distribution of urban residents shows them to have been more youthful than rural residents – over 60 per cent of all urban men were under the age of 40 in 1871. Among the urban-residing native born, over 80 per cent were under the age of 40. In contrast, about half of the urban foreign born in cities, towns, and villages had not reached their fortieth birthday. For the rural areas, of course, the age profile of both natives and immigrants approximates that of all men, since over 80 per cent were rural residents. The still strongly agrarian character of life in Ontario in 1871 is again evident here.

Inferring a process of urbanization from these age distributions reinforces the view of systematic structural change. Such an inference must be tempered by the knowledge that the transition involved immense, and still generally underestimated, individual movement through urban areas. Population turnover, rather than single one-way rural-to-urban moves, characterized the life of nineteenth-century cities and towns. The movement was so large that detailed estimates of the annual volatility of urban populations in the

TABLE A.3
Proportion of adult males in Ontario, 1871, by age, nativity, and rural-urban residence

	Proportion in age group						Sample	
Group	20–29	30–39	40–49	50–59	60–69	70–79	Propor-tion	Number
All	0.335	0.240	0.176	0.120	0.085	0.044	1.000	5,386
Canadian born	0.492	0.251	0.132	0.068	0.042	0.015	0.486	2,618
Foreign born	0.185	0.231	0.218	0.169	0.127	0.070	0.514	2,768
Urban	0.351	0.278	0.176	0.103	0.070	0.022	0.191	1,029
Canadian born	0.583	0.239	0.089	0.050	0.033	0.050	0.067	360
Foreign born	0.226	0.299	0.223	0.132	0.090	0.031	0.124	669
Rural	0.330	0.232	0.176	0.124	0.089	0.048	0.809	4,357
Canadian born	0.470	0.252	0.139	0.071	0.043	0.017	0.419	2,258
Foreign born	0.173	0.209	0.217	0.182	0.138	0.082	0.390	2,099

SOURCE: The film-manuscript sample of 5,386 males over 20 years of age

last century are initially difficult to credit.[16] The process was one of slow accretion, rather than of attracting and retaining large numbers of individuals in any short-term period.

RELIGIOUS AND ETHNIC COMMUNITIES: THE RECORD OF THE 1871 CENSUS

The Canadian census is unique in providing information about both religious affiliation and ethnic or national origin. Ethnicity was assessed with reference to the origin of male ancestors and first appears on the schedules in 1871. In previous chapters we have attempted to exploit the richness of the nominal manuscript records in order to examine the variations in property holding and landed wealth by ethnic origin and religion. Here we describe the basic relationships among ethnicity, religion, economic sector, and nativity for Ontario's adult male population in 1871.

The left-hand side of figure A.2 displays the percentage that each ethnic group made up of the total male population, based on the manuscript sample. For example, the figure shows that men of Irish origin were the largest group among all adult males in 1871, comprising 33.6 per cent of the total sample (34.5 per cent of all persons in the census). The Irish were followed closely by the English and Welsh (28.6 per cent) and then by the Scottish (20.4 per cent). Each of these three groups was larger than all other ethnic groups combined, including those of German and French origin.

FIGURE A.2 Distributions of adult males in Ontario, 1871, by ethnic origin and religion

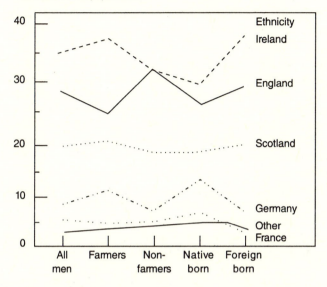

Per cent of total population

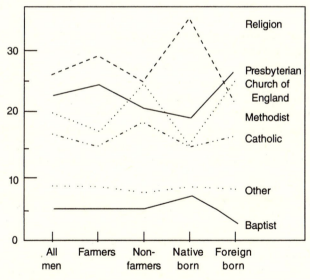

Per cent of total population

SOURCE: See table A.2.

Moving to the right on the figure, one can compare the ethnic distributions of farmers and non-farmers and of the native and foreign born. There is some, but not very striking, ethnic variation between the farm and non-farm sectors and somewhat more variation between the Canadian born and immigrants. Those of Irish, German, and Scottish ancestry were more likely to be farmers, whereas the English clearly tended towards the non-farm economy.

The immigration trends in the decades just before Confederation are reflected in the facts that those of Irish origin constituted three-eighths of all the foreign born by 1871, and the English and Scottish groups were also mainly foreign born. The other three groups tended to be native born, with those of German origin twice as likely to be native Canadians as to have been born in Europe.

Characteristics of the religious groups are displayed graphically in the lower panel of figure A.2. The left side, for all adult men, shows the proportions in the four main church groups, Methodists, Presbyterians, Anglicans, and Catholics. They differed in size by just 10 per cent of the male population, varying from the largest group, the Methodists, at 26.6 per cent, to the smallest of the four, the Catholics, at 16.6 per cent. The Baptists, on the other hand, were a very small, if distinctive, minority, about 5 per cent of the male population (4.8 per cent of the sample and 5.5 per cent of the census enumeration).

Moving to the right on the figure, one can also see that there were only modest differences among the religious groups in the proportions farming and non-farming, with the two largest groups, the Methodist and Presbyterian, slightly more likely to be farmers and the Catholic and Anglican groups somewhat more likely to be non-farmers.

With respect to nativity, there is a clear contrast: among the large churches, only Methodism was mainly a persuasion of the native born, with its adherents twice as likely to be native as foreign born. Presbyterians and Anglicans were more likely to be foreign born. Catholics were nearly evenly split, with only a slightly greater number foreign born. There were also twice as many Canadian as foreign born among the small Baptist group.

NINETEENTH-CENTURY WOMEN HEADS OF HOUSEHOLDS: THE EXCEPTIONAL FEW

As noted in the introduction, the small number of Ontario women in the film-manuscript sample reflects the social and legal practices of the late nineteenth century. Very few women were heads of households. Even as heads of households their rights to own or to inherit property or the products of their own labour were severely restricted. Legally, control of family property remained the exclusive preserve of male heads.[17]

To reiterate, since we aimed to examine the distribution of property ownership and inequality, the sample included adult women (20 years and over) who were recorded as heads of households on the census. There were 313 such sampled women, including ten women property holders who were not heads of households. As in the foregoing analyses, we compare the sample of women with male heads of households.

The numbers and proportions of women and men heads, by age group, are given in table A.4. In some age categories the sample numbers are relatively small and warrant caution in the interpretation of age patterns. Not surprisingly, women heads of households were rather older than male heads on average. The modal age group for male heads was 30–39, with 28 per cent of the sample. For female heads, the modal age groups were the 40–49 and 50–59 groups, each with about 22 per cent. Whereas about 16 per cent of men heads were over age 60, nearly a third of the women were. Of course, the distribution for women reflects the fact that they tended to assume household headship, and some chance of property ownership, mainly on widowhood. A full 84 per cent of the women heads of households in the sample were widows. Just thirty-two members of the sample, or 10 per cent of the women, were single heads and another twenty, about 6 per cent, were married.

In 1871 the law tended, it seems, to favour a widow's inheritance if she was providing for children. One examination of surviving wills suggests that most often children inherited major portions of estates; widows were normally accorded support for their lifetimes.[18] That widows' inheritance of property was linked to the presence of young children in need of care may be reflected in the age distributions of household size. Table A.5 shows the age-specific distribution, as well as the age-specific proportions of foreign born, and of urban residents.[19] Although on average for the province households headed by men were larger (5.57) than those headed by women (4.2), there is a hint in the sample data that among women the younger heads were responsible for larger households, between four and five individuals on average. The households of women over 60 seem to have been comparatively small by nineteenth-century standards.

Given the still very largely rural distribution of families, perhaps the most striking characteristic of women household heads was their tendency to reside in urban areas, as reported earlier and shown in table A.5. Less than

TABLE A.4
Age distributions of female and male heads of households in Ontario, 1871

	Female heads		Male heads	
Age	Proportion	Number	Proportion	Number
20–29	0.067	21	0.164	623
30–39	0.179	56	0.284	1,080
40–49	0.227	71	0.233	888
50–59	0.224	70	0.161	611
60–69	0.182	57	0.110	418
70 and over	0.121	38	0.049	186
Total	1.000	313	1.000	3,886

NOTE: There are ten adult female non-heads in the sample who claimed property in their own name.
SOURCE: The film-manuscript sample of heads of households Ontario, 1871.

20 per cent of male heads, but over a third of the women heads, were urban dwellers in 1871. Both younger men and younger women had a greater tendency to live in villages, towns, and cities, but a much larger proportion of women under 60 years found urban locations either more congenial or, more likely, essential to family sustenance. No doubt maintaining a family farm for any period of time was difficult for widowed women, especially if they did not have adult children or could not hire assistance. At the same time, turning the family home into a source of income by taking in boarders or others' laundry was a likely strategy for widowed women and obviously feasible only in cities and towns.[20]

As shown in table A.5, Ontario's female household heads also tended to be foreign born: 70 per cent were immigrants compared with 58 per cent of the male heads. This finding partly reflects the tendency of immigrants to be older than the native born. On further inspection we find that women heads were also more likely to be Catholic and of Irish origin than male heads of households. Over 40 per cent of the women in the sample were of Irish origin, compared with a third of male heads, and about 22 per cent were Catholic, compared with 16 per cent of the men. The sample allowed us to examine some of the relations between these socio-demographic characteristics and women's property owning in the preceding chapters. We note again that women heads of households in mid-Victorian Ontario were found to be divided between a significant number who were propertied and a larger group who somehow managed without ownership of even their homes or small plots of land.

TABLE A.5
Female and male heads of households in Ontario, 1871, by age, size of household, foreign birth, and urban residence

Age	Average household size		Proportion foreign born		Proportion urban residence	
	Female head	Male head	Female head	Male head	Female head	Male head
20–29	4.0	3.7	0.33	0.32	0.43	0.21
30–39	4.7	5.2	0.50	0.50	0.32	0.22
40–49	5.0	7.0	0.65	0.64	0.41	0.18
50–59	4.6	6.6	0.86	0.72	0.39	0.16
60–69	3.1	5.3	0.82	0.77	0.30	0.16
70 and over	3.0	4.1	0.84	0.84	0.18	0.10
Total	4.20	5.57	0.703	0.584	0.339	0.187

NOTE: See table A.4.
SOURCE: See table A.4.

ONTARIO'S OUT-MIGRATION

If late nineteenth-century Ontario was still known as a land of opportunity for the diligent, it was also a way-station for those continually tempted by the seemingly brighter prospects of life in the United States. The temptation was as great for the Canadian born as for recent immigrants. There is no question that in the second half of the century many people began to migrate to the United States and that many more left than came north to Canada. To complement the specific analysis of the property ownership of Canadian emigrants to the United States reported in chapter 5, we employ the Ontario census sample, similar samples from the U.S census, and aggregate census data to describe the basic parameters of the outflow.

The effects of the out-migration on age distributions in Ontario and the United States can be considered using the data of table A.6. Canadian-born adult males residing in Ontario in 1871 were very young, with an average age of just 33.4 years. As a comparison, consider Ohio, a major U.S. destination for Ontario emigrants. The native Canadian men born in Ontario were four to five years younger than the U.S.-born men in Ohio (33.4–38.2). In part, this difference results from the fact that there were larger numbers of immigrants to Ohio from the north-east of the United States than there were Quebec born in Ontario; both groups of interregional migrants tended to be older, with average ages of 49.9 years and 40.6 years, as shown in the table. On the other hand, the Ontario born in Ontario were the same

TABLE A.6
Average age of adult men in Ontario, 1871, by place of birth

Ontario 1871		United States 1870			
Birth group	Ontario residence	Birth group	U.S. residence	Northwest residence	Ohio residence
All men	39.1	All men	38.8	39.0	39.1
Canadian born	33.4	U.S. born	38.3	38.0	38.2
		Northwest			
Ontario born	32.7	born	32.4	32.4	32.8
Quebec born	40.6	Ohio born	34.7	34.7	32.5
		Northeast			
		born	39.0	42.8	49.9
Foreign born	44.5	Foreign born	38.2	37.4	41.5
		Canadian			
U.S. born	44.2	born	37.2	38.2	–

NOTES: The northwest consists of northern states from Ohio to California. The Ohio sample is of size 360.
SOURCE: The film-manuscript sample of size 5,386 and a partial sample of size 5,726 from the United States manuscripts of the 1870 census.

average age as the Ohio born in Ohio (32.7–32.5). The similarity in average ages is paralleled by the close similarity in the age distributions of the two regions, as revealed in table A.7, which reports census counts of all men in 1870 and 1871 (the Ontario distribution is the same as that presented above).

The similarity reflects the effects of out-migration for both areas: there were many Ohio-born men moving further west, just as there were Ontario-born men moving south and west (indeed, over half of Ohio-born men were living west of that state in 1860 and 1870). Thus, out-migration generated in Ontario, as in Ohio, a very young adult male population born in the region. In contrast, the average age of foreign-born men in Ontario and Ohio was relatively high (44.5 and 41.5). The fact that it was higher in Ontario probably means that the foreign migration rate had decreased more in Ontario than in Ohio. Moreover, the foreign born in Ontario were clearly older than those in the United States to the east and west of Ohio.

Table A.6 also indicates that the Canadian born in the United States were a good deal younger than those who had migrated the other way, 37.2 years on average vs. 44.2 years. Other evidence suggests that the Americans moving north in the few decades prior to Confederation were modestly well off.[21] The age differential between the two groups gives credence to the presumption that the Ontario born moving south were not as well estab-

TABLE A.7
Age distributions of men in Ontario, 1871, and in Ohio,
1870

Age	Ontario residence	Ohio residence
20–29	0.35	0.34
30–39	0.24	0.24
40–49	0.18	0.18
50–59	0.12	0.13
60–69	0.07	0.13
70–99	0.04	0.04
	1.00	1.00

SOURCE: See table A.6.

TABLE A.8
Canadian residents of U.S. birth and U.S. residents of Canadian birth, 1850–71

Canadian residence		U.S. residence	
Year	U.S. born	Year	Canadian born
1871	64,449	1870	493,464
1861	66,356	1860	249,970
1851	56,214	1850	147,711

SOURCE: Various census volumes of each country

lished. The issues were specifically addressed in chapter 5, but we can also turn to the published census data for *all persons* migrating across the border.

Table A.8 demonstrates that the movement north of those born in the United States was slight in the 20 years prior to 1871, while movement in the other direction was dramatic. The magnitude of the southward flow is underscored if one calculates the average annual rate of increase of the Canadian born residing in the United States; the rate was 6.2 per cent from 1850 to 1870 and 7.0 per cent from 1860 to 1870.[22] It has been noted that this outflow represented about 6.6 per cent of the total foreign-born population of the United States in 1850 and 8.9 per cent by 1870.[23] Roughly 10 per cent of all the Canadian born lived in the United States in 1850; the rate climbed to 15 per cent in 1870!

To assess the migration of the foreign born into Ontario, we must turn to less direct census data. The flows for five-year periods are given by the

TABLE A.9
Date of immigration into Ontario of the foreign born living in
the province, 1901

Date	Number of foreign born
Before 1851	50,022
1851–55	22,997
1856–60	19,118
1861–65	12,778
1866–70	20,320
1871–75	26,574
1876–80	17,871

SOURCE: Census of Canada, 1901, vol. I, 450, table XVI

1901 census. The relevant data are presented in table A.9, showing the date
of immigration of the foreign born into the province. Correction of the
figures for deaths would only boost early-year totals relative to those of
later years. At the least, one can conclude that there was no more than a
constant flow of adult males into Ontario.

Given the high rates of out-migration, the Ontario population of 1871
was increasing only very moderately. The rate of increase is known to have
dropped significantly after 1861. For the adult male population we can
calculate that there was an average annual increase of 4.2 per cent from
1851 to 1861 and just 1.4 per cent from 1861 to 1871. One might argue
that the period 1861–5, at least, was one of abnormal conditions caused by
the Civil War.[24] On the other hand, there was a concerted drive after mid-
century towards national unity and autonomy, expressed in its political and
economic forms in the drama of Confederation and in the subsequent National Policy of 1879. On the face of it, these political and economic changes
might have been expected to stem the tide of out-migration.[25] In getting
on with their daily lives, however, ordinary individuals often do not see the
implications of national movements in the same light as do those who stand
to benefit directly from them. Despite the continuing attraction of the Ontario economy to European immigrants, in the 1850s and 1860s a 'back
door' had opened widely through which many Ontario born moved to the
United States. The broad outlines of this story are well known. We still
lack detailed accounts of the social composition of the migrants and their
families, both immigrant and emigrant, and we know little of their actual
social and economic circumstances. Our substantive analysis in chapter 5
revealed a surprising lack of relative economic success among Canadians
who had tried their luck south of the border.

Notes

CHAPTER 1 Concepts and Contexts

1 For Ontario, see Michael B. Katz, *The People of Hamilton, Canada West: Family and Class in a Mid-Nineteenth-Century City* (Cambridge, Mass.: Harvard 1975); David Gagan, *Hopeful Travellers: Families, Land, and Social Change in Mid-Victorian Peel County, Canada West* (Toronto: University of Toronto Press 1981); Gordon Darroch, 'Occupational Structure, Assessed Wealth, and Homeowning during Toronto's Early Industrialization, 1861–1899,' *Histoire sociale / Social History* 16 (November 1983) 381–410, and 'Early Industrialization and Inequality in Toronto, 1861–1899,' *Labour / Le Travailleur* 11 (Spring 1983) 31–61.

2 Livio Di Matteo and Peter George, 'Canadian Wealth Inequality in the Late Nineteenth Century: A Study of Wentworth County, Ontario, 1872–1902,' *Canadian Historical Review* 73 (December 1992) 453, 483.

3 Ibid., table 1, 460, and table 2, 461. It may be noted that, in a recent study of Nova Scotia, Gwyn and Siddiq also report in 1871 that 44 per cent of net worth was real estate, though in 1851 the figure had been over 63 per cent. Julian Gwyn and Fazley Siddiq, 'Wealth Distribution in Nova Scotia during the Confederation Era, 1851 and 1871,' *Canadian Historical Review* 73 (December 1992) table 3, 449.

4 Gagan, *Hopeful Travellers*, 99. Even in the late twentieth century, land and housing are the major sources of wealth in North America. In 1990 in Canada, for example, these two assets represented 36 per cent of total value, with housing comprising just less than a quarter of aggregate total worth. James B. Davies, 'The Distribution of Wealth and Economic Inequality,' in *Social Inequality in Canada: Patterns, Processes, Policies*, ed. James Curtis, Edward Grabb and Neil Guppy (Scarborough, Ont.: Prentice-Hall 1993).

5 Di Matteo and George, 'Canadian Wealth Inequality,' 466, 482.

6 Darroch, 'Occupational Structure,' 384–8; Bruce S. Elliott, 'Sources of Bias in Nineteenth-Century Ontario Wills,' *Histoire sociale / Social History* 18 (May 1985) 125–32; DiMatteo and George, 'Canadian Wealth Inequality,' 456–9.

7 Davies, 'Distribution of Wealth' 107.

8 Ibid., 108.

9 Di Matteo has begun a promising study that attempts to construct wealth estimates for the entire province of Ontario in 1892 from probate and census records.

10 Gordon Darroch and Michael Ornstein, 'Ethnicity and Occupational Structure in Canada in 1871: The Vertical Mosaic in Historical Perspective,' *Canadian Historical Review* 61 (September 1980) 227.

11 John McCallum, *Unequal Beginnings: Agriculture and Economic Development in Quebec and Ontario until 1870* (Toronto: University of Toronto Press 1980) 22, 48, and 87; William Marr and Donald Paterson, *Canada: An Economic History* (Toronto: Gage 1980) table 2.3; Jacob Spelt, *Urban Development in South-Central Ontario* (Toronto: University of Toronto Press 1972); Gregory Kealey and Bryan Palmer, *Dreaming of What Might Be: The Knights of Labor in Ontario, 1800–1900* (Toronto: New Hogtown Press and Cambridge University Press 1987 [1982]) 27–8.

12 David Gagan and H.E. Turner, 'Social History in Canada: A Report on the "State of the Art," ' *Archivaria* 14 (Summer 1982) 32; Douglas McCalla and Peter George, 'Measurement, Myth, and Reality: Reflections on the Economic History of Nineteenth-Century Ontario,' *Journal of Canadian Studies* 21 (Fall 1986) 77, 80; Gregory S. Kealey, 'Labour and Working Class History in Canada: Prospects for the 1980s,' *Labour / Le Travailleur* 7 (Spring 1981) 68.

13 Chad Gaffield, 'Children, Schooling, and Family Reproduction in Nineteenth-Century Ontario,' *Canadian Historical Review* 72 (June 1991) 157–91. Gaffield notes the exceptions to this urban focus, especially the work of Gidney, Lawr, and Millar, for example, 'From Voluntarism to State Schooling: The Creation of the Public School System in Ontario,' *Canadian Historical Review* 66 (1985) 443–73.

14 Leo Johnson, 'Land Policy, Population Growth, and Social Structure in the Home District, 1793–1851,' *Ontario History* 63 (1971) 41–60; H. Clare Pentland, ' The Development of the Capitalistic Labour Market in Canada,' *Canadian Journal of Economics and Political Science* 25 (1959) 450–61.

15 Marvin McInnis, 'The Size Structure of Farming, Canada West, 1861,' *Research in Economic History*, Supplement 5 (1989) 313–29, especially 314–15.

16 See Gordon Darroch and Michael Ornstein, 'Ethnicity and Class, Transitions

over a Decade: Ontario, 1861–1871,' Canadian Historial Association, *Historical Papers* (1984) 111–37. On the question of the settlement of Irish immigrants, see Donald Harmon Akenson, *The Irish in Ontario: A Study in Rural History* (Kingston and Montreal: McGill-Queen's University Press 1984).

17 For example, Gilbert Stelter and Alan Artibuse eds., *The Canadian City: Essays in Urban History* (Toronto: McClelland and Stewart 1977).

18 Two books emerged from the larger project: Katz, *People of Hamilton* and, with Michael J. Doucet and Mark J. Stern, *The Social Organization of Early Industrial Capitalism* (Cambridge, Mass.: Harvard University Press 1982). Methodologically, the studies broke new ground in the analysis of institutionally generated nominal records, city directories, tax records, and the manuscript censuses.

19 In the second volume produced by the Hamilton project, *Social Organization*, the authors' make comparisons with Buffalo, New York, and its Erie county hinterland. The comparative strategy was a valuable extension. It would also have served Canadian social history if the comparison had included Hamilton's immediate rural region.

20 The criticisms are reviewed in Gregory Kealey, 'The Writing of social history in English Canada, 1970–1984,' *Social History* 10 (1985) 347–65.

21 Bryan D. Palmer, *A Culture in Conflict: Skilled Workers and Industrial Capitalism in Hamilton, Ontario, 1860–1914* (Kingston and Montreal: McGill-Queen's University Press 1979) and Gregory S. Kealey, *Toronto Workers Respond to Industrial Capitalism, 1867–1892* (Toronto: University of Toronto Press 1980).

22 The most frequently cited works are David Bercuson, 'Through the Looking Glass of Culture: An Essay on the New Labour History and Working-Class Culture in Recent Canadian Historical Writing,' *Labour / Le Travailleur* 7 (1981) 95–112, and Kenneth McNaught, 'E.P. Thompson versus Harold Logan: Writing about Labour and the Left in the 1970s,' *Canadian Historical Review* 63 (1981) 141–68.

23 Bettina Bradbury, 'Pigs, Cows, and Boarders: Non-Wage Forms of Survival among Montreal Families, 1861–91,' *Labour / Le Travail* 14 (Fall 1984) 9–46, and *Working Families: Age, Gender, and Daily Survival in Industrializing Montreal* (Toronto: McClelland and Stewart 1993).

24 Gordon Darroch, 'Migrants in the Nineteenth-Century: Fugitives or Families in Motion?' *Journal of Family History* 6 (Fall 1981) 257–77; Bruno Ramirez, *On the Move: French-Canadian and Italian Migrants in the North-Atlantic Economy, 1860–1914* (Toronto: McClelland and Stewart 1991).

25 John Herd Thompson, 'Writing about Rural Life and Agriculture,' in *Writing*

about Canada: A Handbook for Modern Canadian History, ed. John Schultz (Scarborough, Ont.: Prentice-Hall 1990) 101.

26 David Gagan, *Hopeful Travellers*.

27 Graeme Wynn succinctly summarizes the arguments in 'Notes on Society and Environment in Old Ontario,' *Journal of Social History* 13 (Fall 1979) 49–65.

28 Peel county after mid-century was part of a south-central subregion of Ontario that was quite distinctive in several respects, being early settled, with a continuously large number of men aspiring to land ownership and a highly productive wheat and mixed-farming economy.

29 See Akenson, *The Irish*. Unique among the authors of local urban and rural studies in Ontario, Akenson provides a systematic provincial context for his analysis by employing McInnis's 1861 farm sample. Though this study reveals that in terms of material attainment the Irish of Leeds and Landsdowne surpassed their fellow Irish immigrants across the province, the differences are not so great as to make the locale exceptional, and this fact strengthens Akenson's case for the wider significance of his local study.

30 Chad Gaffield, *Language, Schooling and Cultural Conflict: The Origins of the French-Language Controversy in Ontario* (Kingston and Montreal: McGill-Queen's University Press 1987) 183.

31 Thompson notes that, despite its descriptive value, 'local' history has generally been a term of contempt among professional historians, since the amateur genre has offered them so little of importance. 'Writing about Rural Life,' 104.

32 See, for example, R. Cole Harris and John Warkentin, *Canada Before Confederation: A Study in Historical Geography* (New York: Oxford University Press 1974) chap. 4; McCalla and George, 'Measurement, Myth, and Reality.'

33 Hal S. Barron, 'Rediscovering the Majority: The New Rural History of the Nineteenth-Century North,' *Historical Methods* 19 (Fall 1986) 141–52; Thompson, 'Writing about Rural Life.'

34 The only variables from the first schedule not employed in the analysis were whether the persons enumerated were born or married within the previous year, whether they attended school, or whether they were considered 'deaf, dumb, blind or of unsound mind.'

35 The variables given on these schedules, but not employed in the analysis, are the specific tabulations of farm products, for example, acres and bushels of spring and fall wheat, peas, potatoes, and so on, and the counts of particular farm equipment, such as ploughs, cultivators, and fanning mills.

36 The Census of Industrial Establishments for 1871 provides information on the ownership of manufacturing establishments and on capital and employment. These records, however, are not linked by line and page to others,

which means that a nominal linkage procedure needs to be devised. The poor quality of the name entries and the absence of other identifiers makes this a thoroughly daunting task. For these reasons we have not undertaken it.

37 Peter Laslett, *The World We Have Lost* (London: Methuen 1965) 148; Katz, *People of Hamilton* ch. 2.

CHAPTER 2 Landownership and Land Occupancy in Nineteenth-Century Ontario

1 'Acres of Your Own,' in *Poems and Songs* (Toronto 1874), cited by Allan Smith, 'Farms, Forests and Cities: The Image of the Land and the Rise of the Metropolis in Ontario, 1860–1914,' in *Old Ontario: Essays in Honour of J.M.S. Careless*, ed. David Keane and Colin Read (Toronto and Oxford: Dundurn Press 1990) 72.

2 Marvin McInnis, 'The Size Structure of Farming, Canada West, 1861,' *Research in Economic History*, Supplement 5 (1989) 313–29.

3 David Gagan, *Hopeful Travellers: Families, Land, and Social Change in Mid-Victorian Peel County, Canada West* (Toronto: University of Toronto Press 1981) ch. 3. For an earlier and more general view, see H. Clare Pentland, 'The Development of a Capitalistic Labour Market in Canada,' *Canadian Journal of Economics and Political Science* 25 (November 1959) 450–61.

4 See, for example, Lee Soltow, *Men and Wealth in the United States: 1850–1870* (New Haven, Conn.: Yale University Press 1975); and for Canada, Michael Katz, *The People of Hamilton, Canada West: Family and Class in a Mid-Nineteenth Century City*, (Cambridge, Mass.: Harvard University Press 1975) 44–93; and Lars Osberg and Fazley Siddiq, 'The Inequality in Wealth in Britain's North American Colonies: The Importance of the Relatively Poor,' *Review of Income and Wealth* 34 (June 1988) 143–64.

5 Assessment records can be found in national and provincial archives and in county offices. Generally, the units of assessment were properties; occupants were normally listed, whether owners or tenants. The rolls have a number of limitations that bear note. In many areas, substantial numbers of vacant lots were not assigned an owner. More seriously, many adults were simply excluded from municipal assessments. An income exemption was common, and occupants of premises frequently had no real or personal estate. Further, properties within a township were not collated by owner's name. Ownership figures for real estate in different townships and counties are not readily available, although some early lists did have entries for each piece of property classified by owner's name. An example is Alfred township in the Ottawa district in 1839.

For the historical study of wealth distributions, probate records and estate inventories are a valuable source, with their own limitations. See ch. 1, n6. Finally, the use of the non-census sources are complicated by definitions of assessment that are often difficult to interpret. See, for example, *Statutes of Ontario, Canada*, Cap. 36, 32 Vic. 1868–9, 180, 181.

6 Michael B. Katz, Michael J. Doucet, and Mark J. Stern, *The Social Organization of Early Industrial Capitalism* (Cambridge, Mass.: Harvard University Press 1982) ch. 2; Gordon Darroch, 'Early Industrialization and Inequality in Toronto, 1861–1899,' *Labour / Le Travailleur* 11 (Spring 1983) 31–61; Gagan, *Hopeful Travellers*, 99–109; Donald H. Akenson, *The Irish in Ontario: A Study in Rural History* (Montreal and Kingston: McGill-Queen's University Press 1984) 246–9, 339–44; Livio Di Matteo and Peter George, 'Canadian Wealth Inequality in the Late Nineteenth Century: A Study of Wentworth County, Ontario, 1872–1902,' *Canadian Historical Review* 73 (December 1992) 453–483.

7 Gustavus Myers, *A History of Canadian Wealth* [1914]; first Canadian edition with an introduction by Stanley Ryerson (Toronto: James Lewis and Samuel 1972).

8 Cited in Gagan, *Hopeful Travellers*, 31.

9 Ibid.; Leo Johnson, 'Land Policy, Population Growth and Social Structure in the Home District, 1793–1851,' *Ontario History* 67 (March 1971) 41–3; Gary Teeple 'Land, Labour, and Capital in Pre-Confederation Canada,' in *Capitalism and the National Question*, ed. Gary Teeple (Toronto: University of Toronto Press 1972) 44–66.

10 Lillian Gates, *Land Policies in Upper Canada* (Toronto: University of Toronto Press 1968) 155, 258, 304. We thank Steven Baranyi of York University for helpful comments.

11 See Graeme Wynn, 'Notes on Society and Environment in Old Ontario,' *Journal of Social History* 13 (Fall 1979) 49–65.

12 Allan Smith, 'The Myth of the Self-made Man in English Canada, 1850–1914,' *Canadian Historical Review* 59 (May 1978) 189–219.

13 Gagan cites numerous references to land ownership as the quintessential measure of the promise of life in Ontario after mid-century; see *Hopeful Travellers*, ch. 5.

14 See 'Instructions to be issued to officers taking the 1871 Census,' *Report of the Department of Agriculture*, 1870, no. 19, 125–42, especially 134.

15 Specifically, the reference is to land owned 'no matter where situated in the territory of the Dominion'. For the purpose of assessing wealth distributions in land this is clearly the measure preferred, say, to one limited to ownership in a given county, township, or town. *Report of the Department of Agriculture*, 136.

An almost identical proportion of white adult male farmers held real estate in the United States in 1870; Soltow, *Men and Wealth*, 33. We consider amount of acreage owned later. The census of 1901 is apparently the first to give dollar values for real estate while differentiating land and buildings. Land owned was 56 per cent of the total value of land, buildings, implements, and livestock on hand for farm property in Canada; *Fifth Census of Canada*; 1911, vol. 4, *Agriculture*, vii. There is likely a quite high correlation between amount of land owned, its value and the value of other farm property.

16 The first compelling analysis of landlessness and the rise of wage labour was H. Clare Pentland's, 'Development of the Capitalistic Labour Market,' 450–61. Also see his *Labour and Capital in Canada 1650–1860* (Toronto [1960]: James Lorimer 1981). Leo Johnson also developed the thesis and brought evidence to bear for the 1850s for several counties of Ontario's Home district, 'Land Policy, Population Growth.'

17 *Manual Containing "The Census Act" and The Instructions to Officers Employed in the Taking of The First Census of Canada (1871)* (Ottawa: Department of Agriculture 1871) 27.

18 Gagan, *Hopeful Travellers*, 53–4.

19 As we noted, farmers made up over half of Ontario's labour force in 1871 (51.6 per cent of the sample). The sample shows that even outside the urban areas over a third of adult men were not farmers; about 11 per cent were labourers and a quarter were rural skilled and semi-skilled workers.

20 Age standardization hypothetically equalizes the age distributions of two groups, generating expected rates, such as ownership proportions, based on the hypothetical age distribution. The differences between the observed and expected rates can be attributed to the effect of the age differences between the groups. In the present case, the rates are the age-specific proportions of land owners and the hypothetical age composition is that of the combined native- and foreign-born populations. They are multipied to yield overall standardized rates of ownership. Five-year age intervals were used.

21 In our sample of 5,386 men, 2,029 (37.7 per cent) reported owning acreage in the dominion, but of this group only 2,008 (37.3 per cent) reported owning land that they occupied in the census district in which they were enumerated. The other twenty-one men presumably were 'absentee' land owners of some description, living in Ontario but not on land they owned.

22 'Enumerators must not forget that the products recorded in the schedule may be, and often are, raised by families not engaged in carrying on farming – say, on patches of land or gardens attached to tenements, even in the middle of large cities,' *Manual Containing "The Census Act"*, 28.

23 William L. Marr, 'Tenant vs. Owner Occupied Farms in York County, Ontario, 1871,' in *Canadian Papers in Rural History* 3, ed. Donald H. Akenson

(Gananoque, Ont.: Langdale Press 1982) 50–1, citing the author of the most comprehensive history of Ontario agriculture, R.L. Jones, *History of Agriculture in Ontario, 1613–1880* (Toronto: University of Toronto Press 1946) 62.

24 Marr, 'Tenant vs. Owner,' and 'The Distribution of Tenant Agriculture in Ontario, Canada, 1871,' *Social Science History* 11 (Summer 1987) 169–86. Ontario's overall rate of tenancy for farms was considerably higher than the rates of the other three provinces (15 per cent compared with just 5 per cent in Quebec and 7 per cent in Nova Scotia and New Brunswick) but apparently lower than the average rate for the northern United States (26 per cent in 1880). Rates for the mid-western states were more variable. Marr reports they varied from 9 per cent in Wisconsin to 31 per cent in Illinois. See 'Distribution of Tenant Agriculture,' 177.

25 D.L. Winters, *Farmers Without Farms: Agricultural Tenancy in Nineteenth-Century Iowa* (Westport, Conn.: Greenwood Press 1978) especially 83, 91. Also see the income and profitability of tenant farming in comparison with owner-occupied farms in the rural North, J. Atack and F. Bateman, *To Their Own Soil: Agriculture in the Antebellum North* (Ames, Iowa: Iowa State University Press 1988) 131–4, 239–40, 258–9. They find wide interstate variations in the productivity and in the relative economic standing of tenant farmers in comparison with yeoman farmers.

26 There is some question of what the census meant by tenant, since no precise definition was provided and the instructions simply referred to 'the capacity in which the person occupying the property holds it,' distinguishing specifically owner, tenant and employee. See *Manual Containing "The Census Act"*, 28. Studies in the United States prior to 1880 have inferred tenancy by comparing population, agricultural, and real estate schedules. Both farmers operating farms, but reporting no real estate holdings, and farmers with farms worth more than their own recorded real estate have been considered tenants. See A. Bogue, *From Prairie to Corn Belt: Farming on the Illinois and Iowa Prairies in the Nineteenth Century* (Chicago: University of Chicago Press 1963) 63–4; Atack and Bateman, *To Their Own Soil*, 110.

27 *Census of Canada, 1870–71*, vol. III, 20–49.

28 Bettina Bradbury, 'Pigs, Cows and Boarders: Non-Wage Forms of Survival among Montreal Families 1861–91,' *Labour / Le Travail* 14 (Fall 1984) 9–46; Peter DeLottinville, 'Joe Beef of Montreal: Working-Class Culture and the Tavern, 1869–1889,' *Labour / Le Travail* 8/9 (Autumn/Spring 1989–90) 9–40.

29 Atack and Bateman, *To Their Own Soil*, 111.

30 See Robert V. Wells, 'On the Dangers of Constructing Artificial Cohorts in Times of Rapid Social Change,' *Journal of Interdisciplinary History* 9 (Summer 1978) 103–10.

31 Gérard Bouchard, 'Transmission of Family Property and the Cycle of Quebec Rural Society from the Seventeenth to the Twentieth Century,' in *Canadian Family History: Selected Readings*, ed. Bettina Bradbury (Toronto: Copp Clark Pitman 1992), 112–34, trans. Jane Parniak.

32 Gagan, *Hopeful Travellers*, 58, 123–5.

33 Ibid., 111.

34 For the alternative evidence see Akenson, *The Irish*; Bruce S. Elliott, *Irish Migrants in the Canadas: A New Approach* (Kingston and Montreal: McGill-Queen's University Press 1988); Gordon Darroch, 'Class in Nineteenth-Century, Central Ontario: A Reassessment of the Crisis and Demise of Small Producers during Early Industrialization, 1861–1871,' in *Class, Gender and Region: Essays in Canadian Historical Sociology*, ed. Gregory Kealey (St John's Nfld.: Committee an Canadian Labour History 1988); Chad Gaffield, 'Children, Schooling and Family Reproduction in Nineteenth-Century Ontario,' *Canadian Historical Review* 72 (June 1991) 157–91.

35 Di Matteo and George, 'Canadian Wealth Inequality,' 470.

36 Soltow first considered the application of the binomial model to wealth distributions in 'The Wealth, Income and Social Class of Men in Large Northern Cities of the United States in 1860,' in *The Personal Distribution of Income and Wealth*, National Bureau of Economic Research 39 (New York: Columbia University Press 1975) 245–52.

37 *Census of Canada, 1871*, vol. V, 110–15.

38 Life expectancy for males 20 and older in 1871 was 47.9 years; M.C. Urquhart and K.A.H. Buckley, *Historical Statistics of Canada* (Toronto: Queen's Printer 1965) Series B, 65–74.

39 For adult male farmers 20 and older in the United States, 39 per cent of all free males reported no real estate in 1850 and 43 per cent reported none in 1860, while 42 per cent of free whites reported no real estate in 1870. Caution should be exercised in comparing figures for Ontario and the United States; the comparisons at least provide some context for interpretation. The landowner proportions for Ontario for ages 20–29, 30–39, 40–49, 50–59, 60–69, and 70 and up are 0.249, 0.670, 0.851, 0.838, 0.882, and 0.773 respectively. The same vector for white farmers with real estate in the United States in 1870 was 0.269, 0.628, 0.751, 0.791, 0.796, 0.734. For farmers in northern states in 1870 it was 0.269, 0.650, 0.762, 0.833, 0.807, and 0.741. Thus, except for the youngest group (ages 20–29) the chance of ownership of land was greater for Ontario residents than for those in the United States as a whole or for the northern states. The U.S. samples are described in Soltow,

Men and Wealth. Also see Soltow, 'Distribution of Wealth and Income,' in *Encyclopedia of American Economic History* 3, ed. Glenn Porter (New York: Scribner's 1980), and 'Wealth Inequality in the United States in 1790 to 1860,' *Review of Economics and Statistics* 66 (August 1984) 444–51.

40 Gaffield, 'Children, Schooling, and Family Reproduction,' 166.

41 The variance in acreage owned that is accounted for by age in these linear equations is low: 12 and 1 per cent, respectively. Since our purpose here is to establish an estimate of the slope or relationship for the two portions of the curve, we are not concerned with the overall variance explained but with the coefficients we can employ in our estimating procedure.

42 *Census of Canada, 1871,* vol. V, 110–15.

43 See John Clarke, 'Aspects of Land Acquisition in Essex county, Ontario, 1790–1900,' *Histoire sociale / Social History* 11 (May 1978) 98–119

44 Bittermann presents a rare study of how the timing of arrival translated into significant rural stratification among families in Cape Breton, 'The Hierarchy of the Soil: Land and Labour in a 19th-Century Cape Breton Community,' *Acadiensis* 18 (Autumn 1988) 33–55. Bittermann notes: 'Each successive wave of settlers encountered the diminishing crown assets left by the choices of those who had preceded them' (39). The distinction between foreign and native born does not directly reflect the timing of entry into Ontario's land market, of course. Early immigrants entered the market before younger natives. But family inheritance and assistance patterns would still have tended to confer advantages on the latter from a preceding wave of settlement. For exactly such a case in Ontario see Gaffield's analysis of the differences between anglophone and francophone communities in the Ottawa valley, *Language, Schooling and Cultural Conflict: The Origins of the French-Language Controversy in Ontario* (Kingston and Montreal: McGill-Queen's University Press 1987) 68–72.

45 See H. Clare Pentland's early interpretation, 'The Development of a Capitalistic Labour Market'; and more recently, Bryan D. Palmer, *Working Class Experience: The Rise and Reconstitution of Canadian Labour, 1800–1980* (Toronto: Butterworths 1983) especially 10–12.

46 Akenson, *The Irish,* 240–263.

47 The results of the standardization are confirmed by an ordinary least squares multiple regression equation predicting the proportion of farmers owning land. The age groups, 30–39, 40–49 ... 70–79 were treated as dichotomous variables, with the youngest group taken as a reference category. The sixth variable was the nativity dichotomy with native born as the reference. The R^2 for the equation was 0.28 for $N = 2,777$. The coefficients for the age variables range from 0.42 for the 30–39-year age group to 0.63 for the 60–69-

year-olds, and all were statistically significant at 0.001 or better, indicating a significantly greater probability of the older groups owning property in comparison with the youngest reference group. The native born / immigrant difference was not statistically significant and the coefficient was only 0.013.

48 Perhaps there were disadvantaged foreign born in the cities or at least among non-farmers. Later analysis of urban-rural patterns bears on this question. The fact remains that greater proportions of the foreign born were landowners in Ontario in 1871, and there was no nativity difference in landowning, even when age differentials are considered.

49 Computed from the census sample for adult males reported by Soltow, *Men and Wealth*. It is possible that the foreign born in Ontario were systematically located on less valuable land, even within local communities, given chain migration and clustering of related households. In this case, a detailed analysis of real estate values, rather than merely acreage owned, might reveal a greater differential.

50 Akenson, *The Irish* 254–63.

51 Ibid., 233. Though Akenson worries about the accuracy of census tabulations for religious groups, it is not clear that the census data he uses were insufficient to explore economic and social differentials at the local level.

52 Katz, Doucet, and Stern, *Social Organization*, 136-48.

53 Weber reasoned that the ethic of Protestantism breaks with traditionalism by granting an essential, morally charged conception to material acquisition. See Max Weber, *The Protestant Ethic and the Spirit of Capitalism* [1905] (New York: Scribner's 1958). Weber's thesis was not intended mainly to distinguish among specific congregations in a variety of historical circumstances. It posited how the ethic of Protestantism lent legitimacy and moral force to capitalism at a very specific juncture in Europe in the sixteenth and seventeenth centuries. Nevertheless, it has often been used to distinguish specific church groups. A still useful account is Ephraim Fischoff, 'The Protestant Ethic and the Spirit of Capitalism,' *Social Research* 11 (1944) 53–77. Also see Richard Bendix in his article on Max Weber in the *International Encyclopedia of the Social Sciences*, vol. 16 (Macmillan and Free Press 1968).

54 Leonore Davidoff and Catherine Hall have provided a penetrating analysis. *Family Fortunes: Men and Women of the English Middle Class, 1780–1850* (London: Hutchinson 1987) ch. 1.

55 Paul E. Johnson, *A Shopkeeper's Millennium: Society and Revivals in Rochester, New York, 1815–1837* (New York: Hill and Wang 1978); Mary P. Ryan, *The Cradle of the Middle Class: The Family in Oneida County, New York, 1790–1865* (Cambridge: Cambridge University Press 1981).

56 Neil Semple, 'The Quest for the Kingdom: Aspects of Protestant Revivalism

in Nineteenth-Century Ontario,' in *Old Ontario: Essays in Honour of J.M.S. Careless*, ed. David Keane and Colin Read (Toronto and Oxford: Dundurn Press 1991) 95–118.

57 R. Cole Harris and John Warkentin, eds., *Canada before Confederation: A Study in Historical Geography* (New York and Toronto: Oxford University Press 1974) 112.

58 S.D. Clark, *Church and Sect in Canada* (Toronto: University of Toronto Press 1948); William Westfall, 'The Dominion of the Lord: An Introduction to the Cultural History of Protestant Ontario in the Victorian Period,' *Queen's Quarterly* 83 (Spring 1976) 47–70.

59 The appendix to the book provides a detailed socio-demographic profile of the province, employing the full manuscript sample.

60 The statistical evidence is given by several multiple regression equations involving age, nativity, and the religious groups as independent variables predicting ownership.

61 Clark, *Church and Sect*, ch. 7.

62 For example, John Bodnar, *The Transplanted: A History of Immigrants in Urban America* (Bloomington: Indiana University Press 1985); Bruno Ramirez, *On The Move: French-Canadian and Italian Migrants in the North Atlantic Economy, 1869–1914* (Toronto: McClelland and Stewart 1991).

63 Gaffield, *Language, Schooling and Cultural Conflict*; John Mannion, *Irish Settlements in Eastern Canada: A Study of Cultural Transfer and Adaptation* (Toronto: University of Toronto Press 1974); Elliott, *Irish Migrants.*.

64 David Gagan reviews this tendency in urban studies in 'Class and Society in Victorian English Canada: An Historiographical Reassessment,' *British Journal of Canadian Studies* 4:1 (1989) 77–8.

65 Generally, throughout the analysis both ordinary least squares regression (OLS) and logit regression analyses were conducted when the dependent variable was dichotomous, for example, owner and not owner. The latter is the strictly more appropriate specification. In virtually every case, however, the results were very close or identical. To illustrate, we record the OLS regression results.

 Simple dichotomies are employed as independent variables for various age categories and for religion, ethnic origin, and nativity, predicting landownership proportions. An example of the coding is that age 30–39 is 1.0 if an individual is 30–39; otherwise it is zero. If all explicit variables are zeros, we have the regression value for an individual 20–29 who is a member of the Church of England and whose origin is English or Welsh. The equation is as follows:

$$P_{AC>0} = 0.166 + 0.417age_{30-39} + 0.597age_{40-49} + 0.585age_{50-59}$$
$$(0.222) \qquad (0.024) \qquad (0.026)$$

$$+ 0.626age_{60-69} + 0.517age_{70-99} + 0.050Cath + 0.084Bapt$$
$$(0.030) \qquad (0.042) \qquad (0.029) \qquad (0.041)$$

$$+ 0.070Meth + 0.052Pres + 0.079otherreligion + 0.009Scot + 0.064Iri$$
$$(0.024) \qquad (0.028) \qquad (0.034) \qquad (0.028) \qquad (0.022)$$

$$+ 0.002German + 0.024Fr + 0.020otherethnic + 0.017foreignborn$$
$$(0.029) \qquad (0.047) \quad (0.054) \qquad (0.018)$$

$$N = 2{,}777 \text{ and } R^2 = 0.29.$$

The coefficients indicating the difference between the English and Welsh group and other origin groups are very weak, with the single exception of the Irish. In terms of variance explained, the age variables have much the greatest effect, followed by the origin and religion variables, which are barely different in effect, followed finally by nativity. The comparable logistic model for assessing the effects of sets of independent variables duplicated the result, with age having by far the greatest influence, and origin and religion having similar, weaker, but statistically significant (at 0.05) effects. Nativity did not significantly affect landowning.

66 Akenson, *The Irish*, especially chs. 1 and 7. Also see Gordon Darroch and Michael Ornstein, 'Ethnicity and Occupational Structure in Canada in 1871: The Vertical Mosaic,' *Canadian Historical Review* 61 (September 1980) 305–33.

67 Gordon Darroch, 'Half Empty or Half Full: Images and Interpretations in the Historical Analysis of the Catholic Irish in Nineteenth-Century Canada,' *Canadian Ethnic Studies*, 25:1 (1993) 1–8.

68 See n 65 on forms of regression analysis.

69 The results of additional regression analyses reveal that the effects of Irish origin are significant and independent of those of religion, even when a cross-product term is included to represent the interaction of Irish origin with the Protestant-Catholic divide.

70 Katz, *People of Hamilton* 81–91.

71 See, for example, Gagan on Peel County's quite productive farms, *Hopeful Travellers*, 44, table 8, where over 70 per cent of occupiers held over fifty acres in 1871 and nearly that proportion in 1851. In the less rich Ottawa valley Gaffield reports that substantial majorities of farmers held over fifty acres in 1861 and 1871, *Language, Schooling and Cultural Conflict*, 77, table 16. Also see Marvin McInnis, 'A Reassessment of Wheat as a Staple in Upper Canada,' paper presented to the Canadian Historical Association, Guelph 1984. Using his sample of farms for Ontario in 1861, McInnis indicates that only about half the acreage occupied by farmers was cultivated and of that

about a fifth was devoted to the major export and cash producing staple, wheat (10, table 1). A standard farm was about 100 acres and on average some eleven acres were devoted to wheat production although wheat was grown on over 90 per cent of all Ontario farms.

72 As indicated earlier, over 70 per cent of Irish-origin farmers were Protestant and less than 30 per cent were Catholic in the provincial sample.

73 In this case OLS is the appropriate specification, since the dependent variable, acreage owned, can be taken to be continuous.

74 Paul Craven and Tom Traves, 'The Class Politics of the National Policy, 1872–1933,' *Journal of Canadian Studies* 14 (Fall 1979) 14–38.

75 The Gini index is the most commonly employed measure of inequality. It has a value between 0 and 1, where 0 denotes perfect equality in the distribution, and 1 denotes perfect inequality. See F.A. Cowell, *Measuring Inequality: Techniques for the Social Sciences* (Oxford: P.A. Allen 1977).

76 Di Matteo and George, 'Canadian Wealth Inequality,' table 4.

77 Gordon Darroch 'Early Industrialization and Inequality in Toronto 1861–1899,' *Labour / Le Travailleur* 11 (Spring 1983) 31–61, especially table III. The data *excluded* the unassessed population. It is probable that half or nearly half of the adult men in Ontario's cities held no taxable wealth at all. For Hamilton, see Katz, *People of Hamilton*, and Katz, Doucet, and Stern, *Social Organization*, ch. 2, especially tables 2.4, 2.5.

78 For the antebellum period in the United States, see Soltow, *Men and Wealth*, 101–46. For Nova Scotia in 1871, see Fazley Siddiq, "The Size Distribution of Probate Wealthholding in Nova Scotia in the Late Nineteenth Century,' *Acadiensis* 18 (Autumn 1988) 136–47.

79 See also Soltow, *Patterns of Wealthholding in Wisconsin since 1850* (Madison: University of Wisconsin Press 1971) 76, 80.

80 Compare Gagan, *Hopeful Travellers*, ch. 3, and Akenson *The Irish*, ch. 5, especially 258.

CHAPTER 3 Home Ownership, Secure Property, and the Propertyless: Structural Patterns and Cultural Communities

1 Michael Doucet and John Weaver, 'Material Culture and the North American House: The Era of the Common Man, 1870–1930,' *The Journal of American History* 72 (1985) 560–87, cited by Richard Harris and Chris Hamnett, 'The Myth of the Promised Land: The Social Diffusion of Home Ownership in Britain and North America,' *Annals of the Association of American Geographers* 77 (1987) 173.

2 Bettina Bradbury, 'Cows, Pigs and Boarders: Non-Wage Forms of Survival

among Montreal Families, 1861–1881,' *Labour / Le Travailleur* 14 (Fall 1984) 9–46. Richard Bushman, 'Family Security in the Transition from Farm to City, 1750–1850,' *Journal of Family History* 6 (Fall 1981) 238–56; Richard Harris, 'Housing in Canadian Cities: An Agenda and Review of Sources,' *Urban History Review / Revue d'histoire urbaine* 14 (February 1986) 259–66 and 'Homeownership and Class in Modern Canada,' *International Journal of urban and Regional Research*, 10 (1986) 67–86.

3 Michael B. Katz, Michael J. Doucet, and Mark J. Stern, *The Social Organization of Early Industrial Capitalism* (Cambridge, Mass.: Harvard University Press 1982) 131.

4 See the two views expressed in ibid., 131–57 and Matthew Edel, Elliot D. Sclar, and Daniel Luria, *Shaky Palaces: Homeownership and Social Mobility in Boston's Suburbanization* (New York: Columbia University Press 1984). The latter argue that investment in homes compared badly with investment in stocks. But the comparison is a narrow one, especially for those of modest means. The debate is thoughtfully reviewed by Michael J. Doucet and John Weaver, *Housing the North American City* (Montreal and Kingston: McGill-Queen's University Press 1991) ch. 4, especially 171–2.

5 Soltow, *Men and Wealth in the United States* (New Haven, Conn.: Yale 1975) ch. 3; Gordon Darroch, 'Early Industrialization and Inequality in Toronto, 1861–1899,' *Labour / Le Travailleur* 11 (Spring 1983) 31–61; David Gagan, *Hopeful Travellers: Families, Land, and Social Change in Mid-Victorian Peel County, Canada West* (Toronto: University of Toronto Press 1981) 100; Livio De Matteo and Peter George, 'Canadian Wealth Inequality in the Late Nineteenth Century: A Study of Wentworth County, Ontario, 1872–1902,' *Canadian Historical Review* 73 (December 1992) tables 3 and 4. Julian Gwynn and Fazely Siddiq estimate wealthholding for Nova Scotia from probate records in which real estate was a declining proportion of total estate between 1851 and 1871, primarily for non-farming groups. 'Wealth Distribution in Nova Scotia during the Confederation Era, 1851 and 1871,' *Canadian Historical Review* 73 (December 1992) table 3.

6 For each household the 1871 census recorded the number of 'dwelling houses' owned and the enumerator's instructions specified that 'All properties belonging to the same family are to be entered under one reference to the head of the family.' Department of Agriculture, *Manual Containing "The Census Act" and the Instructions to Officers Employed in the Taking of the First Census of Canada (1871)* (Ottawa: Department of Agriculture 1871) 25.

7 Within the over-50 group, the rates are 0.71, 0.78, and 0.59 for those aged 50–59, 60–69, 70 and over, respectively.

8 The age-standardized rates were achieved by applying the age composition of

the Ontario male population in 1871 to the specific groups to obtain adjusted home ownership proportions. Six age categories were used: 20–24, 25–29 ... 50–99.

9 The major Ontario city studies are, Michael J. Doucet, 'Working Class Housing in a Small Nineteenth-century Canadian City: Hamilton, Ontario, 1852–1881,' in Gregory Kealey and Peter Warrian, eds, *Essays in Working Class History* (Toronto: McClelland and Stewart 1976) 83–105; Katz, Doucet, and Stern, *Social Organization*, 131–57; Gordon Darroch, 'Occupational Structure, Assessed Wealth and Homeowning During Toronto's Early Industrialization, 1861–1899,' *Histoire sociale / Social History* 16 (November 1983) 381–410; Richard Harris, Gregory Levine, and Bryan S. Osborne, 'Housing Tenure and Social Classes in Kingston, Ontario, 1881–1901,' *Journal of Historical Geography* 7 (1981) 271–89. The studies reporting some rural rates are Gordon Darroch, 'Class in Nineteenth-Century Central Ontario: A Reassessment of the Crisis and Demise of Small Producers during Early Industrialization,' in *Class, Gender and Region: Essays in Canadian Historical Sociology*, ed. Gregory Kealey (St John's: Committee on Canadian Labour History 1988) 49–72, and Gagan, *Hopeful Travellers*, ch. 5. Recently Doucet and Weaver have provided a varied, rich, and often provocative account of North American urban home ownership. The study ranges widely in its topics and inferences, but centres on evidence for Hamilton, Ontario. Nineteenth-century data for Hamilton, mainly from assessment rolls, are integrated into more general interpretations. *Housing the North American City.* See especially ch. 4 on property ownership as a North American cultural phenomenon and ch. 7 on social patterns of ownership in Hamilton.

10 Legal incorporation of urban places was not directly tied to population size, though the two are related. A little less than 20 per cent of the population lived in incorporated places in 1871. There were five cities (Toronto, Hamilton, London, Kingston, and Ottawa), forty-three towns, and sixty-five villages. In 1871 11 per cent of the province's population lived in municipalities of over 5,000. *Census of Canada, 1891*, vol. I, table VII.

11 Without a closer analysis we cannot say why the rates reported for three of the cities in other studies are higher than the 0.22 rate reported here. One reason may be that they are population rates, rather than rates for male heads, but this fact seems insufficient, since male heads were the great majority of owners. There may be significant variation between the census-enumerated and tax-assessed populations, and it may be that home ownership in London and Ottawa was less common.

12 The data come from a systematic study of the five largest land surveys in Hamilton conducted by Michael Doucet. See Katz, Doucet, and Stern, *Social Organization*, 148–9.

13 Harris and Hamnett, 'The Myth of the Promised Land,' 180, and Richard Harris, 'The Growth of Home Ownership in Toronto, 1899–1913,' paper presented at the Housing Tenure Workshop, Centre for Urban and Community Studies, University of Toronto, February 1987.

14 In addition to wage work and entrepreneurial opportunities, the larger towns and cities had become centres offering a range of services to local areas, such as banks, newspapers, high schools, and medical and legal services. After 1850 they were also the nodes of the rapidly expanding railway network. See Jacob Spelt, *Urban Development in South-Central Ontario* (Toronto: McClelland and Stewart 1972) ch. 4.

15 Katz, Doucet, and Stern, *Social Organization*, 141; Gagan, *Hopeful Travellers* 136, table 54.

16 Katz, Doucet, and Stern, *Social Organization* 131.

17 Bruce Elliott, *Irish Migrants in the Canadas: A New Approach* (Kingston and Montreal: McGill-Queen's University Press 1988) 198.

18 To this point the analysis has been based on a consideration of all adult men, whose rate of home ownership was 0.473. The difference is accounted for by the extremely low proportion of home owners among men who were not household heads, merely 0.008. The only non-heads to own homes were a few men between ages 50 and 59 (8 per cent). The majority of the non-heads, of course, were single young men (about 75 per cent were 20–29 years).

19 Although the female sample is relatively small, in most cases the numbers in any category are fifty or more. Where they are not, we report the numbers in parentheses in the text.

20 The simple differences in proportions discussed in the following text are statistically significant at least at the 0.05 level unless otherwise noted.

21 R. Cole Harris and John Warkentin, *Canada before Confederation: A Study in Historical Geography* (New York and Toronto: Oxford University Press 1974) 130–5. In appendix B of this chapter we consider the implications of the unusual census data on 'shanties' reported in the 1851–2 census because they provide a rare view of housing stock in the last century. These detailed data indicate that 45 per cent of houses in that year were log, 37 per cent were frame, and only about 7 per cent were brick or stone; 12 per cent were classified as shanties. Unfortunately there are no comparable 1871 data.

22 The index summarizes the deviation from a perfectly equal distribution of property (index value 0), in which houses would be owned in exact proportion to the distribution of the population; conversely, an index of 1 would mean that only one person owned all the houses.

23 Katz, Doucet, and Stern, *Social Organization*, 136–7; Gagan, *Hopeful Travellers*, 136.

24 Improved land was defined simply as 'the portion of land on which some work of measurable importance has been done, such as, for instance, under-brushing or chopping trees, or breaking up marshes, meadows, pastures, or plains.' Note again that the instructions to enumerators indicated, 'All proper-ties belonging to the same family are to be entered under one reference to the head of the family.' See *Manual Containing "The Census Act,"* 28, 29.

25 Michael Katz, *The People of Hamilton, Canada West: Family and Class in a Mid-Nineteenth Century City* (Cambridge Mass.: Harvard University Press 1975) 95–111.

26 Elliott, *Irish Migrants*, especially ch. 8.

27 We believe the distributional divisions drawn here would have had fairly ob-vious social and cultural implications in nineteenth-century Ontario. At the same time we do not presume that even the most carefully defined categories or boundaries represent class formations in the absence of a study of property relationships, the labour process, and concomitant ways of social life. Detailed studies of class formation in Ontario cities have appeared only relatively re-cently. For example, Bryan Palmer, *A Culture in Conflict: Skilled Workers and Industrial Capitalism in Hamilton, Ontario 1860–1914* (Kingston and Mon-treal: McGill-Queen's University Press 1979); Gregory Kealey, *Toronto Work-ers Respond to Industrial Capitalism, 1860–1892* (Toronto: University of Toronto Press 1980); Gregory Kealey and Bryan Palmer, *Dreaming of What Might Be: The Knights of Labor in Ontario, 1880–1900* (New York: Cambridge University Press 1982). We need complementary studies of the extent and implications of petty property ownership within these communities, say, of shops and of homes among master craftsmen and journeymen. We know even less about class relationships in rural communities. Kevin Burley reports an interesting study of the changing conditions of small property and petit bour-geois production in one Ontario town, ' "Good for All He Would Ask:" Credit and Debt in the Transition to Industrial Capitalism – The Case of Mid-nineteenth Century Brantford, Ontario,' *Histoire sociale / Social History* 20 (May 1987) 79–100.

28 See Elliott, *Irish Migrants*, chs 8 and 9, and Gagan, *Hopeful Travellers*, 53.

29 See Spelt, *Urban Development*, 109–15, 122–3; Bryan Palmer, *Working Class Experience: The Rise and Reconstitution of Canadian Labour, 1800–1980* (To-ronto: Butterworths 1983) 60–91.

30 Of the sample population, 67.9 per cent were married, which matches exactly the aggregate census report. Among them, 89.3 per cent of the heads of households were married and 8.9 per cent of the male non-heads. Fewer than 5 per cent of men reported being widowed. Katz, Doucet, and Stern, *Social Organization*, 290, and Gagan, *Hopeful Travellers*, 93 report the tendency for rapid remarriage among widowed men.

31 Rather to their surprise, Atack and Bateman conclude that, in historical perspective, the egalitarian ideals of a Jeffersonian landed democracy were quite
closely met in the United States rural north before the Civil War. Jeremy
Atack and Fred Bateman, *To Their Own Soil: Agriculture in the Antebellum
North* (Ames, Iowa: Iowa University Press 1987), especially ch. 6 and
268–70.

32 Rosemary R. Ball, ' "A Perfect Farmer's Wife": Women in 19th-Century Rural Ontario,' *Canada: A Magazine* 3 (1975) 3–21. Gagan, *Hopeful Travellers*,
55–6.

33 Elliott, *Irish Migrants*, 198. Also see Lisa Wilson Waciega 'A "Man of Business": The Widow of Means in Southeastern Pennsylvania, 1750–1850,' *William and Mary Quarterly* 44 (1987) 40–64.

34 There is a manufacturing schedule for the 1871 census that gives capital and
numbers of workers employed (the schedule for industrial establishments).
One might attempt to collate these data with the general tabulation of shops,
stores, and warehouse and factory ownership to classify manufacturing establishments by size. Beyond the tediousness of the collation, there is the problem that this is the only schedule in 1871 that does not provide a direct
nominal link to the other schedules. Thus, a name-linkage procedure would
have to be employed and is complicated by the poor quality of the nominal
information recorded on the manufacturing schedule. We have explored the
linkage in other work; it is troublesome. We have forgone the pleasure here.

35 Palmer, *A Culture in Conflict*; Kealey, *Toronto Workers Respond*.

36 Logistic regression is the appropriate model for dichotomous dependent variables. The logarithm of the variable is employed as a probability function, and
the procedure estimates the odds of, say, being propertyless from the characteristics of the population.

37 The model has nineteen simple dichotomies representing the variables, that is,
five age variables (30–39, 40–49 ... 70–99), foreign birth, three residence variables (in villages, towns, or cities), five ethnicity variables (Scottish, Irish,
German, French, and other origin), and five religious variables (Roman Catholic, Presbyterian, Methodist, Baptist, and other religions). Each variable is
defined as a dichotomy with an appropriate comparison category; they are, respectively, ages 20–29, native-birth, rural residence, English or Welsh origin,
and Anglican religion. So, a characteristic is evaluated in terms of its measured effect on the chance of owning secure property or not (or being propertyless in the second model) *in comparison* with those in the reference
category.

38 The magnitude of the difference between the value of the test statistic for the
baseline case and for each separate model provides a measure of the relative
importance of the *excluded* variable. The test statistic is analogous to a chi-

square statistic comparing actual values of the dependent variable with values predicted from the specific model. The statistic is −2 times the logarithm of the likelihood ratio. See John Fox, *Linear Statistical Models and Related Methods with Applications to Social Research* (New York: Wiley 1984) 307–10. We thank Frank E. Harrell Jr, Duke University, for consultation on this logistic procedure as presented in The SAS Institute Inc., *SAS User's Guide*.

39 In the statistical models presented, the specific contrast employed was between each religious group and the Church of England, rather than, say, a Catholic-Protestant divide.

40 William Westfall, *Two Worlds: The Protestant Culture of Nineteenth-Century Ontario* (Kingston and Montreal: McGill-Queen's University Press 1989) 10.

41 Westfall, *Two Worlds*, and John Webster Grant, *A Profusion of Spires: Religion in Nineteenth-Century Ontario* (Toronto: University of Toronto Press 1988).

42 Also, the difference was much less striking between the Protestant Canadian born in cities and their Protestant Irish-born neighbours. The rates of home ownership for all urban areas were 0.26 and 0.34 for these two, respectively.

43 'The development out of a frontier population of an enterprising business class and a sober, steady working class could not come through an emphasis upon traditional values of decorum and moral decency. It required the sort of rigid discipline provided by religious asceticism.' 'The rise of the Baptists and Methodists to positions of importance in the business life of Canada during the latter half of the nineteenth century offers an illustration of the close relation between the development of religious asceticism and the growth of capitalism.' Clark, *The Developing Canadian Community*, 2nd edition (University of Toronto Press 1968) 158, 157.

44 S.D. Clark, *Church and Sect in Canada* (Toronto: University of Toronto Press 1948) 350, quoting the *Canadian Baptist*, 18 December 1873.

45 *Minutes of the 48th Annual Conference of the Wesleyan Methodist Church in Canada 1871* (Toronto: Wesleyan Book Room 1871) 128.

46 *Canadian Temperance Advocate*, a monthly magazine advertising in the *Colonial Protestant* and *Journal of Literature and Science* 1:8 (Montreal 1848). Clark, *Developing Canadian Community*, 153.

47 We note that neither Katz, Doucet, and Stern nor Gagan report any relationship between religious affiliation and home ownership in Hamilton and Brampton in 1871, though they considered the question. Katz, Doucet, and Stern, *Social Organization*, 140; Gagan, *Hopeful Travellers*, 140.

48 The differences between native and foreign-born groups across church affiliations were greater. For the native born, the home-owner proportions vary from a low rate of just over a third among Anglicans to a high of 45 per cent among Baptists and 'other' denominations. This 11 per cent difference

(0.45 – 0.34) is well beyond the possibility of a chance result in the sample and is surprising in terms simply of whether men of different Protestant denominations had acquired a family residence or not: a third more native-born Baptists owned homes than did native-born Anglicans.

49 Clark, *Developing Canadian Community*, 152; *Church and Sect*, 355.

50 Westfall, *Two Worlds*, and Grant, *Profusion of Spires*.

51 Doucet and Weaver develop the same point in *Housing the North American City*, ch. 4.

52 Leonore Davidoff and Catherine Hall, *Family Fortunes: Men and Women of the English Middle Class, 1780–1850* (London: Hutchinson 1987) 362.

53 Davidoff and Hall, *Family Fortunes*, 74. The authors unravel the profound implications of the ideology for the social construction of gender and for gender relations among middle-class families.

54 Mary P. Ryan, *Cradle of the Middle Class: The Family in Oneida County, New York, 1790–1865* (Cambridge: Cambridge University Press 1981).

55 Peter Knights reports for samples of entirely ordinary nineteenth-century Boston men that they were engaged in very frequent real-estate transactions. *Yankee Destinies: The Lives of Ordinary Nineteenth-Century Bostonians* (Chapel Hill and London: University of North Carolina Press 1991) 205.

56 Westfall, *Two Worlds*, 22 summarizing passages from John Strachan's letters.

57 It should be noted that the model requires one to choose a comparison or reference category among the religious, ethnic, or other such groups. The choice is to some extent arbitrary. In choosing the Anglican church and the English and Welsh group, we take it that the claim of some members to high social status had not entirely faded by 1871 – at least among the church and ethnic group elites. Of course, choosing one group ignores the fact that there were important variations among their members in wealth, as in perception of their social place and sense of common heritage. The arbitrary combination for census purposes of the English and Welsh is an obvious example.

58 Lee Soltow, 'The Distribution of Income in the United States in 1798: Estimates Based on the Federal Housing Inventory,' *Review of Economics and Statistics* 69 (February 1987) 183, and *Distribution of Wealth and Income in the United States in 1798* (Pittsburgh: University of Pittsburgh Press 1989) chs 3 and 4.

59 Harris and Warkentin, *Canada before Confederation*, 130.

60 A microfilm was placed on the reel and a ruler placed vertically on the screen in the reader bin. The film was spun through the machine at two-second intervals using the motorized winder. If a page from the housing schedule encompassed the left-hand side of the ruler, all shanties on the page were selected for the sample. All houses were recorded on every fifth two-second

possibility if the ruler edge lay on a page of the housing schedule. The first film was fed forward through the machine, the second backward, and so on. Lee Soltow has pursued the analysis in more detail in 'Inequalities in the Standard of Living in the United States, 1798–1875,' in *American Economic Growth and Standards of Living before the Civil War*, ed. Robert E. Gallman and John Joseph Wallis, National Bureau of Economic Research Conference Report (Chicago: University of Chicago Press 1992) 121–71.

61 Soltow, *Men and Wealth*, 78.

62 Bureau of Industries, *Annual Report of the Bureau of Industries for the Province of Ontario, 1887*, printed by order of the Legislative Assembly (Toronto 1888) 61.

63 Katz, Doucet, and Stern, *Social Organization*, 155–6.

64 An advertisement to potential emigrants claimed, 'Boys of twelve years of age and upwards readily get employment at proportionate wages.' Authority of the Government of Ontario, *Emigration to Canada*, pamphlet number 15, Archives of Ontario (Toronto 1871) 33.

65 Bureau of Industries, *Annual Report*, 61

66 Katz, Doucet, and Stern, *Social Organization*, 240–1 and Peter Oliver, ' "A Terror to Evil Doers": The Central Prison and the "Criminal Class" in Late Nineteenth-Century Ontario,' in *Patterns of the Past: Interpreting Ontario's History* ed. Roger Hall, William Westfall, and Laurel Sifton MacDowell (Toronto and Oxford: Dundurn Press 1988) 206–237.

67 Katz, Doucet, and Stern, *Social Organization* 210, 237; Oliver, ' "A Terror" ' 208–20.

68 Report on the Common School System in the United States and Canada, *British Parliamentary Papers*, 1867 [3857] XXVI, 235, Rev. James Fraser; obtained from *Area Studies Series* (Shannon, Ireland: Irish University Press 1971).

69 Alison Prentice, *The School Promoters: Education and Social Class in Mid-Nineteenth Century Upper Canada* (Toronto: McClelland and Stewart 1977) 75. The School Act of 1841 and the Amendment in 1843 had made provisions for the establishment of separate Protestant and Catholic schools if a group of inhabitants in a school district so desired.

CHAPTER 4 Literacy and Illiteracy in Ontario in 1871: Trends, Social Patterns, and Property Holding

1 Carlo M. Cipolla, *Literacy and Development in the West* (Harmondsworth: Penguin 1969); Lawrence Stone, 'Literacy and Education in England, 1640–1900,' *Past and Present* 42 (February 1969) 61–139; Kenneth A. Lock-

ridge, *Literacy in Colonial New England: An Enquiry into the Social Context of Literacy in the Early Modern West* (New York: Norton 1974); Harvey J. Graff, *The Legacies of Literacy: Coninuities and Contradictinos in Western Culture and Society* (Bloomington and Indianapolis: Indiana University Press 1987); Lee Soltow and Edward Stevens, *The Rise of Literacy and the Common School in the United States* (Chicago: University of Chicago Press 1981).

2 See Egil Johansson, *The History of Literacy in Sweden, in Comparison with Some Other Countries* (Umea, Sweden: 1977) and Lockridge, *Literacy in Colonial New England.*

3 We note the implications and limits of the 1871 census definition in the analysis. Graff has defended judicious use of the census data for Ontario. Harvey Graff, 'What the 1861 Census Can Tell Us about Literacy: A Reply,' *Histoire sociale / Social History* 8 (November 1975) 337–49. Graff was replying, in part, to questions raised about the adequacy of the 1861 census by H.J. Mays and H.F. Manzl in 'Literacy and Social Structure in Nineteenth-Century Ontario: An Exercise in Historical Methodology,' *Histoire sociale / Social History* 7 (November 1974) 331–45. Also see Allan Greer, 'The Pattern of Literacy in Quebec, 1745–1899,' *Histoire sociale / Social History* 11 (November 1978) 295–335, and for a general discussion of the measurement of literacy, Roger Schofield, 'The Measurement of Literacy in Pre-Industrial England,' in *Literacy in Traditional Societies*, ed. Jack Goody (Cambridge: Cambridge University Press 1968) 311–25.

4 See Harvey J. Graff, *The Literacy Myth: Literacy and Social Structure in the Nineteenth-Century City* (New York: Academic Press 1979) 56ff.

5 On the emergence of this cultural amalgam in the United States in which a literate public had become an ideological imperative, an urgent social cause, and of significant commercial value, see Soltow and Stevens, *Rise of Literacy*, especially chs. 1, 3, and 6. On the Ontario case and the 'moral basis of literacy,' see Graff, *Literacy Myth*, ch. 1.

6 Graff, *Literacy Myth.*

7 Harvey J. Graff, *Literacy and Social Development in the West: A Reader* (New York: Cambridge University Press 1981); *The Legacies of Literacy*; Soltow and Stevens, *Rise of Literacy*, especially chs 4 and 5; Greer, 'Pattern of Literacy.'

8 Greer, 'Pattern of Literacy,' 326–30.

9 *The New Zealand Official Yearbook*, 1902, 242.

10 Cipolla, *Literacy and Development*, 89.

11 U.S. Bureau of the Census, *Historical Statistics of the United States*, 206, 214, Series H407; Charles Warren, *Illiteracy in the United States in 1870 and 1880* (Washington DC: 1884); U.S. Bureau of the Census, *Illiteracy in the United States* (Washington, DC: 1905).

12 Soltow and Stevens, *Rise of Literacy*, chs 4 and 5.

13 There were a good many Canadian migrants to the northern counties of the state, six of which bordered on Ontario. In 1875 they had between 3 and 17 per cent of their population classified as Canadian born. *Census of State of New York for 1875* (Albany: Weed, Parsons and Co. 1877) 29.

14 In addition to the provincial figures for males and females, the census reports illiteracy rates for each of the 206 counties in Ontario in 1871. We note that the highest rates, over 10 per cent, were recorded east and north of Port Hope, a town on Lake Ontario's northern shore.

15 As it is in other respects reported in the introduction, the sample proves to be an excellent representation of the Ontario male population as judged from the comparisons with the published counts for illiteracy. The proportion of males *21 and over* in Ontario reported to be unable to write was 0.113, and the corresponding figure in the sample was 0.111.

16 Cipolla, *Literacy and Development*, 93 and Bureau of the Census, *Illiteracy in the United States*, Bulletin 26. If one applies 1871 Ontario population weights to the age-specific illiteracy rates in the above countries, one can obtain a standardized illiteracy rate for males 21 and older for each country. These rates are 0.28 for Belgium (inability to read), 0.53 for Italy (inability to read), and 0.10 for the Austrian region, as contrasted to the Ontario illiteracy rate of 0.11.

17 Graff, *Literacy Myth*, 269, citing Grove, *A Search for America* (Toronto: 1927; reprinted by McClelland and Stewart 1971) 302.

18 Greer, 'Pattern of Literacy,' 327, table 10.

19 Graff, *Literacy Myth*, 65–9, and, especially, *Legacies of Literacy*, 366–72.

20 Graff, *Legacies of Literacy*, 337–8.

21 Graff, *Literacy Myth*, 57.

22 Ibid., 59.

23 The value of the R^2 statistic, indicating the proportion of variance explained in illiteracy by age, is relatively high (74 per cent) because we are fitting only twelve age-specific illiteracy rates for the groups 20–24, 25–29 ... 75–79.

24 James Thompson, *The Literacy of the Laity in the Middle Ages*, University of California Publications in Education, vol. 9. (New York: Franklin Press 1960); Edward Reisner, *Nationalism and Education Since 1789* (New York: Macmillan 1922) 410–17; Graff, *Legacies of Literacy*, especially chapters 6 and 7.

25 Soltow and Stevens, *Rise of Literacy*, 75–7.

26 R.D. Gidney, D.A. Lawr, and W.P.J Millar have established that the intentions of the school promoters, led by Egerton Ryerson, to put in place a centralized and relatively bureaucratized school system after 1846 was

counterbalanced to at least 1870 by strong local influence and management of the common schools. See, among other articles, Gidney, 'Elementary Education in Upper Canada: A Reassessment,' *Ontario History* 65 (1973) 169–85; Lawr and Gidney, 'Who Ran the Schools? Local Influence on Educational Policy in Nineteenth-Century Ontario,' *Ontario History* 72 (September 1980) 131–43; Gidney and Millar, 'Rural Schools and the Decline of Community Control in Nineteenth-Century Ontario,' Fourth Annual Agricultural History of Ontario Seminar, *Proceedings*, 70–91. Also see Chad Gaffield, *Language, Schooling and Cultural Conflict: The Origins of the French-Language Controversy in Ontario* (Kingston and Montreal: McGill-Queen's University Press 1987) ch. 4.

27 Soltow and Stevens, *Rise of Literacy*, ch. 5, especially 176, for the southern states.

28 This standardization was achieved by applying twelve population weights (for the six age groups 20–29, 30–39, ... 70–99, for each of the Canadian born and foreign born) to the farm and non-farm groups.

29 *Rise of Literacy*, ch. 5.

30 In part the discrepancy may derive from the fact that Graff reports 1861 data, and the census of that year assessed illiteracy in terms of the inability to read *or* write, thus categorizing more adults as literate. Further, Graff's focus on ethnicity as a primary source of urban illiteracy refers to combinations of birthplace and religion, highlighting the high urban Irish-Catholic rates. The differences between reading and writing ability for 1871, as given in table 1 of this chapter, suggest that a rate of writing illiteracy of about 0.11, for our urban Canadian-born sample, would be equivalent to a rate of about 0.08 as defined by ability to read. This figure is still over twice Graff's reported rate for the native born ten years earlier in Hamilton.

31 H. Clare Pentland, 'The Development of the Capitalistic Labour Market in Canada,' *Canadian Journal of Economics and Political Science* 25 (November 1959) 450–61; Ruth Bleasdale, 'Class Conflict on the Canals of Upper Canada in the 1840s,' *Labour / Le Travailleur* 7 (Spring 1981) 9–39; William N.T. Wylie, 'Poverty, Distress, and Disease: Labour and the Construction of the Rideau Canal, 1826–32,' *Labour / Le Travailleur* 11 (Spring 1983) 7–29.

32 *Census of Canada*, 1871, vol. I, table X, 207.

33 Johansson, *History of Literacy in Sweden*.

34 See the early work of Stone, 'Literacy and Education in England'; Lockridge, *Literacy in Colonial New England*; and Johansson, *History of Literacy in Sweden*. Harvey Graff traces religious influences and variations for many centuries in *Legacies of Literacy*.

35 Stone, 'Literacy and Education in England,' 76–7.

36 Cipolla, *Literacy and Development*, 72–3.
37 Harvey J. Graff, *The Labyrinths of Literacy: Reflections on Literacy Past and Present* (London and Philadelphia: Falmer Press 1987) 250ff.
38 John Webster Grant, *A Profusion of Spires: Religion in Nineteenth-Century Ontario* (Toronto: University of Toronto Press 1988), and Susan Houston and Alison Prentice, *Schooling and Scholars in Nineteenth-Century Ontario* (Toronto: University of Toronto Press 1988). The quotation is from Grant, 145.
39 Graff, *Legacies of Literacy*, 286.
40 Standardization values were obtained by applying Ontario population weights to Protestant and Catholic illiteracy averages for six age groups, as in table 9, and for thirty-two age-occupation-nativity cells. Empty cells have been eliminated from calculations.
41 Disproportionately large numbers of Catholics of Irish and French-Canadian heritage were common labourers in both urban and rural Ontario (28 per cent versus 12 per cent of Protestants in urban areas; 17 per cent versus 11 per cent of Protestants in rural areas), and much larger proportions of Canadian-born Catholics were illiterate than Catholic immigrants in both rural and urban areas of the province, as we found for farmers and non-farmers. Again to our surprise, in the province's cities, towns, and villages taken together, the native-born Catholics were more likely to be illiterate than the Irish-Catholic immigrants, just as we found among all non-farmers, though both rates are slightly lower in the urban areas. This finding contrasts with the results of Graff's study of three of the Ontario cities.
42 *Profusion of Spires*, 160.
43 Gaffield, *Language, Schooling*, especially ch. 4.
44 Donald Harmon Akenson, *The Irish in Ontario: A Study in Rural History* (Kingston and Montreal: McGill-Queen's 1984) 268–77.
45 Akenson, *The Irish* 276.
46 *Profusion of Spires*, 149–50. He notes, too, that beyond the elementary schools, the Catholic hierarchy intended that universities serve only as training for the priesthood for a tiny elite of families in a predominately working-class community. They were to be 'little seminaries,' focused on classical and philosophic studies for a select few.
47 William Westfall, 'The Dominion of the Lord: An Introduction to the Cultural History of Protestant Ontario in the Victorian Period,' *Queen's Quarterly* 83 (Spring 1976) 47–60.
48 Alison L. Prentice and Susan E. Houston, eds, *Family, School and Society in Nineteenth-Century Canada* (Toronto: Oxford University Press 1975) 128–33.
49 Alison Prentice, *The School Promoters: Education and Social Class in Mid-Nine-*

teenth Century Upper Canada (Toronto: McClelland and Stewart 1977) 71. Strachan, the influential Anglican bishop of Toronto, was a formidable supporter of denominational education from the 1820s to the 1860s. Ryerson became Ontario's dynamic and determined chief superintendent of schools in the public system's most formative period through 1876.

50 Grant, *Profusion of Spires*, 56–8.

51 Much has been made of Ontario Methodists' involvement in both popular and formal education, especially given Ryerson's prominence. Much less, if anything, is known about literacy among members of the other major denominations, especially within the small, rural, and very independent Baptist community. Grant considers the Ontario Baptists to have been 'orthodox heirs of the Puritan tradition' and resistant to any tendency to dilute their inherited Calvinism. Thus, their intimate knowledge of the New Testament as a blueprint for congregational life likely assumed an elementary reading ability among adherents. It may also be assumed that Ontario's Presbyterians generally shared in the early enthusiasm for literacy of the Scottish Calvinist Reformation. See Grant, *Profusion of Spires*, 31.

52 The census manuscripts record remarkable denominational diversity at this relatively late date. There were Episcopal Methodists, New Connection Methodists, Bible Christian Methodists; there were members of the Kirk and Canadian Presbyterians, as well as members identifying as Reformed and Evangelical Union Presbyterians; and there were Free Will Baptists, Christian and Union Baptists. Among the proselytizing sects, there were Irvingites, Swedenborgians, and Tunkers. The groups varied, too, in their origins, some European, some American.

53 The terms liturgical and pietistic, orthodox and evangelical refer to different aspects of a church-sect typology. In this typology the church tends to be inclusive in membership, impersonal, bureaucratic, accepting of the social order and appealing to the propertied and well placed. The sect tends to be the opposite in every respect, exclusive, demanding commitment, locally organized, rejecting of secular society, and appealing to the marginal and poor. Of course, the typology refers only to tendencies in historical patterns.

54 Michael B. Katz, Michael J. Doucet, and Mark J. Stern, *The Social Organization of Early Industrial Capitalism* (Cambridge, Mass.: Harvard University Press 1982) 268, table 7.8.

55 Edwin Cannan, 'Editor's Introduction,' to Adam Smith, *The Wealth of Nations* (New York: Modern Library, Random House, 1937) xxxiii, xxxiv.

56 Graff, *Legacies of Literacy*, 286.

57 The very small foreign-born segment of the French group (less than 1 per cent of the provincial population and 20 per cent of the French-origin group)

had a still high, but comparatively modest, rate of 0.125 compared with that of the native born. France as a whole had achieved considerable movement towards national literacy throughout the nineteenth century.

58 Graff, *Literacy Myth*, 56.

59 Ordinary least squares regression with a dichotomous dependent variable generates unbiased estimates of the regression coefficients – the estimates of the net effect of an independent variable. Statistical tests of the significance of these coefficients are not possible, however, since the standard errors of the regression coefficients are biased. Logistic regression employing maximum likelihood estimates provides for appropriate tests of significance. See E.A Hanushek and J.E Jackson, *Statistical Methods for Social Scientists* (New York: Academic Press 1977) ch. 7.

60 All variables are drawn from the census as discussed in the previous analysis (see ch. 3).

61 This analysis is a formal analogue to the more familiar variance explained in a least squares regression model.

62 A least squares equation predicting illiteracy from age, ethnicity, and religion led to an equivalent interpretation. Though not directly comparable, the coefficients of the ordinary least squares and logit models generally agreed, and we would make similar inferences from each: religion and ethnicity and age were major independent conditions affecting illiteracy in nineteenth-century Ontario, with French origin and Catholic faith especially salient among the cultural factors.

63 A similar logistic regression for the sample of heads of households that included women heads indicated that gender was *not* a statistically or substantively significant predictor of the odds of being illiterate, taking all the other factors into account; ethnicity and religion retained their primary explanatory power.

64 See Graff, *Literacy Myth*.

65 Ibid., 137; Graff has extended his analysis and critique to a wide array of historical periods and materials, for example, *Literacy and Development*. In Ontario he found urban illiterates in 1861 to be somewhat more likely than the literate to hold unskilled jobs and to be out-migrants from Ontario cities, but they were not seriously disadvantaged occupationally, nor did their lack of literacy deny them modest economic and property accumulation or a measure of occupational mobility between 1861 and 1871. See *Literacy Myth*, 69–102, 132–53.

66 Some second thoughts concerning early Scottish literacy are expressed in R.A. Houston, *Scottish Literacy and Scottish Identity: Illiteracy and Society in Scotland and Northern England, 1600–1800* (New York: 1985) 33, 72, 142, 256–7.

67 *Report of the Department of Agriculture*, 1870, no. 19, 125–42, 'Instructions to be issued to officers taking the 1871 census,' 134.

68 Carroll Wright and William Hunt, *History and Growth of the United States Census, 1790–1890* (Washington, D.C.: 1900) 159.

CHAPTER 5 Property Ownership among Emigrants, 1860 and 1870: Canadians in the United States and Americans in Ontario

1 Thomas White, Jr, *A Lecture on Canada as a Field for Emigration*, Special Emigration Commissioner to Great Britain, Liverpool, 30 June, 1869 (Toronto: Hunter Rose 1869) pamphlet 1869, row 6, Provincial Archives of Ontario. The concern over emigration to the United States is well documented. It runs throughout the debates on land policy, for example. See Lillian Gates, *Land Policies of Upper Canada* (Toronto: University of Toronto Press 1969).

2 Jacob Spelt, *Urban Development in South-Central Ontario* (Toronto and Montreal: McClelland and Stewart 1972) 55.

3 William L. Marr and Donald G. Paterson, *Canada: An Economic History* (Toronto: Gage 1980) table 6.7 and 178. Marcus Hansen, *The Mingling of the Canadian and American Peoples* (New Haven, Conn.: Yale University Press 1940). Leon Truesdell, *The Canadian Born in the United States* (New Haven, Conn.: Yale University Press 1943) 10, 13.

4 See Tamara Hareven, *Family Time and Industrial Time: The Relationship Between the Family and Work in a New England Industrial Community* (Cambridge, Mass.: Harvard University Press 1982); Bruno Ramirez and Jean LaMarre, 'Du Québec vers les Etats Unis: L'étude des lieux d'origine,' *Revue d'histoire de l'Amérique Française* 38 (1985) 409–22; Randy William Widdis, 'Scale and Context: Approaches to the Study of Canadian Migration Patterns in the Nineteenth Century,' *Social Science History*, 12 (Fall 1988) 269–304; Bruno Ramirez, *On the Move: French-Canadian and Italian Migrants in the North Atlantic Economy, 1860–1914* (Toronto: McClelland and Stewart 1991).

5 Public Records Office, London, *Correspondence CO-42–693*, letter from W.C. Murdoch, 16 June 1870.

6 Ibid.

7 Hansen, *The Mingling*.

8 Ibid., 120.

9 Ibid., 160–2.

10 See ibid., 123–4; John McCallum, *Unequal Beginnings: Agriculture and Economic Development in Quebec and Ontario until 1870* (Toronto: University of Toronto Press 1980) 44. Migration to the United States has been a subject of greater interest in the history of Quebec than of Ontario, owing to the considerable social and political significance attached to outflow in the former

province. Among more recent studies see Ralph Vicero, 'The Immigration of French-Canadians to New England, 1849–1900: A Geographical Analysis,' doctoral thesis, University of Wisconsin 1968; Yolande Lavoie, *L'émigration des Québecois aux Etats-Unis de 1840 a 1930* (Québec: Gouvernement du Québec 1979); Frances H. Early, 'The French-Canadian Family Economy and Standard-of-Living in Lowell, Massachusetts, 1870,' *Journal of Family History* 7 (Summer 1982) 180–99; Gilles Paquet and Wayne Smith, 'L'émigration des Canadiens français vers les Etats Unis, 1790–1940: problématique et coups de sonde,' *L'Actualité économique* 59 (1983) 423–53; Hareven, *Family Time*; and Ramirez and La Marre, 'Du Québec vers les Etats Unis'; Jacques Rouillard, *Ah les Etats!: les travailleurs canadiens-français dans l'industrie textile du la Nouvelle-Angleterre d'après le témoignage des derniers migrants* (Montréal: Boréal Express 1985). The review essay by André E. LeBlanc, 'French Canada's Diaspora and Labour History,' *Labour / Le Travail* 20 (Fall 1987) 213–20, is a valuable source. Bruno Ramirez puts the diaspora in the context of the North Atlantic economy in *On the Move*.

11 Among a larger literature, see Fernand Ouellet, *Economic and Social History of Québec 1760–1850: Structures and Conjonctures* (Toronto: Gage 1980) 186–95; McCallum, *Unequal Beginnings*, 25–44; R.M. McInnis, 'A Reconsideration of the State of Agriculture in Lower Canada in the First Half of the Nineteenth Century,' In *Canadian Papers in Rural History*, ed. Donald Akenson vol. 3 (Gananoque, Ont.: Langdale Press 1982) 9–49; Allan Greer, *Peasant, Lord, and Merchant: Rural Society in Three Quebec Parishes 1740–1840* (Toronto: University of Toronto Press 1985) 209–17.

12 Greer, *Peasant, Lord, and Merchant*, 216.

13 McCallum, *Unequal Beginnings* 113–14.

14 Gates, *Land Policies*, 309.

15 David Gagan, *Hopeful Travellers: Families, Land, and Social Change in Mid-Victorian Peel County, Canada West* (Toronto: University of Toronto Press 1981) ch. 3.

16 Marr and Paterson, *Canada*, 178–180. Also see Widdis, 'Scale and Context.'

17 See the instructions to the marshals of the 1860 and 1870 censuses. The details of the samples are given in Lee Soltow, *Patterns of Wealthholding in Wisconsin since 1850* (Madison: University of Wisconsin Press 1971); 'The Wealth, Income, and Social Class of Men in Large Northern Cities of the United States in 1860,' in *Personal Distributions of Income and Wealth*, ed. James D. Smith, vol. 39, Series in Income and Wealth, National Bureau of Economic Research; *Men and Wealth in the United States: 1850–1870* (New Haven, Conn.: Yale University Press 1975).

18 Ibid.

19 Paul A. David and Peter Solar, 'The History of the Cost of Living in America,' in *Research in Economic History*, ed. Paul Uselding, 2 (1977) 25. The price indexes, with 1860 prices equal to 100, are 1870 = 157, 1871 = 147 (and, for comparison, 1980 = 984; 1983 = 1,190).

20 See R.K Vedder and L.E. Gallaway, 'Settlement Patterns of Canadian Emigrants to the United States, 1850–1960,' *Canadian Journal of Economics* 3 (August 1970) 476–86.

21 These age breaks are limited, of course, so that there are large enough sample numbers in each category from which to draw tentative analysis (about seventy and fifty in the smallest categories for each group).

22 See ch. 4.

23 *Census of Rhode Island*, 1875 (Providence 1877) xciv.

24 Soltow, *Men and Wealth*.

25 Harris, 'The Family Home in Working Class Life,' Research Paper No. 171, (Toronto: Centre for Urban and Community Studies, University of Toronto 1989).

26 The sample size is 1/760 of the population. Year of immigration is given for the foreign born in the great majority of cases. To have limited the Canadian group to those entering, say, between 1860 and 1871 or to those over age 20 in 1871, however, would have severely restricted the sample size. A multivariate regression analysis shows that ethnicity, age, and year of immigration all are relevant to explained variation in illiteracy. The origin of parents, on the other hand, adds little to the statistical account.

27 Very similar results emerge if the members of the 1900 census sample are classified by place of birth of their fathers or of their mothers. The relatively small sample of non-French males over age 35 whose parents were Canadian born had an illiteracy rate of 0.075; the comparable French-Canadian males with French-Canadian parents had a rate of 0.397. These are people who tended to emigrate in the very early 1870s.

28 Hansen, *The Mingling*, 148, 150.

29 The result conforms with findings reported by Darroch and Ornstein for the U.S. residents of central Ontario in terms of occupations, where rather larger than average numbers of U.S. emigrants were merchants, manufacturers, professionals, and other non-manual workers in 1861 and 1871. See Gordon Darroch and Michael Ornstein, 'Ethnicity and Class: Transitions over a Decade, Ontario, 1861–1871,' Canadian Historical Association, *Historical Papers* (1984) 111–37, tables 1a, 1b.

30 Hansen, *The Mingling*, 167. Ramirez's fine-grained study of the migrant Quebec families (and Italian migrants to North America) has revealed how family migration strategies revolved about childrens' work and education. Initially

marginal Quebec farm families sought opportunities for children's employment in the unskilled labour pools of New England, as vital, temporary, contributions to household income. Later, as Franco-American communities
developed and the opportunities for children's educational and job prospects
grew, families turned from sojourning to permanent residence. *On the Move*,
chs 3 and 5.

31 Ramirez, *On the Move*.

CHAPTER 6 Estimating the Distribution of Propertied Wealth in Victorian
Ontario: Provincial Patterns and Comparisons

1 In chapter 2 we were able to apply a known relation between farm values and
farm acreage for the northern United States to Ontario farm acreage. In that
case, the resulting Gini indices of inequality were in the order of 0.66–0.70
and were quite close to similar indices for the northern states in 1870.

2 Public Archives of Ontario has microfilm holdings for many subdistricts for
1871, provided by the Genealogical Society of Salt Lake City. The records
are not complete. Records of the county treasurers might be accessed for
other regions.

3 Dollar assessment values for subdistricts and districts in 1870 are found in
Sessional Papers of Canada, No. 1, First session of the Second Parliament, Session 1873, *Miscellaneous Statistics of Canada for the Year 1870–71*, Part I, Municipal Returns, Ontario (Ottawa 1872) 3–21, and *Miscellaneous Statistics of
Canada for the year 1870*, Part II, Municipal Returns, Ontario (Ottawa 1873)
2–18. The definitions of real and personal estate, as given in the *Ontario Statutes*, Cap. 36, 32 Vict. Assessment of Property, 180, are: real estate, land, and
real property 'include all buildings or other things erected upon or affixed to
the land, and all machinery or other things so fixed to any building as to form
in law part of the realty, and all trees or underwood growing upon the land,
and all mines, minerals, quarries and fossils in and under the same, except
mines belonging to her majesty.' Personal estate and personal property 'include all goods, chattels, shares in incorporated companies, interest on mortgages, dividends from bank stocks, money, notes, accounts and debts at their
actual values, income and all other property, except land and real estate, and
real property as above defined.'

4 Published aggregate counts for individual subdistricts were not conveniently
given for males 20 and older. Males of age 20 were given only for the province. The twelve cities and towns for which data are given are Hamilton,
Kingston, London, Ottawa, Toronto, Belleville, Brockville, Cobourg, Peter-
borough, Port Hope, Saint Mary's, and St Thomas.

5 An intractable problem arose in trying to unravel the relations of RE, NTP, and NAC for subdistricts. For example, we hoped that the coefficients derived from multiple regression would suggest acreage values and housing values within urban and rural areas classified by latitude and longitude. They did not, and we were forced to use RE_NAC and RE_NTP of each subdistrict, in spite of the obvious overlap.

6 Inter University Consortium for Political and Social Research, *Historical Demographic and Social Data*, 1870 set for assessed value. See also Lee Soltow, *Men and Wealth in the United States 1850–70* (New Haven, Conn.: Yale University Press 1975) 157.

7 *Census of Canada*, 1871, vol. I, xxviii. The figures in parentheses in the equation are the standard errors of the coefficients.

8 Lee Soltow, *Distribution of Wealth and Income in the United States in 1798* (Pittsburgh, Pa: University of Pittsburgh Press 1989) 43, and data set for 1870 described in Lee Soltow, *Men and Wealth*, 108; 1870 data are technically for farmers and non-farmers, not for the rural and urban sectors.

9 It proved extremely difficult to establish any meaningful relationships among the variables for the tax data in the urban sector. The tax acreage reported varied very substantially from one urban area to another. We employed the following simple rule in establishing wealth of an urban individual: $W_{RE} =$ RE_NTP $\times$ (AC/30) + RE_NTP $\times$ HO. The 1,029 men in the urban areas in our 1871 sample reported an aggregate number of acres amounting to thirty times the aggregate number of homes owned. The above equation is an attempt to give acreage and housing about the same importance in the urban sector. This 30 to 1 rule actually means that 40 per cent of aggregate dollar value is allotted to acreage and 50 per cent to housing. These proportions are very similar to those found in the urban sector in the United States in 1798. See Soltow, *Distribution*, table D, 263.

10 The lower average values in Ontario compared with those of the United States may also simply reflect the different sources. The one set of figures is derived from tax estimates, while the other was derived from a general census, one whose declarations were not to be divulged to tax authorities.

11 The editorial was a comment on the debate regarding immigration and free land grants in the Ontario legislature. *St Thomas Weekly Dispatch and County of Elgin General Advertiser*, 30 January 1868.

12 John McCallum writes in this context, 'As late as 1875 a British trade unionist remarked that, on the whole, "farm labour for hire is in Canada only a transient avocation, there being in this country no large body of men who expect to devote their lives to working for wages, as every healthy and sober man can easily become a landholder" ' *Unequal Beginnings: Agriculture and*

Economic Development in Quebec and Ontario Until 1870 (Toronto: University of Toronto Press 1980) 97. The original source is Harold Innis and A.R.M. Lower, *Select Documents in Canadian Economic History, 1783–1885* (Toronto: University of Toronto Press 1933) 535–6.

13 David Levine, 'Production, Reproduction, and the Proletarian Family in England, 1500–1851,' in *Proletarianization and Family History*, ed. David Levine (New York: Academic Press 1984) 87–127.

14 Schumpeter treated tenants in an agricultural society as entrepreneurs. To the extent that they managed their farms well, by hiring resources and meeting expenses, he thought of them as essential to capitalism. The more successful stepped up the agricultural ladder to purchase land and join the owner-occupier category. Even if they did not join the class of landed owners, Levine suggests that in the sweep of the capitalist reorganization of rural England from the sixteenth to the eighteenth century, 'Tenant farmers, like remora fish, swam along with their landlords, also enjoying the gains.' 'Production, Reproduction,' 90. However central they were to the operation of agricultural capitalism or however they benefited from the concentration of wealth, tenant farmers were one large step removed from the yeoman ideal.

15 *Parliamentary Papers,* Irish University Press, British-Irish Censuses, vol. 8, summary tables, 1851, ccxxiii, and vol. 9, 909. See also *Parliamentary Papers,* 1854–5, XLVII, 686–7, and Lee Soltow, 'Inequality of Wealth and Land in Scotland in the Eighteenth Century,' *Scottish Economic and Social History* (1990) table 5.

Perhaps the earliest count is that given for males 20 and older in agriculture in England in 1831. The number of occupiers was 236,343 (141,460 of whom were employed labourers) and 744,407 labourers. See J. Marshall, *Digest of All the Accounts Relating to Population, Production, Revenues, etc., Great Britain and Ireland* (London: 1833) 10.

The situation in England, Wales and Scotland from 1848 to 1871 and earlier may have been distinctly different from other places on the continent. See in particular John Stuart Mill, *Principles of Political Economy*, ed. Sir W.J. Ashley (April 1929; from the first, 1848, edition to the seventh edition of 1871, reprinted New York: Augustus M. Kelley 1965) Book II, chs VI and VII, titled, 'Of Peasant Proprietors' and 'Continuation on the Same Subject,' 256–96.

16 *Census of Canada,* 1871, vol. II, Table 13, 245.

17 Levine, 'Production, Reproduction,' 90.

18 Parliamentary Papers, 1854–5, XLVII, 686–7; Soltow, 'Inequality of Wealth,' table 5, and 'Wealth Distribution in England and Wales in 1798,' *Economic*

History Review, Second Series, 34 (February 1981) 70.

19 *Parliamentary Papers*, 1863, LX, pencilled pagination 353, Census of Ireland, 1861.
20 Soltow, 'Inequality of Wealth,' table 5.
21 See David Gagan, ' "The Prose of Life": Literary Reflections of the Family, Individual Experience and Social Structure in Nineteenth-Century Canada,' *Journal of Social History* 9 (January 1976) 368.
22 Throughout the analysis we have attempted to examine the relation of property ownership, literacy, and wealth to a number of independent variables. There is considerable measurement error associated with the wealth measures presented here when wealth is attributed to the sample individuals, as we have indicated. For consistency, we present one multivariate analysis expressing the relationships. The results follow in the appendix to this chapter.

CHAPTER 7 Property, Families, and Class in Victorian Ontario: Some Conclusions

1 David Gagan, 'Class and Society in Victorian English Canada: An Historiographical Reassessment,' *British Journal of Canadian Studies* 4:1 (1989) 75.
2 David Gagan, ' "The Prose of Life": Literary Reflections on the Family, Individual Experience and Social Structure in Nineteenth-Century Canada,' *Journal of Social History* 9 (January 1976) 368.
3 Giddens neatly expresses the relation of individual mobility and class formation in the following terms: 'In general, the greater the degree of "closure" of mobility chances – both intergenerationally and within the career of the individual–the more this facilitates the formation of identifiable classes.' *The Class Structure of Advanced Societies* (New York: Harper Torchbooks 1973) 107.
4 Gagan, ' "The Prose of Life," 369.
5 Gregory S. Kealey and Bryan D. Palmer, *Dreaming of What Might Be: The Knights of Labor in Ontario, 1880–1900* (Cambridge: Cambridge University Press 1982; Toronto: New Hogtown Press 1987). See chapter 1 for a clear account of the urban structural changes and working class movements. Also see the debate on the character of the working-class movements presented in Gregory S. Kealey 'Labour and Working Class History in Canada: Prospects in the 1980s,' *Labour / Le Travailleur* 7 (Spring 1981) 67–94, and David J. Bercuson, 'Through the Looking Glass of Culture: An Essay on the New Labour History and Working-Class Culture in Recent Canadian Historical Writing,' *Labour / Le Travailleur* 7 (Spring 1981) 95–112.
6 Kealey and Palmer, *Dreaming*, 27–36.

7 Michael B. Katz, Michael J. Doucet, and Mark J. Stern, *The Social Organization of Early Industrial Capitalism* (Cambridge, Mass.: Harvard University Press 1982) ch. 9.
8 The first general narrative and analytic account of the economic history of the province is Ian Drummond with Peter George, Kris Inwood, Peter W. Sinclair, and Tom Traves, *Progress Without Planning: The Economic History of Ontario from Confederation to the Second World War* (Toronto: University of Toronto Press 1987).

APPENDIX: Demographic and Social Patterns among Adult Males and Female Heads of Households, Ontario, 1871: A Census Re-analysis

1 Donald Harman Akenson, *Irish In Ontario: A Study in Rural History* (Kingston and Montreal: McGill-Queen's University Press 1984) 203.
2 *Census of Canada, 1870–71,* vol. 1.
3 William L. Marr and Donald G. Paterson, *Canada: An Economic History* (Toronto: Gage 1980) 170.
4 We note that the mean age of the adult male population as reported in the census is 38.9 years and the mean age of the film-manuscript sample is 39.1 years, reflecting the sample's close match to the population. These averages are just slightly greater than the mean age of the free adult male population of the United States twenty years earlier, which was 37 years. Lee Soltow, *Men and Wealth in the United States: 1850–1870* (New Haven, Conn.: Yale University Press 1975) 9.
5 Michael R. Haines, 'The Use of Model Life Tables to Estimate Mortality for the United States in the Late Nineteenth Century,' *Demography* 16 (May 1979) 289–312; Kevin McQuillan, 'Ontario Mortality Patterns, 1861–1921,' *Canadian Studies in Population* 12 (1985) 31–48.
6 *Census of Canada,* 1871, vol. 5, table A, 2–6. The population of Upper Canada in 1851 was 952,004 and of Ontario in 1871 was 1,620,851. Thus, for the twenty year period the growth rate was $1,620,851 = 952,004 \ (1.027)^{20}$ or an annual rate of 2.7 per cent.
7 Marr and Paterson, *Canada,* 151–1 and table 6:2.
8 See ibid., table 6:2 and 178–80; Warren E. Kalback and Wayne W. McVey *The Demographic Bases of Canadian Society,* second ed. (Toronto: McGraw-Hill Ryerson 1979) 53–4 and table 2:4.
9 Gordon Darroch and Michael Ornstein, 'Ethnicity and Occupational Structure in Canada in 1871: The Vertical Mosaic in Historical Perspective,' *Canadian Historical Review* 61 (September 1980) 305–33. In this study age and nativity had a statistically independent association with occupation, as did national origin or ethnicity.

10 Marr and Paterson, *Canada*, table 6:7.
11 See F.H. Leacy, ed., *Historical Statistics of Canada* (Ottawa: Statistics Canada 1983) tables D86–106, M12–22.
12 Lee Soltow, *Men and Wealth*, table 1.2.
13 Ibid., 17.
14 Leacy *Historical Statistics*, table D86–106.
15 Urban areas are defined as all incorporated places, regardless of size or function. Others have indicated the limits and advantages of this legal definition, but without a locational analysis of industry, institutions, and services, it is the only serviceable one. Akenson points out in a local analysis of Leeds and Lansdowne township that the definition probably does not seriously underestimate the numbers of urban dwellers, since the population of very small incorporated places more than offsets the larger centres of 2–3,000 that were not incorporated. Akenson, *The Irish*, 36, n43. The best analysis of urban places and urbanization is still Jacob Spelt, *Urban Development in South-Central Ontario* (Toronto and Montreal: McClelland and Stewart 1972).
16 There is a large literature on urban 'transiency.' The early analysis of Boston by Thernstrom and Knights established the parameters of this incessant movement. Their estimates indicate that about 1.5 million people streamed through Boston in the decade between 1880 and 1890, but the city had only 363,000 enumerated residents in the first year and 448,000 a decade later. See Stephan Thernstrom and Peter Knights, 'Men in Motion: Some Data and Speculations about Urban Population Mobility in Nineteenth-Century America,' in *Anonymous Americans: Explorations in Nineteenth-Century Social History*, ed. Tamara Hareven (Englewood Cliffs, NJ: Prentice-Hall 1971) 17–47. A reassessment is Donald H. Parkerson, 'How Mobile were Nineteenth-Century Americans?' *Historical Methods* 15 (Fall 1982) 99–109. For Ontario see Michael Katz, *The People of Hamilton, Canada West: Family and Class in the Mid-Nineteenth Century* (Cambridge, Mass.: Harvard University Press 1975) ch. 3; David Gagan, *Hopeful Travellers: Families, Land, and Social Change in Mid-Victorian Peel County, Canada West* (Toronto: University of Toronto Press 1981) ch. 5.
17 Single women had such rights in law, but, of course, being single was for most a temporary, early stage of the life cycle. The 1871 census was taken just prior to the Married Women's Real Estate Act, 1873, which allowed married women for the first time to dispose of real estate as if they were unmarried, that is, without a trustee. *Ontario Statutes*, Cap. 18, 36 Vict.
18 According to a small, local study of wills by Cohen for three Ontario townships in the earlier periods, 1800–11 and 1850–8, husbands' wills normally set out specific conditions of inheritance for widows, often including specification that remarriage was a condition of disinheritance and that the inherit-

ance was limited to a portion of the estate only for the women's lifetime. Marjorie Griffin Cohen, *Women's Work: Markets and Economic Development in Nineteenth-Century Ontario* (Toronto: University of Toronto Press 1988) 49–54. For the limitations of the study of wills, see Bruce Elliott, 'Sources of Bias in Nineteenth-Century Ontario Wills,' *Histoire sociale / Social History* 17 (May 1985) 125–32.

19 The differences in total proportions between the male and female samples are statistically significant (at least at the 0.05 level), although not all of the differences for specific age categories are. We refer to the general patterns.

20 Bettina Bradbury, 'Cows, Pigs and Boarders: Non-Wage Forms of Survival among Montreal Families, 1861–1881.' *Labour / Le Travailleur*, 14 (Fall 1984) 9–46.

21 Gordon Darroch and Michael Ornstein, 'Ethnicity and Class: Transitions over a Decade, Ontario, 1861–1871,' *Canadian Historical Association, Historical Papers* (1984) tables 1a, 1b.

22 To be specific, the 1870 population was 493,464 and the 1850 population was 147,711; so $493,464 = 147,711(1.062)^{+20}$ for the twenty years, representing an annual rate of increase of 6.2 per cent.

23 R.K. Vedder and L.E. Gallaway, 'Settlement Patterns of Canadian Emigrants to the United States, 1850–1960,' *Canadian Journal of Economics* 3 (August 1970) 476–86.

24 See Robin W. Winks, *Canada and the United States, The Civil War Years* (Baltimore: Johns Hopkins University Press 1960).

25 Gagan, *Hopeful Travellers*, 152–3.

Illustration Sources and Credits

Index

acreage: estimated dollar value of, for Ontario 192–4; secure property and 85–6; size inequality of 203; value of, estimated 192–4. *See also* land

age: as factor in wealth acquisition 199; composition and inferences for social trends 117; condition of property ownership 203; distributions and ownership 15; illiteracy and, in multivariate analysis 151; profiles of adult males in Ontario 210–15; propertylessness and 89; secure property and 88; standardization procedure for 233 n20; standardized rates for, in landholding, by nativity 46, for farmers 26–32

agrarian economy: structural continuity of, in Ontario 83

agrarian life: dominant feature of Ontario 216

Akenson, Donald H. 11, 44, 47, 48, 55, 57, 140, 209

Americans: age among, in Ontario 224–5; land and home ownership among, in Ontario 180–2

Anglicans. *See* Church of England

anti-Catholicism 102

assessment records 4–5; as a main source in analysis of wealth 20–1; for subdistricts, used in estimating wealth 13, 18; limitations of 231–2 n5; problems of individual records 184–5; use of, estimating wealth 184

Atack, Jeremy 31

Atlantic provinces: emigration to United States from 163

Austria: age patterns of illiteracy in 117

Baptists: advantage in houses owned 102; encouraging literacy among 142; expressions of frugality among 94; great underrepresentation in prisons among 109; home ownership among 94–5; household size among 107–8; illiteracy and, in multivariate analysis 151; in old Ontario's business life 96; landownership among farmers 50–3, 59–60; literacy and 135–6; overrepresentation among teachers 110–11; remarkable housing accumulation among 95

Barrie Northern Advance 164